Slawomir Dębski (Ed.)

Transatlantic Perspectives on Security Imperatives

AF185500

Transatlantic Public Policy Series

edited by

Eberhard Bohne
Professor of Public Administration
German University of Administrative Sciences Speyer

Charles F. Bonser
Dean Emeritus
Indiana University
School of Public and Environmental Affairs, Bloomington

Kenneth M. Spencer
Professor of Public Policy
University of Birmingham
School of Public Policy

Volume 3

LIT

Transatlantic Perspectives on Security Imperatives

edited by

Slawomir Dębski

LIT

Bibliographic information published by the Deutsche Nationalbibliothek
The Deutsche Nationalbibliothek lists this publication in the Deutsche
Nationalbibliografie; detailed bibliographic data are available in the Internet at
http://dnb.d-nb.de.

ISBN 978-3-8258-0655-2

A catalogue record for this book is available from the British Library

© LIT VERLAG Dr. W. Hopf Berlin 2007
Auslieferung/Verlagskontakt:
Fresnostr. 2   48159 Münster
Tel. +49 (0)251–62 03 20   Fax +49 (0)251–23 19 72
e-Mail: lit@lit-verlag.de   http://www.lit-verlag.de

Distributed in the UK by: Global Book Marketing, 99B Wallis Rd, London, E9 5LN
Phone: +44 (0) 20 8533 5800 – Fax: +44 (0) 1600 775 663
http://www.centralbooks.co.uk/acatalog/search.html

Distributed in North America by:

Table of Contents

Transatlantic Community and Challenges of the Broader Middle East

Human Security – Transatlantic Approach?

Acknowledgments

The present volume would have never been published but for kindness, assistance and commitment of many people. Organizing a transatlantic meeting of experts, followed by preparation of the joint publication, was by no means an easy task. Otherwise, would the debate about current state and prospects for transatlantic relations still be so endlessly fascinating? It is impossible to mention all those who contributed to the success of the TPC Colloquium 2006, but everyone of them deserves a very warm expression of thanks. Primarily, I would like to thank the members of the Executive Committee of the Transatlantic Policy Consortium, who had decided at the 2005 meeting that the next colloquium would be held at The Polish Institute of International Affairs in Warsaw, and the subject of the discussion would be security issues in transatlantic relations. I would like to thank particularly Chuck Bonser, Ken Spencer and my two predecessors at the post of the Director of The Polish Institute of International Affairs, Ryszard Stemplowski and Roman Kuźniar, who substantially contributed to the organization of the meeting in Warsaw, as well as Adrian Zdrada and Katarzyna Kołakowska who supervised all the organizational matters in Warsaw.

The publication of this volume, containing papers prepared by the participants of the meeting, was quite a different and not even easier task. We hand its results to readers thanks to the commitment and consistency of Eberhard Bohne, co-editor of the Transatlantic Public Policy Series, Karin Schmid and Małgorzata Krystyniak. Karin Schmid of Speyer University prepared the camera-ready copy of the manuscript. Grand acknowledgments are due to all authors of this volume, who made their contribution to a better understanding of the challenges for the security of the states in the transatlantic area, and to a strengthening of the ties between Europe and North America in this regard. I would also like to thank all participants of the colloquium who spoke in the debate as well as in the unofficial part of the meeting, possibly becoming a source of inspiration for the authors who are solely responsible for the presented theses. This publication was supported by a grant from the Polish Institute of International Affairs. Any errors or omissions are the fault of the editor alone.

Warsaw, June 2007   *Sławomir Dębski*

1

Introduction

Sławomir Dębski

The ensuring of security to its citizens is one of the fundamental responsibilities of the state. However, each state operates in an international environment. So when seeking to guarantee the security of their own citizens states have to take into account the fact that other states have similar needs. Past experience shows that the endeavors of states for security is a never-ending process that requires constant effort. Things are further complicated by the fact that the assessment of the state of security is always a subjective one. Each state and each society makes this assessment independently, frequently taking different factors into account. Some of them are determined by geographical location, the economic situation or military potential, while others pay more attention to history, political culture or psychology. The issue is complicated enough to make a problem of international security a perfect subject of considerations, not only for decision makers but also for experts and academicians,

The United States, the hegemony of the world system, and its European allies are the most developed countries in the world, so they form the centre of the system. That is why the transatlantic area exerts a decisive influence on the course of most global processes and on the level of world security in particular. This is due to the fact that the states in or near the centre of the system, hence in the optimum position, are interested first of all in the stabilization of the system. So they maintain and enhance the status quo. The same goal is furthered by the endeavors of semi-peripheral actors to improve their own situation by securing admission to integration institutions that arrange relations between the most developed states of the world, the core of the system, i.e. NATO and the European Union.

The threats to the stability of the system come from the striving of semi-peripheral powers to take over the hegemonic role or build an alternative hegemonic system. In addition, new challenges continue to emerge. The stability of the system can also be endangered by actions designed to change the principles that govern the system. This can be attained first and foremost by attacking the core of the system, its values, principles and sense of security. One such phenomenon is no doubt transnational terrorism. Its sources are traced back to unbalanced development, the Middle East conflicts, social tensions arising in the context of relations between the state and religion, the rivalry between religious and social models in the Muslim world, or the accelerated flow of ideas and faster communication, associated with globalization but made possible by advances in technology. The response of the states, occupying a central position in the world system, to these challenges shall determine the stability of that system.

The transatlantic area is, therefore, central to the deliberations over the security of the contemporary world, over the ways of raising the level of security on a global scale, but also over the negative consequences of the efforts to harmonize security on a global scale.

The Transatlantic Policy Consortium (TPC), affiliating American and European universities and research institutions, organized a Colloquium on Security and Transatlantic Relations in Warsaw from 4 to 6 June 2006. The meeting was an opportunity for discussing

- different perceptions of the threats on both sides of the Atlantic,
- the state and directions of evolution of the institutions set up to ensure security in the transatlantic area,
- the challenges related to the situation in the Middle East, including the prospects of closer cooperation between the United States and its European allies in order to establish peace in that region of the world and, last but not least,

- the impact of the process of the harmonization of security on a global scale, as illustrated by the ever more widespread use of ever more stringent security procedures, on civil rights and liberties.

The articles published in this volume are not, however, a collection of transcripts of conference papers. Some of them were written months after the colloquium ended, but were, beyond doubt, influenced by the debates that took place and the arguments that had been invoked there. We divided them into three chapters. The foci of them are the future of NATO, the Middle East problems, the possibilities of transatlantic cooperation in promoting peace in that region, and the challenges to human security, both those ensuing from the new threats and from the attempts to oppose such threats. The collection does not make up a coherent picture, even though the authors' views on many issues are convergent. But it can serve as an illustration of the state of the debate on security problems in transatlantic relations in the broad sense at this specific time. We hope that the views presented in this book shall become a source of inspiration for other students of these problems, and that this will contribute to greater synergies of thinking and studies of global security pursued in American and European institutions. Consequently, this will serve the purpose for which the TPC was established ten years ago. I am certain that, in one form or another, the TPC discussions of security problems in transatlantic relations and on a wider, global scale will continue. This will contribute to a better understanding of the challenges that the contemporary world is facing, and to the devising of ever more effective tools of ensuring security.

Future of NATO – A Transatlantic Conundrum?

2

NATO's Role in the US War on Terrorism: Implications for the Future

Renée de Nevers

Since the end of the Cold War, the North Atlantic Treaty Association's (NATO's) future has been the subject of much debate. NATO's practical response, during the 1990s, was to redefine its mission in two ways. The alliance sought to revise its mission and priorities to encompass a broader range of concerns, based on the logic that it must go "out of area or out of business", and NATO expanded by incorporating former communist- ruled states to the East. The lure of NATO membership, it was argued, would help cement democratic values in the new member states.[1] Three central issues of threat, institutional benefits, and identity are evident in these efforts, as NATO strove to focus on emerging threats and chronic security problems while it relied on institutional mechanisms and norms to build trust in cooperation and to reshape East European identities. These practical measures were accompanied, however, by a growing unease within the alliance about the increasing disparity of power between the United States and its European allies by the late1990s.[2]

The war on terror that followed the attacks of September 11, 2001 shifted the terms of the debate, as cooperation against terrorism took center stage. Nonetheless, tensions over the interplay of threats, institutions and identity remain central to understanding NATO's role in the international system, and its utility to its member states. Although NATO's mission has expanded dramatically since the end of the Cold War and alliance members agree on the threat posed by terrorism, NATO's role in the struggle against terrorists is somewhat ambiguous. This could have long-term implications for alliance unity. Moreover, the "capabilities gap" that has hounded NATO for decades has magnified due to the US's adoption of increasingly sophisticated weaponry and communications systems.

What role does NATO play in the US war on terror? Certainly NATO is not just a "tool" of US policy. However, terrorism is perceived by the United States as the key national security threat it will face for the foreseeable future. Just as the US is working to transform its own strategies in response to this threat, we would expect it to evaluate key alliances and security relationships with this measure. To understand how the war on terror has affected NATO efforts to cooperate, we must keep in mind that the war on terror is a US creation, and NATO has been forced to adjust to this fact.

First, NATO actions contribute in a largely supportive role to US efforts to combat terrorism. NATO's contribution to efforts to quell terrorism is somewhat elusive. Both the European "fight against terrorism" and the US "war on terror" are carried out elsewhere. Second, to the degree that NATO members participate in offensive efforts to respond to terrorism, this is done not through NATO, but outside it, through bilateral activities or loose coalitions of the willing.

Why is NATO's role so limited? Two factors help explain this: the increasing capabilities gap between the US and its NATO allies, and the US's increasing resistance to alliance constraints. These highlight an additional issue confronting NATO: the question of whether a military alliance is the appropriate instrument to confront terrorism. If not, then this raises questions about NATO's future, given the changes in the central security threats confronting its members today.

In this chapter, I will first briefly describe and compare NATO and US strategies regarding terrorism. I then evaluate NATO actions in terms of their contribution to the US strategy to fight terrorism. Third, I discuss possible explanations and implications for the patterns found through this examination.

To begin with, it is important to keep in mind that NATO today is more than a classical military alliance. Alliances have been defined as "formal associations of states for the use (or nonuse) of military force, in specified circumstances, against states outside their own member-ship".[3] NATO is more than this. It is commonly described as a politi-cal-military alliance, with its key political function of guiding mem-bers' foreign and security policy and providing a forum for alliance consultation, and the operational function of ensuring that members can cooperate militarily.[4] NATO's dual role is part of the reason it has endured. The key question is whether its members continue to agree on its value, and what its core tasks should be.

Comparing the US and NATO's Responses to Terrorism

While terrorism emerged as a shared concern by the late 1990s, and was incorporated as a factor contributing to security challenges confronting NATO in its 1999 Strategic Concept, it was not a core fo-cus of alliance policy.[5] Terrorism crystallized as a central threat to al-liance members after September 11, 2001. NATO's initial response to these attacks was twofold: almost immediately, the Alliance invoked Article V of its Charter, declaring the attack on the US an attack on all alliance members. It followed this shortly with agreement on practical steps to assist the US coalition as it took on Al Qaeda and the Taliban in Afghanistan in October 2001. These included:
- Greater intelligence sharing
- Assistance to states that might be threatened due to their support for the coalition
- Increased facilities security
- "backfilling" allied assets need for supporting anti-terrorist efforts
- overflight rights
- access rights for ports and airfields
- naval deployment in the eastern Mediterranean
- NATO Airborne Warning and Control System (AWACS) aircraft deployed to the US.[6]

The alliance also moved quickly to develop military guidelines for responding to terrorism. The new "Military Concept for Defense Against Terrorism" was endorsed as official NATO policy at the No-vember 2002 Prague Summit. Four military roles are identified for alliance operations against terrorism: anti-terrorism or defensive measures, consequence management in the event of an attack, counter terrorism, meaning offensive measures, and military cooperation with non-military forces in the fight against terrorists.[7]

How does this compare to US efforts to combat terrorism? The US *National Security Strategy* (*NSS*), published in March 2006, specifies four policy elements to address terrorism: preventing terrorist attacks before they occur; denying rogue states and terrorist groups weapons of mass destruction (WMD); denying terrorist groups sanctuary or support from rogue states; and preventing terrorist groups from controlling any nation that they could use as a base of operations.[8]

There is clear overlap between the goals set forth in these two strategies. Each seeks to prevent attacks from occurring, and NATO's counterterrorism strategy shares with US policy the recognition that preventing attacks may require offensive action against terrorists or states that support them: "allied nations agree that terrorists should not be allowed to base, train, plan, stage, and execute terrorist actions, and the threat may be severe enough to justify acting against these terrorists and those who harbor them".[9] NATO's military guidelines appear to be more defensive and reactive than those of the US, however. Emphasis is placed on reducing vulnerability and enhancing capabilities to respond quickly to potential attacks, and on ensuring appropriate force protection in all military activities. While the guidelines suggest that NATO forces could play either lead or supportive roles in offensive operations against terrorists, more planning is recommended for NATO-led operations, with more concrete suggestions evident in the recommendations for support missions.

NATO's Role in the US War on Terrorism

Looked at through the lens of US goals in the war on terror, then, what role does NATO play in efforts to combat terrorism? Representatives of the US government invariably reiterate NATO's importance and value to the US. NATO is widely regarded as the most important institution that the US works with, the "premier alliance". Government officials also point out how much the alliance is doing and has done to support US activities against terrorists, which I discuss below.

US recognition of the importance of allies in this struggle was stressed in US President George W. Bush's second inaugural address in January 2005, and it is reiterated in the 2006 NSS, which states that to win against terrorism, "we need the support and concerted action of friends and allies".

At the same time, US strategy documents suggest that NATO is not the preferred model for multilateral cooperation in the war on terror, and NATO appears to be less central to US policy than it was previously. There is a notable decline in attention to NATO in the most recent NSS – and more critically, the NSS makes explicit the US preference for the model of the Proliferation Security Initiative (PSI) established in 2003:

> Establishing results-oriented partnerships on the model of the PSI to meet new challenges and opportunities. These partnerships emphasize international cooperation, not international bureaucracy. They rely on voluntary adherence rather than binding treaties. They are oriented towards action and results rather than legislation or rule-making.[10]

The NSS also states that "existing international institutions have a role to play, but in many cases coalitions of the willing may be able to respond more quickly and creatively, at least in the short term."[11] Similarly, the 2006 Quadrennial Defense Review (QDR) highlights the distinction between "static alliances versus dynamic partnerships", and the Pentagon's preference for the latter.[12] Some in the Pentagon insist that this criticism is aimed at organizations such as the Organization for American States (OAS), which has resisted US efforts to revise its charter in order to isolate Venezuela's President, Hugo Chavez, for example. But some NATO allies have taken note of the tone, and may not be reassured by this clarification, particularly in light of suggestions within the policy-making community that the US should treat NATO as a toolbox, and "cherry-pick" its partners from the alliance depending on their support for US policy goals.[13] Secretary of Defense Donald Rumsfeld's comments that the US is "rethinking" what role alliances like NATO should play, while working to establish "more flexible partnerships with foreign militaries" can only reinforce the impression that US leaders see NATO's value waning, in favor of flexible coalitions and bilateral arrangements.[14]

A second factor to keep in mind is the turnover in membership in the US Congress. While not younger than previous members of Congress, about two-thirds of the current members entered Congress after the end of the Cold War. The average length of service now is ten years in the House of Representatives, and slightly over thirteen years in the Senate. Fewer representatives have a military background than previously.[15] This all implies that there is less institutional memory in Congress of NATO's importance to the US, and the central role it has played in US security policy.[16] Moreover, many Congressional staffers are younger, and many of those with experience working on NATO issues have left, sometimes moving to positions in the executive branch. This suggests that Congress may prove less willing in the future to support NATO, unless the executive branch does more to explain to Congress what NATO is doing and how it helps the US.[17]

Within the executive branch as well, however, NATO's centrality in US foreign and security policy may be questioned. Many National Security Council (NSC) staffers have little memory of the Cold War, and their political perspectives have been shaped by America's strength, conflict in the Middle East, and problems of terrorism and the spread of WMD. As one staffer noted, "not being encumbered with all this baggage from the Cold War is a huge advantage". He was referring in specific to the Anti-Ballistic Missile (ABM) treaty, from which the US withdrew in December 2001 in order to expand and accelerate efforts to develop missile defense capabilities; but similar sentiments toward NATO do not seem out of the question.[18] This could further erode political support for working through the alliance to address core security problems.

I evaluate NATO's contribution to the US "war on terror" through the lens of US strategic goals, by examining three categories: prevention, denial of access to WMD, and denying terrorists state support, sanctuary, or territorial control. The latter combines two elements of US strategy noted earlier; the denial of support, and keeping terrorists from gaining outright control over a state. These are combined because the tactics intended to achieve these goals overlap.

Examining NATO actions in this way is not meant to imply that NATO is a tool of US foreign policy. The US has been preoccupied with its campaign against terrorism since 2001, however, and US dominance and its leanings toward unilateralism have already caused concern in the alliance. US views of NATO's value are likely to be influenced by its perceptions of the support NATO has provided to US efforts in this campaign. At the same time, the alliance clearly states its goal of responding to member state efforts to address terrorism; and the US is focused intently on this struggle.

Prevention

NATO's role in preventing terrorist attacks encompasses two areas: intelligence sharing and active patrolling to detect preparations for an attack. NATO has done some of each of these, primarily through Operation Active Endeavor (OAE). OAE is NATO's only Article V operation, and was the first substantive military action the alliance took after the September 11 attacks to address the terrorist threat.[19] This activity corresponds directly both to the US's goal of preventing terrorist attacks, and to NATO's anti-terrorism strategy. After deploying in the eastern Mediterranean in October 2001 as a deterrent and surveillance measure in support of the US intervention in Afghanistan, OAE evolved into a broader counter-terrorism initiative. OAE expanded to cover the entire Mediterranean in 2003, and during the US invasion of Iraq it escorted ships through the straits of Gibraltar, at the US's request, to alleviate concerns that such ships might be targeted by terrorists in the Straits. The Operation has focused on monitoring shipping and the safety of ports and narrow sea-lanes. A second goal of OAE, particularly since 2003, has been to expand participation by non-NATO states, both NATO Partners and countries participating in NATO's Mediterranean Dialogue.[20]

Much of OAE's work has been done through expanded intelligence sharing activities, and intelligence sharing within the alliance has been enhanced through OAE activities. Intelligence sharing operations include efforts to develop a network for tracking merchant shipping throughout the Mediterranean, and improving means to share this with relevant governments. This should help address not only terrorist concerns, but also drug interdiction and efforts to prevent the spread of weapons of mass destruction.[21]

OAE has clear military objectives, and the alliance has developed valuable experience in maritime surveillance and interdiction. At the same time, the Operation has had other goals as well. Expanding cooperation with NATO partners, in particular, has both strategic and political aims. NATO's effort to include Russia in OAE, for example, was intended to gain Moscow's agreement to extend OAE activities into the Black Sea. This has not yet happened, due to objections from both Russia and Turkey, but Russia participated in OAE in 2006.[22] Efforts to include more Mediterranean countries were designed to improve cooperation and, if possible, to share the burden for sustaining the operation with a greater number of countries. This corresponds to the Alliance's current effort to explore expanded partnerships with countries around the globe.[23]

Just as it plays a critical role in OAE, intelligence sharing would appear to be a second critical element of cooperation in prosecuting the war on terror. Indeed, many experts view intelligence as the most important tool in fighting terrorism.[24] The United States cooperates with a broad range of countries around the globe to share intelligence regarding terrorist activities. NATO's intelligence contribution to US efforts against terrorism is limited, however, for several reasons. First, most of the military intelligence NATO relies on, which is shared through the NATO Special Committee, is provided by the United States to the alliance. The Multinational Battlefield Information and Exploitation System (BICES), for example, is a "near-real-time all-source system" by which the US feeds information to NATO commands.[25]

Second, the US and its European allies appear to have diverging views about the role of military intelligence. From the US perspective, military intelligence is an increasingly important component of battlefield military activities. The Department of Defense (DOD) emphasizes that military intelligence is no longer a staff function, but rather a war fighting function that soldiers on the battlefield will be actively engaged in at all times. As part of its broader interest in information warfare, the DOD is pushing to establish a fully "networked battlespace", with the goal of "information dominance" in any conflict.[26] NATO's European members do not place the same emphasis on military intelligence.

NATO created the Terrorist Threat Intelligence Unit (TTIU) shortly after September 11 in order to enable Alliance members to share information and develop common views of the terrorist threat. This is perceived by many as critical to NATO's cooperation against terrorism, because without a shared sense of threat, the Alliance will find it difficult to agree on appropriate responses. The TTIU does not focus on military intelligence, but instead relies on open-source information to conduct its analyses, with the goal of improving political cooperation against terrorism. Indeed, the United States appointed an FBI official as its representative to the TTIU, in the belief that his experience was most appropriate for the Unit. The TTIU is still quite small, but is generally perceived to be doing good work. Its contribution is likely to be primarily to the political process of developing consensus within NATO.

Third, the capabilities gap that has presented a chronic problem for NATO is increasing in the intelligence area. This presents growing problems for interoperability. Already in the 1990s, the US military had to maintain "legacy" communications systems to enable it to operate with other NATO members, and allied forces depended heavily on US communications and intelligence during the 1999 Kosovo bombing campaign.[27] The US spends far more on research and development than its allies; the DOD's budget request for research and development for FY 2007 is $ 57.9 billion, while the entire defense budget for the United Kingdom, NATO's next largest spender, was $ 51.1 billion in FY 2005.[28] The US can also draw on a more vibrant domestic technology industry than can its European allies. One reason the US rejected some European offers of military assistance in its intervention in Afghanistan in 2001 was the difficulties presented by different levels of technological sophistication.[29]

To be sure, the alliance is well aware of the need for improvements in intelligence capabilities and interoperability. NATO adopted an initiative on developing new capabilities, particularly in areas such as intelligence and surveillance, in November 2002, and some alliance members are working to improve their information warfare capabilities.[30] That this continues to be problematic is evident in repeated references to the need for improved intelligence sharing both among national agencies and internationally.[31]

Fourth, far more intelligence sharing within Europe, and between the United States and European states, happens bilaterally or among small groups of states, and at varying levels of intelligence. The US maintains the most in-depth intelligence cooperation with the United Kingdom, and its cooperation with those states participating in the UK-USA network is far more intensive than is its intelligence sharing with the rest of the alliance.[32] Moreover, the most vital terrorist-related intelligence information generated in Europe is outside NATO's scope, but comes from police and domestic intelligence agencies. The central mechanism for sharing this information is the Berne Group, a club of European intelligence organizations – to which the US does not belong. Greater cooperation in non-military intelligence sharing is hindered by two issues: the problem of ensuring protection of sources when information is dispersed, and differences between the United States and many European allies over appropriate domestic privacy standards.[33]

NATO's contribution to ongoing efforts to prevent terrorist attacks is thus important, but one could question how central the alliance is to US efforts in this area. To be sure, US officials agree that many NATO members have strong intelligence capabilities, and can provide intelligence that the US doesn't have. But this cooperation is likely to be bilateral. While OAE's surveillance activities are important to tracking potential terrorist movements, the intelligence developed through OAE may be more directly relevant to law enforcement activities than to military missions. Similarly, some of the most important elements of intelligence gathering in Europe take place outside NATO itself, conducted by domestic intelligence organizations. Bilateral intelligence sharing among key allies has continued even when political relations were severely strained in the months prior to the US invasion of Iraq, as recent revelations about German intelligence cooperation with the US make clear.[34] But NATO as such does not generate much raw intelligence useful to preventing terrorism. The alliance has recently established a new intelligence "fusion center" to ensure that needed intelligence can be distributed to troops in the field. This does not appear to represent new intelligence gathering or analysis, but rather better means to share information.[35]

Denying Terrorists Access to WMD

Preventing the spread of WMD is one of NATO's core goals. However, it has been difficult to determine what NATO's role should be in international efforts to confront the problem of proliferation. Two central issues are involved. First, should denial efforts be primarily bilateral or multilateral? Moreover, what is NATO's "value added" as a multilateral organization seeking to address proliferation problems? Some NATO members have been actively involved in cooperative threat reduction efforts in Russia and other former Soviet republics. The United Kingdom, for example, is working with the Russian government on projects ranging from nuclear submarine dismantlement to developing sustainable employment for scientists and engineers formerly employed in Soviet WMD programs. Germany, France, and Canada have been involved in efforts to develop plutonium disposition methods.[36] Several core NATO countries, France, Germany, and the U.K., have also sought since 2004 to induce Iran to end its nuclear enrichment program. These nonproliferation efforts have been conducted bilaterally or by small groups of states, however, rather than as a multilateral NATO initiative. To the degree that combined alliance efforts have been undertaken, these have focused on political dialogue, through forums such as the NATO-Russia Council and consultations with other partner states.

Second, what means are appropriate for preventing terrorists from acquiring WMD: denial or pre-emption? This question was at the heart of the bitter debate over invading Iraq in 2002 – 2003. Notably, there was relatively widespread agreement within the alliance about Iraq's suspected WMD capabilities.[37] The differences were over the response, and core NATO allies disagreed about whether pre-emption was an appropriate counter to state efforts to develop WMD. This is not a new debate, but it was sharpened by the fight over Iraq policy.

One of NATO's central efforts in responding to terrorism has been the development of consequence management capabilities. To this end, it is developing defensive measures to respond to WMD attacks. NATO agreed at the November 2002 Prague Summit to several measures to protect against WMD attacks, which included creating an event-response team, a deployable laboratory to analyze samples of potential WMD, and a multinational Chemical Biological Radiological Nuclear (CBRN) defense battalion which participated in security operations at the 2004 Athens Olympics.[38] The alliance enhanced its efforts to develop defense stockpiles to protect against chemical or biological attacks, and a disease surveillance system.[39] The alliance is also developing new defense technologies to protect against terrorist threats through its established mechanisms for cooperation on national armaments.

While the US urges NATO to do more to confront the problem of WMD proliferation, NATO is not central to US counterproliferation activities. Rather, US policy favors preemption, as stated clearly in the 2006 NSS. Moreover, to the degree that it relies on multilateral efforts to prevent proliferation, the current administration has stated its preference for more flexible partnerships like the PSI, an activity established by the US and eleven other countries in 2003 to strengthen nonproliferation efforts by interdicting exports of potential WMD materials destined for countries seeking to acquire such weapons.[40] The advantages of the PSI, from the US's perspective, are that it is a coalition of the willing, involving only those who share PSI goals; and it is a "results-oriented" activity that emphasizes international cooperation rather than legislation or rule-making.[41] In other words, it allows the US the freedom to do what it wishes, with only those partners that agree to its goals. While many NATO members are involved in the PSI, this is not an alliance activity.

Differences between the US and some core NATO allies about appropriate means to achieve desired ends are starkly apparent in confronting the problem of WMD. While NATO members share a strong interest in preventing the spread of WMD, the question of whether preemption is an appropriate tool remains unresolved. The US preference for working in different forums suggests that it wants to avoid alliance constraints in efforts to confront the WMD threat. The example of recent efforts to deal with Iran's suspected nuclear weapons program only reinforces this point.

Deny State Support or Sanctuary to Terrorists

In contrast to those areas discussed above, NATO's contribution to the US goal of denying support or sanctuary from rogue states to terrorist groups, and ensuring that such groups do not gain control over states, is significant. NATO's peacekeeping mission in Afghanistan, the International Security Assistance Force (ISAF) is in the process of assuming control over international military forces throughout the country, taking over in the south and east from US troops. NATO forces are also involved in ongoing efforts to train Iraqi security forces.

The US intervention in Afghanistan that began in October 2001 was initially a source of some tension within the alliance. While several NATO states offered to contribute troops to this mission, and NATO declared that the September 11 attacks constituted an Article V attack against all alliance members, the US did not seek NATO's participation in its invasion of Afghanistan. This apparently reflected Bush's desire to avoid having allies dictate how the war would be fought, and the preference among some in the Pentagon to avoid the headaches of gaining allied consensus on a strategy that had emerged during NATO's bombing campaign against Serbia in 1999.[42] Equally important was the question of whether NATO allies could contribute the specialized capabilities needed for the campaign the US planned.[43] Nonetheless, a few NATO countries were part of the coalition that attacked Afghanistan – including Denmark, France, Germany, Turkey and the United Kingdom – and NATO AWACS planes patrolled US airspace in the fall of 2001, "backfilling" to ensure US defense while freeing US forces for the campaign against Afghanistan.

ISAF was initially established with United Nations (UN) Security Council authority under British control in October 2001, after the US overthrew the Taliban government. NATO assumed control of ISAF in August 2003.[44] Initially ISAF's mission was limited to patrolling Kabul, but over the last few years, ISAF has expanded its mission into the northern and western provinces of Afghanistan. It has also deployed several Provincial Reconstruction Teams (PRTs), a model developed by the US military that combines security and reconstruction functions in an effort to help stabilize the countryside.[45] By February 2006 NATO was responsible for security in about half of Afghanistan, and current plans call for it to assume full control over the mission by the end of 2006. At that point, ISAF will be one of NATO's largest operations, and it is expected to involve about 25,000 troops.

ISAF is clearly a valuable contribution to the US goal of denying terrorists sanctuary or allies, given Al Qaeda's close ties with the previous Taliban regime, and ongoing efforts to pursue Al Qaeda members in the border region between Afghanistan and Pakistan. All twenty-six NATO members participate in ISAF, as well as ten non-NATO partner countries. At the same time, ISAF has suffered from some notable problems. First, since 2003, the alliance has had trouble getting sufficient troop commitments to meet the target force size. Second, many troops in Afghanistan operate under "national caveats" whereby governments place limits on what military activities their troops are allowed to do, or where they are allowed to go in carrying out their missions. The problem is not unique to ISAF; national caveats caused headaches in NATO's peacekeeping mission in Bosnia as well. Recognition of the operational problems they pose has led to a recent decline in the use of national caveats, but they have made both multinational cooperation and operations in general more difficult in Afghanistan.[46]

A third problem is that the Afghan government remains hesitant about the handover to NATO. Afghanistan fears that the US will abandon it, and it is unsure what NATO authority over both the peacekeeping and counterterrorism mission will mean in the long run. Recent and strengthened Taliban attacks in southern Afghanistan are apparently intended to test the will of NATO member states to sustain their commitment; and this renewed fighting has forced the US to reverse plans to reduce its military commitment in Afghanistan.[47] Notably, US forces, which will be the largest contingent in ISAF, will continue to conduct the bulk of counterterrorism activities. It is not clear whether ISAF's rules of engagement will allow it to do more than peacekeeping, although the range of security problems on the ground in Afghanistan ranges from drug trafficking to counterterrorism without clear delineations.[48] Nor is it entirely clear how well the lines of command within ISAF will work, since the US contingent will retain its counterinsurgency function in addition to peacekeeping.[49]

NATO has played a far smaller role in Iraq. While the Bush administration framed the invasion as part of the war on terror, the Alliance was deeply split on the question of invading Iraq, and did not formally participate in the invasion. Nonetheless, NATO supported the US-led operation in several ways. The Alliance contributed to Turkey's defense against possible Iraqi retaliation during the 2003 invasion, and agreed to Poland's request for allied support when it took over leadership of one sector of the stabilization force in Iraq in May 2003.[50] Fifteen NATO states have contributed forces to the coalition since 2003.[51] And although Germany did not participate in the coalition and strongly opposed the US invasion, hundreds of German CBW detection troops were deployed in Kuwait and Turkey to help aid coalition forces in the event of a WMD attack.[52]

As an Alliance, NATO has done less. In 2004, NATO agreed to play a central role in training Iraqi security forces. This training effort included mentoring of Iraqi military officers, establishing an officer training facility in Iraq; and training Iraqi officers at NATO facilities. NATO has also donated military equipment to Iraq's security forces. NATO's training mission has faced significant difficulties, however. First, efforts to get the mission up and running were hamstrung by the need to gain consensus on every decision along the way, which greatly slowed the process. Second, as in Afghanistan, some troop contributions have operated under national caveats, which hindered commanders' efforts to coordinate NATO's activities. Third, funding for the mission has been a serious problem. Not only are troop contributors expected to cover the costs of their own contributions, but NATO set up a "trust fund" to cover the larger goal of establishing the defense university, and contributions to the fund have been insufficient to meet the task NATO took on. Although the Iraqi government stressed its preference for in-country training, to help gain popular trust and support for the new security forces, NATO has had greater success with training outside the country.[53]

Analysis and Implications

NATO's Secretary General, Jaap de Hoop Scheffer, stated in February 2006 that "more than ever, NATO is in demand, and NATO is delivering".[54] Between its current missions and its recent and expected expansions, the alliance looks vibrant. NATO's role in the war on terror, however, is largely a support role, and to the degree that NATO countries are engaged in key elements of US strategy to combat terrorism, they do so on the basis of bilateral ties or loose coalitions – not through NATO. OAE provides important support for US military operations in the Middle East, but it is not a combat operation. The contribution that NATO members make by providing intelligence in the struggle against terrorists occurs bilaterally, and it is generated primarily by law enforcement agencies, rather than military intelligence.

Similarly, NATO does not have a direct role in preventing WMD from falling into terrorist hands. NATO maintains political dialogues with countries at risk for the theft or sale of weapons related products, and individual members participate in threat reduction activities. The alliance has focused on developing "consequence management" capabilities to respond to a WMD attack. It is split on the use of preemption as a means to prevent the spread of WMD to states that might let terrorists obtain them, however; and the PSI, not NATO, is the US's preferred mechanism for attempting to interdict shipments that could contribute to proliferation activities.

NATO's ISAF mission in Afghanistan directly contributes to ensuring that terrorists can no longer operate there – but again, ISAF is a peacekeeping and stabilization mission. As a counterterrorist activity, it is a support mission, not one in which NATO is in the lead role. Many member states have individually contributed troops to the US-led coalition, but NATO's sole contribution to stabilizing Iraq has been the training of military officers.

What explains the apparent divergence between US activities and NATO actions? Two factors appear central to this: the chronic, yet growing capabilities gap, and the US's increasing rejection of alliance constraints.

The perennial frustration regarding NATO, from the US's perspective, is the difficulty of convincing its European allies to increase defense spending, and thus to improve capabilities. During the Cold War, NATO agreed that defense spending should be roughly 3 % of a state's GDP; today, the minimum spending level set by the alliance is 2 %. Yet only six NATO countries other than the US currently meet that threshold.[55] Furthermore, how this money is spent causes concern in Washington as well. Many states continue to expend much of their resources on manpower, rather than transforming their forces in ways the US hopes they will – and that NATO has agreed to. Some, like Greece and Turkey, still have military forces focused at least in part on one another. US concern with NATO defense spending is evident in the QDR, which notes that "in many European allied states, however, aging and shrinking populations are curbing defense spending on capabilities they need for conducting operations effectively alongside US forces".[56]

The disparity in alliance capabilities has been thrown into stark relief by the very fact that it became engaged in actual military missions rather than training exercise after 1994. As NATO has taken on new tasks, differences in capabilities have hindered the alliance's operational cooperation. Moreover, the willingness of its European members to address the capabilities gap appears limited; while states recognize the problem, defense spending and military transformation remain low domestic priorities in many states.

The US appears increasingly unwilling to be constrained by the principles guiding NATO military cooperation. While it places continued stress on the importance of the alliance, it seems equally clear that the US does not plan to work through the alliance to address central security problems, as noted earlier. Moreover, the US's focus has shifted, with greater attention given to the Middle East, Central Asia, and East Asia. This is evident in planned military redeployments from Europe; it is also clear in recent decisions by the State department to shift at least one hundred diplomatic positions from Europe to other regions, including Africa, South Asia, East Asia, and the Middle East.[57] This is a logical step, but telling of shifts in US policy priorities and focus.

While NATO's chief military officer stresses that NATO mechanisms and political consultation make it valuable, the US appears unwilling to rely on NATO in campaigns that relate directly to defense of the US. Not only do Pentagon leaders want to avoid the effort of working to build consensus within the Alliance, but they see it as compromising the mission and the safety of US forces. Moreover, some US government officials note that the Bush administration sees NATO as unreliable, because of the difficulty in gaining troop commitments from states in recent years; "we 'ad hoc' our way through coalitions of the willing. That's the future."[58]

To the degree that the major states in it do not seek to address their most urgent threats within the alliance framework, the alliance's survival as a military organization may be open to question. Nor can it easily evolve into a collective security arrangement, if key states such as the United States choose not to rely on its collective functions, and if core states do not seek to meet their defense needs through it. The alliance members' shared values may be sufficient to sustain NATO as an organization, assuming its political consultation and dialogue functions continue to thrive. NATO is likely also to remain a strong pull for others.

This raises several questions that deserve further attention. What should NATO's role be in confronting terror? US and European coop- eration against terrorists is substantial – it just is not happening in NATO. How problematic is it for the alliance if this mission occurs elsewhere, which appears to be the case? Second, are NATO's mem- bers prepared to accept more differentiation in their tasks? If the US continues to view terrorism primarily as a military struggle, this may be inevitable, but it is likely to increase strains within the alliance. To be sure, the US preference for unilateral actions or informal coalitions could change in 2009 when a new administration comes to power. Pentagon planning for military operations in the meantime may make it difficult to reorient US policies to operate jointly with its allies, however. Third, if its main states turn elsewhere to address their secu- rity concerns, and NATO's members fail sufficiently to address the growing gap in capabilities, the Alliance's operational capabilities will be constrained. But is a political function for the alliance sufficient to sustain it?

Clearly, the United States continues to value NATO. NATO is the central European forum in which the US has a seat, and it is actively pushing for NATO to be the locus of broader security discussions with Europe. Yet the US's commitment to working through the alliance to address some of its central security concerns is unclear.

Endnotes

[1] On the debate over NATO expansion, see J. M. Goldgeier, Not Whether but When: The US Decision to Enlarge NATO (Washington, D.C.: Brook- ings Institution Press, 1999); S. D. Yost, NATO Transformed: The Alliances New Roles in International Security (Washington, D.C.: US Institute of Peace, 1998). For a contrary view, see D. Reiter, Why NATO Enlargement Does Not Spread Democracy, International Security 25/4 (Spring 2001), pp. 41-67.

[2] To Paris, US Looks like a "Hyperpower", International Herald Tribune, February 5, 1999; S. J. Huntington, The Lonely Superpower, Foreign Affairs 78/2 (March/April 1999).

[3] G. H. Snyder, Alliance Politics (Ithaca, NY: Cornell University Press, 1997), p. 4.

[4] The Alliance's Secretary General, Jaap de Hoop Scheffer, uses this delineation of political and operational functions. J. de Hoop Scheffer, Speech at the 42nd Munich Conference on Security Policy, February 4, 2006, <Hhttp://www.securityconference.deH>, accessed March 16, 2006.

[5] The Alliance's Strategic Concept, April 24, 1999 <Hwww.nato.int/docu/pr/1999/p99-065e.htmH>.

[6] NATO Briefing: Response to Terrorism, March 2005, p. 2.

[7] NATO's Military Concept for Defence Against Terrorism, updated April 14, 2005, <www.nato.int/ims/docu/terrorism.htm>, accessed May 30, 2006.

[8] National Security Strategy, pp. 8-12.

[9] NATO's Military Concept for Defence Against Terrorism.

[10] National Security Strategy of the United States, March 2006, p. 46.

11 Ibid, p. 48.

[12] Quadrennial Defense Review Report, February 6, 2006, p. vii.

[13] J. Hulsman, Getting Real: An Unromantic Look at the NATO Alliance, The National Interest, 75 (Spring 2004), p. 68.

[14] Rumsfeld Touts Nontraditional Partnerships, New York Times, May 4, 2006.

[15] M. L. Amer, Membership of the 109th Congress: A Profile, Congressional Research Service Report RS22007, December 20, 2004.

[16] Congressman Bob Ney, who entered the House of Representatives in 1995, was behind the renaming of French fries as "freedom fries" in Congressional cafeterias in 2003, for example, and referred at the time to "our so-called ally, France"; US Congress opts for "freedom fries", BBC News, March 12, 2003 <Hwww.news.bbc.co.ukH>.

[17] Indeed, the US public as a whole has less understanding of NATO's value and contributions today. Jones, Testimony to the Senate Foreign Relations Committee.

[18] D. Linzer, The NSC's Sesame Street Generation, Washington Post, March 12, 2006.

[19] General J. L. Jones, Testimony to Senate Foreign Relations Committee, Feb. 7, 2006 <http://foreign.senate.gov/hearings/2006/hrg060207a.html>, accessed March 14, 2006.

[20] NATO Elevates Mediterranean Dialogue to a Genuine Partnership, Launches Istanbul Cooperation Initiative, June 29, 2004, <Hhttp://www.nato.int/docu/update/2004/06-june/e0629d.htmH>.

[21] R. Cesaretti, Combating terrorism in the Mediterranean, NATO Review (Autumn 2005), <Hwww.nato.intH>.

[22] Russia was unwilling to agree to this move unless it gained a greater decision-making role over the activity, which NATO was not willing to accept. V. Socor, Russians Not Joining NATO Operation Active Endeavor, Eurasia Daily Monitor 1/136 (November 30, 2004) <Hwww.jamestown.orgH>; Jones, Testimony to Senate Foreign Relations Committee; I. Torbakov, Turkey Sides with Moscow Against Washington on Black Sea Force, Eurasia Daily Monitor, 3/43 (March 3, 2006) <Hwww.jamestown.orgH>, accessed July 11, 2006.

[23] NATO looks to global partnerships, NATO Update, April 27, 2006, <Hwww.nato.int/docu/update/2006/04-april/e0427c.htmH>.

[24] D. S. Reveron, Old Allies, New Friends: Intelligence-Sharing in the War on Terror, Orbis 50/3 (Summer 2006), pp. 453-468.

[25] R. J. Aldrich, Transatlantic Intelligence and Security Cooperation, International Affairs 80/4 (2004), pp. 731-753.

[26] W. G. Boykin, Intelligence Support to Allied and Coalition Operations, 16th Annual SO/LIC Symposium: Strategic Environment for Coalition Warfare, February 3, 2005, <Hwww.dtic.mil/ndia/2005solic/2005solic.htmlH>; Aldrich (En. 25), p. 745.

[27] D. S. Yost, The NATO Capabilities Gap and the European Union, Survival 42/4 (Winter 2000-01), pp. 97-128.

[28] NATO Europe spends about $ 12 billion a year for research and development. Stephen J. Flanagan, Sustaining US-European Global Security Cooperation, Strategic Forum 217 (September 2005), pp. 1-6; Department of Defense Outlays by Title, Center for Strategic and Budgetary Assessments, <Hwww.CSBAonline.orgH> (accessed April 27, 2006); The Military Balance, 2005-2006, p. 101.

[29] This outcome was to some degree predicted by Yost, who argued that the US was not likely to "dumb down" its systems or turn down potential technological advances to ensure allied interoperability. Yost (En. 27), p. 105.

[30] Aldrich (En. 25), pp. 745-748.

[31] Lessons learned from Recent Terrorist Attacks: Building National Capabilities and Institutions, Chairman's Report, October 6, 2005, <http://www.nato.int/docu/conf/2005/050727/index.html>.

[32] UK-USA was established in 1947. Denmark, Norway, Turkey, and West Germany later joined the network. Reveron (En. 24), 460.

[33] Aldrich (En. 25), pp. 738-740.

[34] B. Drogin, German Spies Aided US Attempt to Kill Hussein in Aerial Attack, Los Angeles Times, January 12, 2006.

[35] Launch of the Intelligence Fusion Center in support of NATO, January 17, 2006, <http://www.nato.int/shape/news/2006/01/060117a.htm>.

[36] Global Partnership Annual Report, 2005 (London: 2005) <http://www.dti.gov.uk/energy/nuclear/fsu/GR2005.shtml>; Robin Niblett,

(ed.), Test of Will, Tests of Efficacy: Initiative for a Renewed Transatlantic Partnership, 2005 Report (Washington, D.C.: Center for Strategic and International Studies, 2005), pp. 25-31; Reducing Excess Stockpiles: Russian Plutonium Disposition, Nuclear Threat Initiative, <http://www.nti.org/ e_research/cnwm/reducing/rpdispose.asp>.

[37] It is worth noting that the French government supplied the CIA with contrary information from one of Hussein's Cabinet ministers, who was a French spy, but according to a former CIA official, "he said there were no weapons of mass destruction...so we didn't believe him.", Drogin (En. 34).

[38] E. R. Terzuolo, Combating WMD Proliferation, NATO Review (Autumn 2005).

[39] NATO Briefing: Response to Terrorism, p. 6.

[40] C. Brown and C. Chyba, Proliferation Rings: New Challenges to the Nuclear Nonproliferation Regime, International Security 29/2 (Fall 2004), pp. 5-49; A. Winner, The Proliferation Security Initiative: The New Face of Interdiction, Washington Quarterly, (Spring 2005), pp. 129-143; S. G. Rademaker, Proliferation Security Initiative: An Early Assessment, Hearing Before House International Relations Committee, 109th Congress, 1st Session, June 9, 2005 <http://wwwc.house.gov/international_relations/109/ 21699.pdf>.

[41] National Security Strategy, p. 46.

[42] B. Woodward, Bush at War (New York: Simon and Schuster, 2002), p. 81; T. Terrif, Fear and Loathing in NATO: The Atlantic Alliance After the Crisis over Iraq, Perspectives on European Politics and Society 5/3 (2004), p. 424; T. Valasek, NATO's New Roles: A Vision from Inside the Alliance, CDI Issue Brief, October 19, 2001 <www.cdi.org/terrorism/natio-pr.cfm>.

[43] P. van Ham, Growing Pains, NATO Review (Autumn 2005).

[44] On NATO's role, see <http://www.afnorth.nato.int/ISAF/index.htm>.

[45] While initially designated "provisional", these teams are now called Provincial Reconstruction Teams. R. Borders, Provincial Reconstruction Teams in Afghanistan: A Model for Post-Conflict Reconstruction and Development, Journal of Development and Social Transformation 1 (November 2004) <http://www.maxwell.syr.edu/moynihan/Programs/dev/journal.html>; NGO Concerns Regarding Deployment of US Military Provisional Reconstruction Teams, ACBAR Policy Brief, January 15, 2003 <http://www.care.org/ newsroom/specialreports/afghanistan/a_policypositions.asp> (accessed April 25, 2006).

[46] J. L. Jones, Prague to Istanbul: Ambition versus Reality, in Global Security: A Broader Concept for the 21st Century (Berlin Workshop proceedings, 7-10 May 2004), pp. 27-30; J. Banusiewicz, "National Caveats" Among Key Topics at NATO Meeting, American Forces Press Service, February 9, 2005 <www.defenselink.mil/new/Feb2005>.

[47] E. Schmitt, Springtime for Killing in Afghanistan, New York Times, May 28, 2006.

[48] A. A. Jalali, The Future of Afghanistan, Parameters (Spring 2006), pp. 4-19.

[49] Uncorrected Transcript of Minutes of Evidence, HC 558-ii Defence Committee, House of Commons, March 7, 2006 <www.publications. parliament.uk/pa/cm200506/cmselect/cmdfence/uc558-ii/uc55802>.

[50] Agreement for NATO to aid Turkey was reached in spite of French resistance by taking the decision to NATO's military committee, of which France is not a part. On Poland's request, see: NATO Council Makes Decision on Polish Request, May 21, 2003, <http://www.nato.int/docu/update/2003/05-may/e0521b.htm>.

[51] To be sure, some of these troop contributions are quite small. States contributing include the United Kingdom, Poland, Romania, Bulgaria, Denmark, Estonia, Hungary, Italy, Latvia, Lithuania, Norway, the Czech Republic, the Netherlands, Slovakia, and Spain.

[52] L. H. Daalder and J. M. Lindsay, America Unbound: The Bush Revolution in Foreign Policy (Washington, D.C.: Brookings Institution Press, p. 190.

[53] R. Lynch and P. D. Janzen, NATO Training Mission-Iraq: Looking to the Future, Joint Forces Quarterly, 40/1, (2006), pp. 32-34. The funding problem is not unique to this mission; the NATO Response Force (NRF) has been referred to as a "reverse lottery" because troop contributing nations must bear all the costs. de Hoop Scheffer, Speech at the 42nd Munich Conference on Security Policy; see also Jones, Testimony to Senate Foreign Relations Committee.

[54] de Hoop Scheffer (En. 53).

[55] D.H. Rumsfeld, Speech at the 42nd Munich Conference on Security Policy," February 4, 2006 <www.securityconference.de>.

56 Quadrennial Defense Review, p. 88.

57 Transformational Diplomacy, January 18, 2006, <www.state.gov/r/pa/prs/ps/2006/59339.htm>.

[58] G. Dinmore, US Sees Coalitions of the Willing as Best Ally, Financial Times, January 4, 2006.

3

The United States Policy of Non-Proliferation of Nuclear Weapons in the Age of the War on Terror

Adrian Zdrada

The United States has always regarded the proliferation of nuclear weapons as a serious threat to the stability of the international system, and a threat to US security. In 1945, the United States believed it could remain the only state with a nuclear bomb for as long as possible. The construction by the Soviet Union of its bomb in 1949 altered the situation in strategic terms, and marked the emergence of the bipolar world, which decisively limited the options for exerting pressure on the Soviet Union which, in turn, substantially impacted the shape of the emerging non-proliferation system.

In order to enhance the security of their key ally in Europe and unwilling to deprive them of one of the key attributes of a superpower, the Truman administration agreed to the transfer of American technologies (British scientists had already worked on the Manhattan Project), thus helping the United Kingdom to achieve, in 1953, the status of the world's third superpower with the nuclear bomb in their arsenal. This was practically the only case when an American administration considered proliferation of nuclear weapons to be in the best interest of the United States.

France's accession to this exclusive club, following their first nuclear weapons test in 1960, met with sweeping criticism from the American administration. At the meeting of the North Atlantic Council in 1962, the then US secretary of defense, Robert McNamara, expressed his doubts as to the benefits for Europe from the existence of the French nuclear arsenal independently of NATO. The discord between France and the United States over this issue led to France's withdrawal from the military structures of the Alliance.

In the same year in which the French were launching their first nuclear tests in a deserted area in Algeria, the world found out about the presence of the Israeli nuclear reactor at Dimona in the Negev desert. The news, confirmed by David Ben Gurion, the Israeli Prime Minister of the day, led to the deterioration of relations between the US and Israel, despite Israeli assurances of the peaceful application of their nuclear installations. The attitude of the United States towards Israel and the Israeli nuclear program changed substantially only towards the end of the decade. Despite the fact that the US was later repeatedly defending Israel in the international forum against accusations of running a secret nuclear program, the US was actually deeply skeptical and concerned when the program was launched.

In 1963, president John F. Kennedy made an anxious statement that there might be between 15 and as many as 20 nuclear superpowers within the next ten years.[1] A year later, in 1964, the People's Republic of China carried out its first nuclear test, soon becoming the second communist state with nuclear weapons in their possession.

Nuclear Non-Proliferation Treaty of 1968

As the NPT regime is currently the most important agreement on non-proliferation of nuclear weapons in the world, and it is in the context of this framework that the current US policy is dealt with below, it is reasonable to present the key principles of the Treaty on the Non-Proliferation of Nuclear Weapons.

Although the United States feared the proliferation of nuclear technologies, actions to counter that threat followed cold war logic. Attempts to establish a non-proliferation regime were often looked at in the US as a threat to their ability to defend its interests and ensure security for its allies. At the same time, the regime could strengthen the capabilities of its adversaries. Following many years of negotiations and talks, both between the United States and the Soviet Union, and under the auspices of the United Nations, the parties finally arrived at an agreement that protected the interests of both superpowers, and the states without nuclear technologies in their possession. In 1968, the Treaty on the Non-proliferation of Nuclear Weapons was signed. Initially, the treaty was ratified by the United States, Great Britain and the Soviet Union – states officially considered to be nuclear superpowers. Despite their tests with nuclear weapons prior to 1967, France and China did not sign the agreement but joined the NPT only in 1992. Three years later, in 1995, states-signatories to the treaty decided to extend the Treaty indefinitely. Currently, it covers 187 states. Outside the Treaty remain Israel, India, Pakistan (these have declined to sign it) and North Korea (withdrew from the NPT regime in 2003).

The treaty provides that proliferation of weapons and technologies that enable the production of nuclear weapons outside the five officially confirmed nuclear superpowers, threatens security and stability of the international system. Therefore, the treaty requires those states not to transfer such weapons and technologies to the remaining parties to the treaty. It is further stated that the very existence of nuclear weapons poses a problem. Consequently, article VI of the NPT indicates that all the existing stockpiles should be liquidated, arguing that "only a complete elimination of nuclear weapons is the absolute guarantee that they will not be used". In May 2000, the United States, in conjunction with all other nuclear superpowers, confirmed their intent to liquidate their nuclear stockpiles.[2]

Non-nuclear states may not engage in any actions to obtain nuclear weapons. Simultaneously, the treaty prohibits the use of nuclear weapons against a non-nuclear state, unless the latter attacks the nuclear state in alliance with another nuclear state. In return for their waiver of the right to carry out their own nuclear programs, non-nuclear states were promised to help in obtaining and harnessing nuclear technologies for civilian purposes. The compliance with the provisions of the Treaty was to be supervised by the International Atomic Energy Agency (IAEA).

As pointed out by Michael Ruhle, the NPT had several weaknesses from the very beginning. Firstly, IAEA did not have the right to impose any sanctions in case that infringement on the provisions of the Treaty was identified. Secondly, a rigid division into atomic and non-atomic states led to the situation where, over time, some states of the latter group might want to joint the exclusive club of nuclear super-powers, justifying their actions e. g. by non-compliance of nuclear states with the requirements of Article VI on the general and complete disarmament and liquidation of nuclear arsenals. And finally, the Treaty offers to each state the right to launch a civilian nuclear program. Considering that the differences between civilian and military technologies are negligible, this may lead to a situation where a non-atomic state, without infringing on the Treaty provisions, takes its civilian program to the stage where the transfer to the nuclear weapons production is a fairly easy task. Even more worryingly, the last stage would not be too time-consuming.[3]

Despite the deficiencies of the NPT regime referred to above, the NPT system prevented the proliferation of nuclear weapons until the 1990s. In 1994, the United States still managed to freeze North Korea's military nuclear program, proving the effectiveness of the NPT, while in 1998 the treaty proved totally useless in terms of preventing the non-proliferation of nuclear weapons, with test explosions carried out by two states that were not signatories to the NPT, namely India and Pakistan. The events made the international community, including the United States, aware that the NPT regime could not effectively protect the world against the proliferation of military nuclear technologies. The withdrawal of North Korea from the NPT in 2003, and the subsequent nuclear tests run by the state in 2006, were distinct proofs that even the state with a past record of the Treaty signatory may want to pursue their nuclear ambitions and, in this specific case, the mechanisms intended to prevent the establishment of a military nuclear program in North Korea failed. The weakness of the non-proliferation system became evident for the United States already several years earlier. With the terrorist attacks of September 11, a new, horrifying threat emerged, namely nuclear weapons in terrorists' hands.

Impact of 9/11 Attacks on the Change of US Policy for Nuclear Weapons Non-Proliferation

The terrorist attacks of September 11, 2001, dramatically changed the perceptions in the US of threats resulting from the proliferation of weapons of mass destruction. What seemed an unlikely scenario in the 1990s, suddenly turned out to be a primary threat. G. W. Bush argues that there is an inextricable link between proliferation and the emergence of terrorist organizations and groups of states that support them, which openly threaten to attack the US with weapons of mass destruction. In both US national security strategies published after 9/11, the acquisition by terrorist groups of WMD, including nuclear weapons, is considered as one of the key threats. As argued in the US National Security Strategy of 2006, "the proliferation of nuclear weapons poses the greatest threat to our national security. Nuclear weapons are unique in their capacity to inflict loss of life on a massive scale"[4]. To prevent the proliferation of weapons of mass destruction became one of the key tasks in the war on terror. As a consequence, an entirely new approach to the issue of non-proliferation emerged.

First and foremost, the solutions and ways of dealing with the problem of proliferation employed so far, including the NPT regime, made an implicit assumption concerning the presence of reasonable actors, that is states. The deterrence policy was working, as no leader of any state in the world would decide to use weapons of mass destruction to attack the United States as they knew the consequence would be almost immediate annihilation of their country, following American retaliation. Terrorist organizations do not fear that.

Secondly, the NPT implies that states are responsible for the proliferation of nuclear technologies. The development of communication technologies and effortless mobility of scientists has led to an increased threat that there might be an information leak from a group of scientists, or even isolated individuals, that enables the development of military nuclear programs. A long list of Russian scientists who sold their expertise following the collapse of the Soviet Union in the international free market, or the case of A. Q. Khan, one of the masterminds behind the Pakistani atomic bomb, who was selling his knowledge in Iran, North Korea and several other states, are all good examples of what the problem is about. Although it actually originated prior to 9/11 atrocities, it is those terrorist attacks on New York and Pentagon that made American authorities aware how dangerous this may become. Under the circumstances where terrorist organizations, such as Al Qaeda, have massive funds at their disposal, it is only a matter of time when they get hold of weapons of mass destruction. This may pose a threat to the US and its allies, limited as it is, because primitive, "dirty" bombs would probably be used in the attack. However, the rise to power in Pakistan of radical groups, hostile to the US, with all the state's arsenals and means for carrying nuclear weapons, could have dire consequences.

Finally, states referred to by the United States as "rogue", which support terrorism, as e. g. Iran, can develop their civilian nuclear program without being questioned and, as already mentioned, a full nuclear cycle and production of nuclear weapons is only one step away from that point. The existing NPT control mechanisms do not allow detection of such actions, however, it is up to the UN Security Council to decide whether specific actions are legal and, if not, to take steps to enforce the cessation of such action. And here, as the very case of Iran goes on to prove, there is no agreement on the level of threat that the existence of the Iranian nuclear program poses. What is viewed by the United States as one of the most important challenges to their security, calling for steadfast actions, is looked at by the remaining members of the Security Council as a problem that does not require radical solutions. As pointed out by Michael Ruhle, "being an important crude oil supplier for China and a close trade partner for Russia, Iran feels protected to the extent that the employment of any far-reaching tools of pressure seems unlikely."[5]

Fully aware of not only the new threats, but also of their asymmetrical perceptions in the Security Council, the G. W. Bush administration was in a way forced to reformulate the policy of the United States towards the issue of WMD proliferation. The existing NPT regime continues to be its important element, as it enables, owing to the system of controls in states-signatories, better identification of threats. However, it does not counterbalance the fact that following September 11, 2001, the US deems the NPT regime insufficient, or even ineffective tool for fighting the threats of nuclear weapons proliferation. The inability to reach an agreement on the final document of the NPT Review Conference proved that these concerns were well-founded.[6] As a result, the United States undertook a series of actions, independently, or within the "coalition of the willing", which were to minimize the risk of the "worst weapons being in the hands of the worst people".

In the Strategy for Winning the War on Terror, published in 2006, the Bush administration sets out a number of objectives which, when pursued simultaneously, are to minimize the risk of acquiring and using nuclear weapons by terrorists and rogue states. First and foremost, intentions of terrorist organizations and capabilities to implement them should be determined as early as possible. This translates into the necessity to intensify intelligence actions and find methods for the verification of the collected data. Secondly, access to fission materials, to research funding and to the know-how required to produce the nuclear bombs should be limited. Thirdly, it is necessary to deter terrorists and states that support them from using weapons of mass destruction, including nuclear weapons. The strategy indicates that traditional deterrence methods that were working for states, might not work for terrorist groups, although it mentions an "overwhelming response" directed at state sponsors of the organization that launches such an attack. Fourthly, the strategy emphasizes the need to stop the attempts to smuggle nuclear weapons, and all their components, and to track the movement of individuals who might sell information on how to produce nuclear weapons. And finally, a program of coordinated actions within the country is necessary, in order to minimize the effects of a potential attack.[7]

The Strategy provides that such actions should proceed in cooperation with the international community. However, considering the differences in the perception of threats between the United States and the majority of other states, some of the suggested actions will be taken by the United States only. What was, until recently, the task of the international non-proliferation regime, is now something that the present US administration wants to be able to do on its own. Distrustful of the present regime, President Bush wants to build a proprietary non-proliferation system. The system is based on strengthening the deterrence potential by expanding the US nuclear arsenal, coordinating actions to prevent proliferation within the "coalition of the willing" and finally by implementing the policy of reward for reliable and predictable states outside the NPT system, the cooperation with which is beneficial for the American interests (India or Pakistan), and by isolating or threatening the states that run their own nuclear projects and are considered by the Bush administration as unstable or rogue.

Maintaining the Strategic Edge

The first component of the American strategy to counter shortcomings of the present non-proliferation system is the principle of maintaining the arsenal that would ensure the strategic edge over the remaining states that have nuclear weapons at their disposal. The George W. Bush administration is fundamentally rejecting the concept of qualitative reduction (getting rid of outdated weapons systems is possible, on the condition that they are replaced by more modern and reliable systems), or elimination of nuclear weapons from their arsenal. Article VI of the Treaty on nuclear weapons non-proliferation, which requires nuclear superpowers to engage in negotiations ultimately leading to the elimination of all atomic weapons, has always been a defunct provision. Not only is the United States unwilling to weaken their nuclear powers, but works to modernize its weapons and reinforce its absolute advantage in this respect over other states. The idea is that only the continuous upgrade of atomic weapons is able to ensure security to the United States in a situation where an existing nuclear superpower, currently friendly or neutral to the US, becomes a threat. This line of thinking, prevailing among representatives of the Bush administration, explains why the politicians of the Republican Party and the president himself are not satisfied with Comprehensive Test Ban Treaty (CTBT), and why the missile defense system received such an overwhelming support from them.

The CTBT was signed by President Bill Clinton two weeks after it had been received by the UN General Assembly in September 1996. Clinton called this treaty "the longest sought, the hardest fought prize in the history of arms control".[8] It was to prevent any tests and thus automatically lead to the liquidation of the present nuclear stockpiles in the longer run (without modifications, after some time they would become useless), and prevention of the new ones from emerging (test explosions are the necessary stage of the atomic bomb construction process). The treaty, however, has never been ratified. During the voting in the Senate, 51 senators of the Republican Party rejected it, considering the controls contained in the treaty unreliable, and the treaty itself excessively limiting the freedom of the United States to act. President George W. Bush ruled out the possibility of the repeated submission of the Treaty for ratification in the Senate altogether. In January 2002, representatives of the Department of Defense issued a memo, where they applied for the withdrawal of the American signature from the Treaty. Officials of the National Security Council have not found this proposal worth examining by the president, and the United States are still a signatory to CTBT.[9]

In 1992, the United States introduced a unilateral ban on nuclear weapons tests, arguing that they are able to test new solutions only on the basis of computer simulations. If needed, however, the United States will be able to come back to the real tests. This position of the present American administration enables tests on new types of nuclear weapons, such as tactical nuclear weapons that can destroy underground bunkers. The progress of work on this type of weapons is recommended by the Nuclear Posture Review, published in 2002. Although the political cost of using nuclear weapons on the battlefield would probably be too high, the existence of this type of weapons is to deter leaders of rogue states, or terrorist organizations, making them aware that they are not able to flee from the American retaliatory response. It should also be noted that the threat of using nuclear weapons against the states that do not possess them (e. g. Iran) is a departure from the principle set forth in the Treaty on nuclear weapons nonproliferation.

The program for the strategic missile defense is definitely an inherent part of the new non-proliferation concept, based on the principle of maintaining the edge over all other nuclear states. The United States had supported a similar system even before George W. Bush assumed his presidential duties, although it was this president who withdrew from the ABM Treaty in 2002, opening up the avenue for the United States to develop their system of territorial defense against ballistic missiles in a legal manner. The terrorist attacks of September 11 were yet another proof for the Bush administration that the establishment of the system in the age of potential nuclear terrorism is necessary.

The primary task for the system is to defend the territory against individual ballistic missiles fired by rogue states. The location for the intercepting missiles launcher seems to corroborate this. Both existing launcher facilities are located at the western coast of the United States and are there to intercept missiles fired by North Korea. The planned third element of the system, that is the radar and the interceptors base, is to be located in Europe (negotiations on the issue with Poland and the Czech Republic are currently in progress). This part of the system would be responsible for intercepting missiles fired from the Middle East, most likely Iran, in the direction of the American East Coast.

Undoubtedly, the system, when and if it already exists and works properly, could be regarded as a significant deterrent. Even the most insane state leader would not decide to launch a ballistic missile with the nuclear weapon knowing that the missile will be destroyed en route and the United States, thanks to their reconnaissance satellites, will be able to determine quickly where the missile was launched from, and proceed to the overwhelming retaliatory response.

An effective missile defense system would also pose a challenge to nuclear superpowers, whose nuclear stockpiles are bigger than those in North Korea, as the defense system would give the United States the edge over such superpowers. Theoretically, we can imagine that the US executes a massive nuclear attack on Russia using low-level strategic bombers and submarines. The attack, practically undetectable for the Russian radars, would enable the annihilation of virtually all Russian nuclear weapons already with the first attack.[10] The potential response from Russia would be intercepted by the extensive missile defense system, which would enable the US to leave the confrontation without any civilian casualties. The same operation targeted at China would be even simpler as China has only 18 ballistic missiles at their disposal located in silos and fails to possess any submarines with nuclear weapons carrying capacity, or strategic aircraft capable of bombing American targets in response.[11]

Obviously, the scenarios could not be taken seriously by anyone at the moment. The United States does not have any reason to launch such attacks. Still, this goes on to prove that the American nuclear potential is continuously modified and developed, and to deter rogue states is only a marginal objective of these developmental actions. The establishment of the missile defense system may have different objectives to it, with only one being declared officially. Regarded both as the defensive weapon but, in specific cases, also as offensive weapon, the system is to act as deterrent for all states that could threaten the US security. The missile defense is to be a type of insurance policy in the case that the "good guys" suddenly join the "bad guys".

"Democratic Bomb" Strategy

The statement on deeper cooperation between the US and India in the area of civilian nuclear technologies, issued during the visit of India's Prime Minister Manmohad Singh in Washington in July 2005, marked the launch of the second component of the American non-proliferation strategy, since the agreement with India is the first one entered into with a state that is not a party to the NPT and, implicitly, the Bush administration thus authorizes the existence of nuclear superpowers beyond the NPT regime. The United States has arrived at the conclusion that it is more beneficial for its security to enter into bilateral cooperation with India than to leave the state in an atomic "grey zone".[12] India has announced tighter controls of the fission materials and nuclear technologies. The agreement also provides for subjecting the civilian part of Indian nuclear installations to international control procedures. During Bush's visit to New Delhi in March 2006, details of the agreement were worked out, and the deal was ratified by the Senate of the United States in July 2006. The agreement provides for IAEA controls in 14 out of 22 Indian nuclear installations.[13]

The policy towards India, called by George Perkovich the strategy of the "democratic bomb"[14], represents yet another serious modification of the US non-proliferation position following September 11, since the NPT regime allows cooperation in terms of civilian nuclear installations only with those countries that fail to have nuclear weapons and have declared abstention from such projects. In practice, this departure from the rule undermines the foundations of the present regime. The US has finally decided that the risk of selling fission materials and nuclear technologies, which could end up in the hands of terrorist groups, is too high. Therefore, the Bush administration decided to move away from sanction, towards incentive and cooperation. To take this decision was much easier, as India is a democratic country whose stability and credibility is not questioned by Washington.

A similar, consenting attitude the United States applies to the nuclear program of another non-signatory of the Treaty on nuclear weapons non-proliferation. Still officially unconfirmed by Israel's authorities, but commonly regarded as an open secret, the fact of possessing nuclear weapons by this country posed a problem for the United States only at the beginning stages of development of the Israeli arsenal. However, from the end of the sixties until today, the United States has not only failed to exert pressure on Israel to resign or submit their nuclear installations to international control, but have also consistently defended the Jewish State in the various international forums against all attempts to impose sanctions to force Israel to cooperate in this respect.

Possibly, Australia may also join the group of states for which the United States will make an exception and provide the technologies for uranium enrichment. The Australian government expressed their interest in this type of cooperation and launch of production, both for exports and to be used in the future reactors in Australia. According to a representative of the Bush administration, this should not pose any problems. "Australia is viewed as a totally reliable and trustworthy country, so I don't think there is any issue whatsoever".[15]

Undeniably, the US realizes that making exceptions for India or Australia, and simultaneously demanding tough sanctions for the same activity to be imposed on Iran, may be viewed as hypocritical. Nicholas Burns, the American undersecretary of state, put it this way: "If people are bothered by double standards in the world, they happen all the time. We treat law-abiding democratic countries that are friends of ours differently than law-breaking authoritarian governments".[16] This statement illustrates the essence of the problem. For the United States, proliferation of nuclear technologies is not a threat in itself anymore. As long as the states that have them, or aspire to have them, are stable and reliable democracies and allies of the Unites States, the Bush administration is willing to bend international laws or bypass obligations under the Treaty on non-proliferation of nuclear weapons.

It should be pointed out that Pakistan, a close ally of the US in their war on terror, cannot count on treatment like this yet. The US tolerates Pakistan's nuclear arsenal since it does not have instruments to change the present state of affairs, and imposing sanctions could weaken the position of President Musharaff who remains the warrant of Pakistan's favorable attitude towards American operations against the Taliban in Afghanistan. However, a relatively unstable situation in

Pakistan, and the consequent significant risk of power in Islamabad being taken over by forces hostile to the United States, not even mentioning the non-democratic nature of Musharaff's government, excludes Pakistan from a group of states that the US wants to cooperate with in the area of civilian nuclear programs.[17]

Policy Towards "Rogue States"

Pakistan's nuclear installations are tolerated by Washington, yet the accession of North Korea to the group of nuclear states or the Iranian program for uranium enrichment are treated as key threats to the security of the United States. What is more, it is a threat that the present non-proliferation regime cannot prevent. Representatives of the Bush administration have repeatedly been saying that "they will not tolerate Iran's production of nuclear weapons". Therefore, the US attempt to take advantage of all available tools of pressure on authoritarian governments to prevent the situation where they actually do acquire such weapons. The 2002 US National Security Strategy provides for the rule of pre-emptive attacks as a tool that protects the United States against effects of weapons of mass destruction proliferation, including nuclear weapons. A year later, in March 2003, the United States attacked the Iraqi regime. One of the main reasons behind the intervention was, according to the representatives of the Bush administration, Saddam Hussein's threat to use weapons of mass destruction and a significant risk of the Iraqi actually producing the nuclear bomb.

The very principle of a pre-emptive attack in case of a direct threat is not new to the American strategy and, in the context of weapons of mass destruction, was already employed, also by the Clinton administration (e. g. missile attack on a pharmaceutical plant in the Sudan in 1998, where, based on intelligence, chemical weapons were produced). However, what generates concerns of the international community is that it comes so easy for the Bush administration to say that a particular government poses the threat, and to threaten them with the use of military force even if not all diplomatic tools provided for in international laws have been exhausted. As rightly argued by Lee Feinstein and Anne-Marie Slaughter, the real possibility of using force is often the decisive factor that determines the success of diplomatic actions, such as enforcing inspections to monitor nuclear installations.[18]

In the case of two regimes, regarded as the most serious threat from the standpoint of non-proliferation of nuclear weapons, that is North Korea and Iran, the Bush administration is still attempting not to refer to the necessity of resorting to the ultimate tool of pressure that a military attack is, trying to counter proliferation practices by using sanctions and threats of isolation towards those states. It should be pointed out here that currently the US is much less inclined to act unilaterally, and increasingly often use the mechanisms of multilateral diplomacy, including those established by the NPT regime.

In the case of North Korea, despite the fact that it left the NPT in 2003, diplomatic efforts finally appear to bear more fruit. The agreement signed in February 2007 within the framework of sixlateral negotiations offers hope that the works on the Korean nuclear program will be frozen and the Korean Peninsula will, in the future, be totally free of nuclear weapons. Undeniably, the nuclear test, carried out by the government in Pyongyang in autumn 2006, had big impact on the US position (Bush's consent to bilateral negotiations, which has been the condition for joining the negotiations table by North Koreans). The main reason, however, seems to be the intent to stabilize the situation on the Korean Peninsula, and focus on the emerging threat from Iran.[19]

The case of North Korea is another proof of the NPT system's weaknesses as seen by the Bush administration. The government in Pyongyang, intending to implement their nuclear program without submitting it for international inspections, initially decided not to let IAEA inspectors into their nuclear installations, and subsequently quit the Treaty on the non-proliferation of nuclear weapons altogether. Outside the NPT, no inspections are threatening North Korea. The easy exit from the NPT regime materially undermines the ability to exert pressure by the international community on the states determined in their actions to become nuclear states.

From the perspective of both the US security and the international system of non-proliferation, an even bigger challenge is the Iranian nuclear program. Iranian authorities claim that the program for uranium enrichment serves civilian purposes (ensures independence of fuel sources for Iranian reactors) and, as such, is compliant with international laws, specifically Article IV of the NPT. The article allows non-nuclear states to produce less-enriched uranium to be used as fuel in light water reactors. The same process of uranium enrichment may also be used to produce the highly-enriched uranium (HEU), used to produce nuclear weapons. In addition, some research reactors require small quantities of HEU as fuel. The definite determination of the nature of the Iranian nuclear program is, therefore, extremely difficult.[20]

The United States, failing to believe in the assurances from the government in Teheran of the peaceful nature of the Iranian nuclear program, unilaterally imposed a number of sanctions on Iran. Simultaneously, the US strives to enforce Iran's isolation on the international stage. For a short while, it seemed that the problem might be solved within the framework of negotiations carried out by European states, namely the United Kingdom, France and Germany who, in 2005, received support for their actions from the United States. Iran, however, refused the proposal from the E-3 states. In the face of fiasco of the talks, the European states joined the US and are now opting for more stringent sanctions on Iran. In 2006, two resolutions of the UN Security Council were adopted that order Iran to stop the works which enable the full fuel cycle, but Iran refused to comply with those resolutions, still maintaining that the program is used for civilian purposes, and that it complies with the arrangements under NPT.[21] Under these circumstances, we should expect another resolution by UN Security Council, calling upon Iran again to stop the threatening component of their nuclear program. However, given the reluctance of Russia and China to adopt any determined steps, there are doubts as to the effectiveness of diplomatic actions.

The US is convinced that Iran must be forced to stop their nuclear program, and they will strive to implement the policy of pressure and sanctions along with a group of states within a "coalition of the willing". If their actions fail, the US will probably decide to launch a military operation, intended to liquidate the Iranian nuclear installations. Although the last scenario should be treated as the last resort, it would comply with the doctrine of a pre-emptive attack under the US national security strategy. Iran in possession of nuclear weapons would represent a significant threat both to the US allies in the region (Israel) and, in the time frame of a dozen or so years, also for the United States itself.

Establishment of International Systems for Non-Proliferation Outside of the NPT

The third component of the American strategy for preventing the proliferation of nuclear technologies is the establishment of international cooperation on projects that are to supplement the mechanisms designed by the authors of the Treaty on the non-proliferation of nuclear weapons. The best example of such actions is the Proliferation Security Initiative (PSI). It aims at coordinating the actions of a group of states that join the initiative voluntarily in order to intercept shipments with weapons of mass destructions as well as with means to carry them and the components required for their production. The operations of this type are planned to take place both at sea, in the air and on the ground. So far some 80 states joined the initiative (exact listings are unknown). We know that 19 states, including Poland, are actively participating in PSI operations. The cooperation of the remaining states is of significant importance owing to the sensitive status of some operations, such as searching and seizing goods at sea, where vessels are only bound by the laws of the state in which they are registered. That is why the United States has entered into agreements with "flag of convenience" countries, such as Panama, Belize, Marshall Islands, Liberia, Cyprus or Croatia. This allows them to inspect vessels registered in those countries without infringing on the sea laws.

It appears that the Initiative does serve its purpose and contributes to limiting the proliferation of weapons of mass destruction. The majority of operations under the Initiative are secret, since intelligence must be used. However, a few successful missions have been made public. Among them, there are the 2002 seizure of a North-Korean ship with Scud missiles, heading for Yemen, or the takeover of uranium-enrichment centrifuges en route to Libya in 2003.[22]

Undeniably, the efficiency of the Initiative is undermined by the fact that China and South Korea failed to accede, fearing deteriorating relations with North Korea. If they did accede, this would enable checks on North Korean ships right after they leave their ports, in territorial waters of any of the states. North Korea remains to be one of the states that are most often accused of proliferation of WMD and technologies that enable their production. This example shows a weakness in universal agreements that states participate in based on the "coalition of the willing" principle. On the other hand, it seems that the results of the cooperation have surpassed the expectations of its authors.

Yet another project to supplement the NPT regime is the G-8 Global Partnership Against the Spread of Weapons and Materials of Mass Destruction, announced in 2002 at the G-8 meeting in Kananaskis Canada. A continuation of the Nunn-Lugar program (dealing with the proliferation problem in the Russian Federation), the Global Partnership aims at limiting the proliferation of WMD globally. The task of the initiative is to enable efficient controls over nuclear stockpiles, prevent smuggling, help states with WMDs to maintain control over the export of materials that can be used to produce weapons of mass destruction, as well as to intensify efforts aimed at elimination of superfluous from the defense perspective, fission materials. For that purpose, the US earmarked 10 billion US Dollars, while the rest of G-8 states threw in additional 10 billion US Dollars.[23] Until 2005, 13 states joined the Partnership, next to the initiating group and the European Commission. One of the main receivers of aid, next to Russia, is also Ukraine.[24]

The development of both projects indicates that we could expect more American projects that will strengthen the potential in terms of limiting the proliferation of weapons of mass destruction, including nuclear weapons, without the necessity to abide by rigid regulations that usually accompany multilateral agreements entered into under the aegis of the United Nations.

Conclusions

Following the 9/11 events, the United States has been more than ever interested in stopping the proliferation of weapons of mass destruction, including nuclear weapons. Stating that the possession of those weapons by rouge states and terrorist organizations poses one of the most serious threats to state security, the Bush administration firmly took actions to implement the new strategy for non-proliferation of nuclear weapons. Wherever possible, the US uses the existing non-proliferation regimes, including the mechanisms of the

Treaty on the non-proliferation of nuclear weapons of 1968. President Bush stated, however, that the NPT does not offer sufficient controls in the age of the "war on terror", and therefore embarked on additional actions to ensure security for the US. The new strategy relies on three key principles:

– Firstly, the existing nuclear arsenal should be strengthened and modified, so that the strategic edge over the remaining nuclear states is retained.

– Secondly, the problem to be solved is that of the nuclear states that are not parties to the NPT, or all other states that do not comply with the provisions of the Treaty. To that end, the Bush administration divided the states into two groups – good and bad. The "good" states, in the context of non-proliferation, are stable democracies, where nuclear programs or ambitions do not pose a threat to the US security. President Bush decided that it would be more proper to cooperate with them, even if it defies the provisions of the NPT, than to leave them in a nuclear "grey zone". India is an example of such a state. Another example is Israel, but with this state the circumstances are different, owing to no official confirmation of actually possessing nuclear weapons by Israel. The group of the "bad" states primarily includes Iran and North Korea. Regarding Iran all means, including military force, should be employed in order not to allow the government in Teheran to acquire nuclear weapons. In the case of North Korea, which already has that weapon, tools should be used to liquidate the Korean nuclear program and destroy the already existing nuclear arsenal.

– Thirdly, the US decided to supplement the NPT mechanisms with the various bilateral and multilateral agreements, such as the PSI or the Global Partnership against the proliferation of weapons and materials of mass destruction that contribute to enhanced state security, without restricting the scope of actions taken by the United States.

We should expect that in the future the United States will increasingly more often rely on this flexible strategy, which allows speedy response to the existing and emerging threats, rather than on universalistic agreements such as the NPT. This does not mean that the US will discard the NPT provisions altogether, although they will comply with their provisions in a way that maximizes their security, even at the expense of the letter of the law. This implies a peculiar "*a la carte*" non-proliferation strategy on which the international community will have little impact on. Obviously, the US realizes that it is not possible to counter the proliferation of nuclear weapons by acting unilaterally. Therefore, they will develop initiatives based on the "coalition of the willing" principle which will protect American interests more effectively, and, first and foremost, will be free of limitations derived from the requirement to consult actions within the UN Security Council.

Endnotes

[1] M. Ruhle, Order and Disorder in the Second Nuclear Age, Internationale Politik – Transatlantic Edition 7, No. 4 (2006), p. 19.

[2] G. Perkovich, Bush's Nuclear Revolution: A Regime Change in Nonproliferation, Foreign Affairs 82, No. 2 (2003), p. 3.

[3] M. Ruhle 2006 (En. 1), p. 20.

[4] The National Security Strategy (Washington D.C.: The White House, March 2006), p. 19 <http://www.whitehouse.gov/nsc/nss/2006/>.

[5] M. Ruhle 2006 (En. 1), p. 23.

[6] More on the NPT Review Conference of 2005 in A. Hrynkiewicz-Żabicki, Traktat o nierozprzestrzenianiu broni jądrowej, in L. Kościuk (ed.), Przegląd Światowego Procesu Rozbrojeniowego 2004/2005 rok (Szczecin: P.P.H. Zapol Dmochowski, Sobczyk spółka jawna, , 2006), p. 64-73.

[7] Strategy for Winning the War on Terror, The White House, Nacional Security Council, September 2006, <http://www.whitehouse.gov/nsc/nsct/2006/sectionV.html#wmd>.

[8] Quote from T. Graham Jr. and D. J. LaVera, Nuclear Weapons: the Comprehensive Test Ban Treaty and National Missile Defense, in S. Patrick and S. Forman (ed.), Multilateralism and U.S. Foreign Policy: Ambivalent Engagement (Boulder, Colorado: Lynne Rienner Publishers, 2002), p. 232.

[9] D. G. Kimball, The Status of CTBT Entry Into Force: the United States, VERTIC Seminar on the Comprehensive Test Ban Treaty on the Occasion of The Forth Article, XIV Conference on Accelerating Entry Into Force, New York, 22 September 2005.

[10] The description of the operation and analysis of the effects are presented in K. A. Lieber and D. G. Press, The Rise of U.S. Nuclear Primacy, Foreign Affairs 85, No. 2 (2006), p. 48.

[11] K. A. Lieber and D. G. Press 2006 (En. 10), p. 49-50.

[12] More on the cooperation of the United States with India in A..Zdrada, Polityka Stanów Zjednoczonych wobec Indii, Biuletyn (PISM), No. 68 (313) of 27 September 2005.

[13] US and India seal nuclear accord, BBC, 2 March 2006 <Hhttp://news.bbc.co.uk/2/hi/south_asia/4764826.stmH>.

[14] G. Perkovich, "Democratic Bomb" Failed Strategy, Policy Brief, Carnegie Endowment for International Peace, Washington D.C., November 2006.

[15] G. Perkovich 2006 (En. 14), "Democratic Bomb" Failed Strategy.

[16] G. Perkovich 2006 (En. 14), p. 2.

[17] More on relations between America and Pakistan in: A. Zdrada, Rola Pakistanu w amerykańskiej „wojnie z terroryzmem, Biuletyn (PISM), No. 59 (399) of 6 October 2006.

[18] L. Feinstein and A.-M. Slaughter, A Duty to Prevent, Foreign Affairs 83, No. 1 (2004), p. 142.

[19] Ł. Kulesa, Perspektywy zakończenia północnokoreańskiego programu jądrowego, Biuletyn (PISM), No.10 (424) of 22 February 2007.

[20] M. E. Carranza, Can the NPT Survive? The Theory and Practice of US Nuclear Non-proliferation Policy after September 11, Contemporary Security Policy 27, No. 3 (2006), p. 504.

[21] More on transatlantic cooperation to put an end to the Iranian crisis in Ł. Kulesa, Irański kryzys nuklearny – test dla nowego partnerstwa transatlantyckiego, Polski Przegląd Dyplomatyczny, Vol. 32, No. 4, July-August 2006, p. 15-32.

[22] More on PSI in Ł. Kulesa, Trzecia rocznica Inicjatywy Krakowskiej (PSI) – bilans i perspektywy rozwoju, Biuletyn (PISM), No. 33 (373) of 31 May 2006.

[23] More on the initiative in B. Górka-Winter, Globalne Partnerstwo Przeciwko Rozprzestrzenianiu Broni i Materiałów Masowego Rażenia, Biuletyn (PISM), No. 43 (147) of 31 July 2003.

[24] P. Durys and Ł. Zieliński, Globalne Partnerstwo przeciw proliferacji broni masowego rażenia, in L. Kościuk (ed.), Przegląd Światowego Procesu Rozbrojeniowego 2004/2005 rok (Szczecin: P.P.H. Zapol Dmochowski, Sobczyk spółka jawna, , 2006), p. 170-172.

4

Transatlantic Perspectives on Asymmetric Threats – Their Essence, Nature and Strategic Importance

Marek Madej

Asymmetric Threats – The Problem with the Definition

Starting from the end of the cold war, the international security environment and consequently its perceptions have been changing gradually, but deeply. Within the hierarchy of threats to the stability of the international system and security of individual states, notably the states of the broadly understood West, key threats of the past, related to the military activity of states and the danger of regular, large-scale military aggression, were beginning to be replaced by other security issues. They originated either from actions by non-state actors, or from spontaneous development trends in the contemporary international reality, unrelated to any stimuli from specific actors, such as continuously increasing pollution of the environment, globalization of economies and demographic changes. In order to describe the new challenges and threats, researchers and writers were beginning to look for a new terminology and language that would be useful in analysis of the emerging security environment. One of the key expressions that have been gaining ground recently, following the disaster of September 11, 2001, is the notion of asymmetric threat. The term, originating from military strategists, has from the very beginning been treated as the buzzword and convenient "label" allowing to name and describe the majority, or even all, new (or, alternatively, only recently discerned or acknowledged) problems and challenges to the security of states and the international system as a whole.[1] In effect, within a short time frame, the notion was ascribed several different, often conflicting interpretations and designations, which, as a consequence, has watered down its original meaning. Also, the term is being used jointly with many other, semantically akin, but not interchangeable notions which are sometimes regarded as its synonyms. Among such expressions are "transnational threats", "new" or "non-traditional threats". As argued by some experts, this has deprived the term "asymmetric threat" of any specific meaning and rendered it unfit as a tool for analyzing the international situation.[2] However, given the present popularity of the term and the fact that it has probably entered the jargon of international relations research and political practice permanently, the need to define it in most precise terms has definitely arisen.

In its broadest meaning, the term "asymmetric threat" refers to a threat from a party of a conflict (broadly understood, not necessarily a military conflict) that has a markedly smaller potential than its opponent and, as a result, uses methods, means and techniques of confrontation that differ from the means that represent the customary *modus operandi* for the opponent (that is, those that the opponent prefers, considers acceptable and routine). The application of different methods, tactics and tools is to provide the weaker element in the formula with an opportunity to offset the advantage of the opponent, render impossible, or at least prevent to some extent full employment of his assets, and at the same time should facilitate effective application of its own resources. Undeniably, imbalance of the mutual opponents' potential, similarly to actions to eliminate the opponent's advantage and establish conditions for a better utilization of one's own "assets" is characteristic of parties to almost any conflict. That is why it is generally accepted that the term "asymmetric threat" should apply only to situations where the imbalance of potentials between the opponents is so vast as to rule out, or at least severely limit the opportunities of being successful for the weaker party should it decide to use methods and means similar to those employed by the more powerful enemy.[3]

Such a general perspective on the problem of asymmetric threats generates ambiguities as to its actual scope. Opinions differ among researchers, and the propositions they submit can be subdivided into two basic groups: those that use a broader definition, and those that prefer a more narrowed down approach to the notion of asymmetric threats.

The former, initially more popular, focus on the very aspect of asymmetry (disparity) of methods and means applied by parties to a given conflict. Acknowledging this, an asymmetric threat may be posed be virtually any entity that uses, on account of its relative weakness, methods of confrontation that are markedly different from those employed by the opponent. Thus, it may be a state, or a non-state actor just as well, and individual types of asymmetric threats are then distinguished on the basis of the methods used[4].

This approach, much useful as it is for drawing the various plans to use military force and take defensive actions, loses much of its original potency when applied in the realm of more broadly understood security studies. Three factors are decisive here. Firstly, the focus on methods and means that conflicting parties use carries an inherent danger that the semantic scope of the notion in question will expand too much and finally this notion will be deprived of all its specific, inherent features. In reality, very rarely do we encounter conflicts between two, relatively equal potentials of opponents using similar confrontation techniques. To set a "threshold of relevance" (that is the point from which disparities between methods used by the parties are wide enough to give them asymmetric characteristics) in this case would be difficult and in most cases controversial. A second deficiency of defining asymmetric threats solely through the criterion of methods used is a thorough relativization of the notion. For, in order to recognize the activity of an entity as a source of such threats, we have to compare its potential, measures and techniques used against the resources and methods typical of the entity under threat. Thus, the range of asymmetric threats for a state with a bigger potential (e. g. superpowers such as the US or regional powers, such as India) is different than for a medium, small or weak state. And finally, the third major drawback of the broader interpretation of asymmetric threats is blurring the differences between threats that are rooted in state activity and threats originating from non-state actors. The differences are there even if the threat in both cases results from using the same measures and methods. There will be, for example, different courses of action when weapons of mass destruction are used by the state and when they are used by criminals or terrorists.[5] Moreover, options and requirements for counteracting and neutralization of the threat will also be different for both cases.

Therefore, it appears reasonable to narrow down the semantic scope of asymmetric threats to the activity of non-state actors as this option can be considered free of the above deficiencies. Moving the focus of attention, when defining the threats from methods used by parties to the conflict and the very difference in their potential onto the disparity that exists between them in typological terms, that is that they belong to different types of actors, prevents an excessive expansion of the semantic scope of asymmetric threats, "derelativizes" the concept, and allows emphasis on the peculiar nature of threats to state security from non-state actors.[6]

Among asymmetric threats so understood there are four main categories, in particular in the transatlantic context, and acknowledging the open status of the concept: international terrorism, transnational organized crime (including drug trafficking, sometimes classified as a separate threat), use of weapons of mass destruction by non-state actors and their hostile employment of information technologies.[7]

Characteristics of Asymmetric Threats

Differences that exist between individual types of asymmetric threats, easily identifiable even if the narrowed-down definition is used, make it hard to find a set of characteristic common to all their types. According to some researchers, the only feature that all phenomena that represent asymmetric threats share is, paradoxically enough, the fact that they are so variable, diverse and polymorphic.[8] Nevertheless, for the majority of entities that are sources of asymmetric threats there are certain regularities that can be viewed as typical and characteristic, at least in terms of their mode of development and shape. They are at the same time closely linked with one another, often proceeding sequentially and enhancing one another's operation. The main sources of the regularities are non-state status and the related transnationality and "non-territoriality" of entities that pose such threats (the lack of a clearly specified "area of operation", that is the territory where these entities are sovereign or operate freely).[9]

The marker of fundamental importance for the characteristics of asymmetric threats (narrowly understood) is their quasi-military nature. The threats, even if they do not take the form of a "traditional" military threat (i.e. armed attack of regular units), are associated with violence, and thus break the state's monopoly to use force within its territory.[10] We should, however, remember that the impact of actions by non-state actors that represent the sources of asymmetric threats on the security of individual states is usually not limited to the strictly military aspect. Quite the contrary, it operates primarily outside this sphere, mainly in the psychological dimension, unrelated to physical force in a direct manner.[11] This means that specific actions taken by entities that pose asymmetric threats are usually less focused on the achievement of traditionally understood military success (destruction of the largest possible share of the opponent's military potential) but are primarily intended to involve the civilian realm (public opinion) in the conflict and lead, by exerting direct or indirect influence on public, to dwindling determination of the society and authorities of the attacked state to continue with the conflict.[12]

Transnationality of non-state actors that pose asymmetric threats means that their structures can be developed independently of state borders, in the territory of more than one state. Their actions may penetrate through borders and be implemented in multiple countries, including those that they want to target.[13] As a result, in the case of asymmetric threats the boundaries between external and internal dimensions of state security become blurred.[14] The threat from non-state actors that pose them may, in spite of its external origin, materialize virtually even from within the threatened country. Then the hostile actions against a state that are inspired, planned and organized from outside, would be ultimately prepared and implemented in the targeted state's very territory.[15]

In case of a conflict between an entity that poses asymmetric threats and the threatened state, there is no predefined area of operation (the so-called theatre of war) or frontline. The conflict (and the resultant threat posed by the involved non-state actor) is of total nature in that it may be fought all over the threatened state's territory, or even beyond its border, and the individual hostile (detrimental) actions of non-state actors may adopt a variety of forms and take place at any time. This "totality" of asymmetric threats is further manifested by the fact that entities that pose them intend by their actions to obliterate the boundary between military and non-military (civilian) targets, or even focus on the latter. In other words, the activities of non-state actors are in the majority of cases targeted first of all at the population and civilian institutions of the threatened state, regarded as legitimate (or at least acceptable) targets, as relevant as the military potential of the threatened state, but more readily accessible. All this leads to asymmetric threats being unpredictable in terms of location and timing of their manifestations as well as the form they adopt.

Another important feature of asymmetric threats, notably in the context of their effective combating, is their very low susceptibility to deterrence, or other strategies of threat prevention and combating through coercion.[16] This is primarily (but not exclusively) the consequence of the non-territorial status of entities posing such threats, and their network-like organizational shape which turns them into dispersed objects. In the case where the deterred entity is a non-state, terrorist or criminal group deprived of a geographically specified organizational centre which entails a limited presence of "militarily relevant" ("worth attacking") targets, the credibility of the threatened state in terms of its potential fulfillment of the threat to launch a retaliatory attack, which is of fundamental importance for the effectiveness of the deterring effect, is, for obvious reasons, rather low.[17] A factor that further downgrades the credibility (and consequently the effectiveness) of potential attempts to deter non-state actors that pose asymmetric threats is the difficulty of the threatened states to come up with a response to those threats that is commensurate with them and similar in form (e. g. uses similar means), and that does not lead to excessive collateral damage.[18] Finally, an important reason for this relatively low susceptibility of terrorists, criminals and similar groups to deterrence, are the potential benefits (political or economic) from actions they are involved in, which expands the brackets of tolerance for potential losses as a result of the opponent's counterattack.[19]

Asymmetric threats are also marked by a relatively low intensity, compared against traditional threats for the state security. It appears particularly low if measured by the number of victims, direct property losses, frequency of incidents being manifestations of a given threat, and the capability of entities that represent the threat to maintain a lasting, continuous and highly active presence.[20] In combination with the mostly psychological nature of the asymmetric threat's impact on security, as already indicated above, the result is that the threateners do not essentially represent, in particular if analyzed separately, a serious threat for the traditionally understood security of states as geopolitical entities, i.e. for their sovereignty, territorial integrity or independence.[21] They can, however, be considered as serious threateners for state security if the concept of security is interpreted according to its broader definition, covering also the "soft" security dimension. Such threats may be serious to the soft security because, even if not acute or troublesome for the state system as such, they might be for the population of the threatened state, by contributing to the deterioration of "life quality" and well-being. Moreover, since the operation of asymmetric threats is largely psychological in nature, their negative impact does not have to be based on the actual, objective decrease in the security level of citizens of the threatened state (alternatively, it will be more than just this impact), but rather on the deteriorating sense of security among the citizens, and a change for the worse of their subjective perception of the situation they are in. This, in the longer term, may actually influence political decision of the citizens, impact the allocation of the state resources, and, as a consequence, its opportunities and prospects for development.[22]

What is important in this context is that in the case of asymmetric threats a more peculiar "synergy of impact" is generated than with traditional threats. Impact on state stability may be simultaneously exerted by multiple non-state asymmetric threateners. Owing to the number of such threateners (definitely outnumbering the states), the extent of "overlapping" of their adverse effects, resulting from the concurrence of asymmetric threats, will be substantial, markedly increasing the strategic significance of such threats (interpreted *en bloc*, as one)[23]. What is more, the adverse "synergy of impact" may well emerge also when asymmetric threateners are not collaborating with one another, are not willing to, or even if they are fighting against one another.[24] That is why the "synergy of impact" (intentional or unintentional overlap and mutual enhancement of adverse effects of non-state actors' operation) may be regarded as a characteristic phenomenon for asymmetric threats, or at least one that is more visible in case of such threats. That is why, combined with quasi-military character, impact of primarily psychological nature "totality", relatively low intensity, and finally low susceptibility to deterrence, it represents one of the key markers that decide on the very characteristics of asymmetric threats, as opposed to more traditional threats, and on their present strategic significance.

Strategic Significance of Asymmetric Threats From the Perspective of States of the Transatlantic Area

Many residents of the US, Canada and Europe as well as a sizeable group of security experts share the conviction that asymmetric threats (notably terrorism) are currently one of the most important, if not the most important, challenges for the international system and individual states, in particular Western states.[25] This conviction largely results from the state of shock that the entire world (in particular the West) was in after the events of September 11, 2001, when we could see how vast the opportunities for non-state actors to act are. Undeniably, a role was played here by the massive interest in the actions of non-state actors (notably terrorist groups) from the media, reporting extensively on events of this type and keeping the societies in the state of "emergency standby", leaving them with a sense of insecurity.[26] As a result, the prevention and combating of asymmetric threats has grown to be one of the key priorities for the transatlantic community.[27] Countering such threats was also regarded as a priority task by the NATO, acting as an institutionalized manifestation of the transatlantic security community, and a similar stance could be found in official documents of the European Union.[28]

Perceptions on asymmetric threats as a serious challenge to international security and security of individual states is to some extent justified by worrying transformations within the phenomena that generate such threats. The post-cold war evolution of international terrorism serves as the best example here. The recent rise in importance of religion as a motivation for terrorist actions (notably fundamentalist and, what is important from the perspective of Western states, at the same time anti-Western trends within Islam), accompanied by the development of organizational and operational capabilities of many active terrorist groups (notably in the area of communications, propaganda as well as planning and execution of specific attacks), and greater availability of effective, modern weapons for non-state actors contributed to not only increasing willingness of contemporary terrorists, but also their improved capabilities to launch attacks intended to maximize the damage and number of casualties[29]. This is linked with an increasing use by terrorists of non-selective attack methods (i.e. targeting random individuals), including in particular the suicide tactics which are extremely difficult to counter, and it is partially the result of the changes in the very functions of terrorist attacks.[30]

Similar changes are in progress within the remaining main categories of asymmetric threats. Increased threat from transnational organized crime is evidenced by the rapidly growing number of such organizations, and equally rapid increase of their income. Other changes include, among others, greater organizational effectiveness of such groups (as is the case with terrorists), some of which are also more inclined to resort to brutal violence, and finally the development of new, extremely profitable types of criminal activity (notably in the area of white-collar crime).[31] As far as the remaining two main types of asymmetric threats are concerned, namely the threat to hostile use by non-state actors weapons of mass destruction or information technologies, the argument of their growing importance is corroborated by the rapidly advancing proliferation of technological know-how and, in particular in relation to information technologies, appropriate tools and equipment.[32]

States of the transatlantic area are also characterized by high vulnerability to the impact of entities that pose asymmetric threats. This stems from the complexity of administrative, economic and social structures in those states as well as their dependence on proper functioning of the critical infrastructure. This dramatically increases the number of potential targets for an attack, the destruction or damage of which could materially impact the operation of the entire state.[33] In addition, societies of these states, due to their entry into the post-heroic stage of social development, are marked by a peculiar cultural sensitivity to the psychological impact of entities that represent sources of asymmetric threats.[34]

Still, the actual strategic significance of asymmetric threats for the security of the international system and individual states, notably Western (the most stable and resistant part of the world), has not changed significantly recently and remains at a low level. The assessment is based on two closely interconnected factors: relatively low intensity of actions by non-state actors that are sources of such threats, and insignificant scale of consequences of such activities (even considering the synergy of impact).

The argument of low intensity of asymmetric threateners' actions is justified by a relatively limited number of incidents they have caused and which could adversely affect the security of states. According to the report "Patterns of Global Terrorism" (published until 2003) by the US Department of State, until recently the most often quoted source in the literature on the subject, in the post-cold war period there were up to five hundred acts of international terrorism a year, except 1991 (the vast majority of which were attacks without fatalities).[35] In addition, the number of terrorist attacks (both of international and domestic nature) perpetrated in states of the transatlantic area is, in comparison to other regions of the world, relatively small, especially if we consider incidents with a greater number of casualties.[36] So far, attacks similar to those of September 11, 2001, or March 11, 2004, were still exceptions, while the rule has been the attacks that do not carry any death toll. However, the number of terrorist attacks in other regions of the world, notably in the Middle East and Asia, already substantial and still growing, in particular since the attack on Iraq in 2003, has an anti-Western character (often it is actually anti-American) and is targeted at the interests of the members of transatlantic security community. The very fact that the attacks are launched outside the transatlantic area means, however, that they usually do not represent any serious threat to vital interests of those countries, nor, in objective terms, do they materially affect the quality of life of their residents.

The largely potential nature of threats related to the use of weapons of mass destruction and information technologies by non-state actors indicates that the number of recorded incidents of this type should also be small, in particular with regard on events with serious consequences. Attempts all over the world at using non-conventional means (substances that may be regarded as WMD) by non-state actors have been sporadic and, if executed at all, were in most cases unsuccessful.[37] What is more, they have been unable to trigger off effects on mass scale even if the plans and intentions of their perpetrators have been fulfilled in their entirety[38]. In the post-war period, incidents with the use of information technology aimed at causing damage outside the cyberspace have been negligible in number. Terrorists and other, differently motivated non-state actors, have been launching such attacks rarely and irregularly even against the societies of the West, the most dependent on modern technologies (thus, at least theoretically, most vulnerable to attacks of this type). Of little significance in this context is an undeniably high number of criminal acts that result from the activities of transnational criminal groups. Incidents of this type are not primarily targeted at stability of individual states, which results above all from the indirect nature of criminal activity's impact on state security, and are of importance only in the context of the value of profits generated in this way.

The present low strategic importance of asymmetric threats results, to an even greater degree, also from limited consequences (especially direct – fatalities, property damage) of activities by non-states acting as sources of such threats. The total death toll in over 25,000 terrorist attacks that took place in the world between 1991 and 2006 failed to exceed 41,000 (out of which, only 512 persons died in the European Union states and 3,179 in the United States).[39] The most serious case of using weapons of mass destruction by a non-state actor, namely an attack with Sarin in the Tokyo underground by the Supreme Truth sect (Aum Shinrikyo) in 1995, took the lives of 12 people only, and out of 5,500 injured, over 75 % suffered from the post-traumatic disorder only, without suffering any bodily harm.[40] Thus far, the world has not seen any significant cyberterrorist attack (attack consisting in causing damage or resulting in fatalities in the real world by intentional and politically motivated actions in cyberspace).[41]

Importantly, low intensity of asymmetric threats and relatively small scale of their effects do not result from exceptional resistance of the states to this type of threats, but rather from limited potentials of entities posing those threats, in particular from insufficient potential in terms of development of their resources. Despite the transformations currently in progress, almost no terrorist group, even as affluent and well-organized as Al Qaeda, has managed, since 2001, to wage intensive and heavy human and property loss inflicting terrorist campaign over a longer period of time. The reason has been relative insufficiency of financial, organizational and logistic resources of those organizations, small number of well-trained personnel and, in particular, scarce and, essentially independent of the will of their members, capabilities as regards a substantial reinforcement of the potential they possess (in particular over a shorter period of time and under pressure of state services that combat them).[42] The scale and complexity of technical and organizational problems that accompanied the attempts at acquiring and using in an effective manner a fully operational weapon of mass destruction by those non-state actors, is, in comparison with the resources available to terrorist, criminal and similar groups, so enormous that it prevents successful completion of attempts at WMD acquisition in the majority of cases. In the remaining cases, the efforts and effects do not balance out. The relation between the volume of effort needed (all types of effort, not only financial) and the chance for success of the mission has been so disadvantageous that a much more attractive option, offering a better (not necessarily the best) guarantee of fulfillment of the objectives, would be to employ the potential for actions using more conventional measures. However, this "conventional" activity would definitely pose a significantly smaller threat for the stability of states of the transatlantic area. Technical and operational problems of a similar scale would also afflict entities attempting to launch continuous rather than one-off attacks (which are essentially limited in their potential impact on the security of individual states) using information technologies, trying to inflict losses in the real world, outside cyberspace (e. g. intensive and repeated interference with the operation of the so-called critical infrastructure).[43] And since the obstacles mentioned above, resulting from the necessity to meet the relevant equipment, financial and organizational requirements by terrorists or criminals, are largely of objective nature, even an exceptionally strong determination of a given entity in pursuing its objectives would be of little value when trying to overcome the above problems. Therefore, the inability of the vast majority (if not all) of non-state actors to achieve the effect at a strategic level can arguably be described as lasting. This, in turn, justifies a claim that also in the future the objective importance of asymmetric threats should not change dramatically, in particular from the viewpoint of Western states, although we cannot rule out the possibility that in isolated cases negative effects of actions by non-state actors will prove substantial.

This is not to say that the asymmetric threat represents and will continue to represent in the foreseeable future the relatively highest or at least the most troublesome risk of direct threat to the stability of states in the transatlantic area. Their negative effects will, however, be much less important than the effects of traditional threats which are, luckily enough, more distant today, at least in relation to states of transatlantic security community. This is something to remember, in particular when incorrect perceptions of one's own security status entail incorrect policy or ineffective allocation of the resources, as well as unjustified, increased sense of insecurity among citizens. In other words, it is good to be aware of asymmetric threats as a genuine phenomenon and try to combat them as effectively as possible, but not to overrate them and not to attach more importance to the issue than it actually deserves.

Endnotes

[1] In the US, the concept of *asymmetric threats* was relatively widely used from the middle of the last decade of the previous century, although some components of the more broadly understood concept of asymmetry (e. g. such terms as *asymmetric war* or *asymmetric warfare*) were coined earlier. In other states, the terms began to appear in the second half of the 1990s, but they earned full recognition after September 11, 2001, only. S. Metz, D. V. Johnson II, Asymmetry and U.S. Military Strategy: Definition, Background and Strategic Concepts (Carlisle, 2001); C. Coker, Asymmetrical War (Oslo, 2001).

[2] L. Friedman, Third World War?, Survival 43 (2001/2002), p. 70-71; C. Gray, Thinking Asymmetrically in the Times of Terror, Parameters 32 (2002), p. 5-14.

[3] A. B. Carter and W. J. Perry, Countering Asymmetric Threats, in A. B. Carter and J. P. White (eds.), Keeping the Edge: Managing Defence for the Future (Cambridge, 2001), p. 119-122; I. Arrequin-Toft, How the Weak Win Wars. A Theory of Asymmetric Conflict, International Security 26 (2001), p. 95-96.

[4] Strategic Assessment 1998, Engaging Power for Peace (Washington, 1998), p. 169-184; K. F. McKenzie, The Revenge of the Melians: Asymmetric Threats and the Next QDR (Washington, 2000), p. 1-19.

[5] In the case of states, one of the most likely method for using non-conventional weapons is the attack employing long-range missiles, which at the same time is much less probable with non-state actors.

[6] Asymmetric threats in the narrower meaning should not be, however, interpreted as equivalent to transnational threats. Next to asymmetric threats, by their very definition posed by entities (asymmetry of potentials or methods used must exist between two actors – the source of threat and the threatened entity), transnational threats include also a host of other threats or challenges of transnational character, transcending boundaries of states, but not due to actions of specific entities, but in most cases as a result of unplanned and uncontrolled changes in the international environment (e. g. adverse environmental phenomena, or epidemic). R. A. Matthew, G. E. Shambaugh, Sex, Drugs, and Heavy Metal: Transnational Threats and National Vulnerabilities, Security Dialogue 29 (1998), p. 163-166; P. J. Smith, Transnational Security Threats and State Survival: A Role for the Military?, Parameters 30 (2000), p. 77-91; H. Braun, The non-military threat spectrum, SIPRI Yearbook (2003), p. 33-43.

[7] C. W. Pumphrey, Introduction, in C. W. Pumphrey (ed.), Transnational Threats: Blending Law Enforcement and Military Strategies (Carlisle, 2000), p. 2-4. The above typology focuses primarily on new threats or on those which importance has recently risen from the perspective of developed states (including these of the transatlantic area) and as such it leaves out those threats that are relatively traditional in nature or those that pose a problem for non-Western states, such as activities of the various rebel groups, insurgents, guerrillas, etc. Threats of this type essentially are serious internal threats, while the term asymmetric applies to threats that, at least to some extent. are external in relation to the state they threaten. See: D. A. La Carte, Asymmetric Warfare and the Use of Special Operation Forces in North American Law Enforcement, Canadian Military Journal 2 (2001/2002); F. Osinga, Asymmetric Warfare: Rediscovering the Essence of Strategy, in J. Olson (ed.), Asymmetric Warfare (Oslo, 2002), p. 268-271. The typology was not based on homogenous criteria for the division. Separate itemisation of the last two categories (hostile use of WMD and IT by non-state actors) is justified by the peculiarity of methods and means of this type, notably the consequences of their application as well as, to a large extent, potential rather than actual nature of those threats in relation to the security of states (i.e. the fact that they have not taken the dangerous forms yet, such as terrorist attacks using a non-conventional weapon that lead to mass-scale destruction and many casualties).

[8] R. D. Steele, The New Craft of Intelligence: Achieving Asymmetric Advantage in the Face of Nontraditional Threats (Carlisle, 2002), p. IV-V; W. Schwartau, Asymmetrical Adversaries, Orbis 44 (2000), p. 201.

[9] S. J. Blank, Rethinking Asymmetric Threats (Carlisle, 2003), p. 30-31; M. Pietraś, Bezpieczeństwo państwa w późnowestfalskim środowisku międzynarodowym, in S. Debski and B. Górka-Winter (eds.), Kryteria bezpieczeństwa międzynarodowego państwa (Warsaw, 2003), p. 168-169.

[10] M. Pietraś, 2003, p. 164-165; J. Lepgold, Hypotheses on Vulnerability: Are Terrorists and Drug Traffickers Coerceable?, in L. Freedman (ed.), Strategic Coercion (London, 1998), p. 133-134. Quasi-military nature of asymmetrical threats is reiterated by the fact that relatively regular use of force (broadly understood) in international relations by non-state actors will usually lead to the use of force by states as a countermeasure. D. S. Roper, Transnational Threats: U.S. Military Strategy, in C. W. Pumhrey (ed.) Transnational Threats: Blending Law Enforcement and Military Strategies (Carlisle, 2000), p. 41-51; D. A. La Carte 2001/2002 (En. 7), p. 23, 27-32.

[11] An example of actions taken by non-states in non-military dimensions and having a negative impact on state security, is corrupting state officials by organized crime groups, which significantly reduces the efficiency of countering those groups by states.

[12] L. Freedman, Revolution in Strategic Affairs (London, 1998), p. 41; K. Homan, Countering Terrorism: a Supportive Role for Defense, in P. van Ham et al., Terrorism and Counterterrorism. Insights and Perspectives after September 11 (The Hague, 2001), p. 63.

[13] This is usually linked with the adoption by such groups of a network-like internal organization model, more flexible and offering greater adaptive capabilities than hierarchical structure, prevailing in earlier times. More in J. Arquilla, D. Ronfeldt (eds.), Network and Netwars: The Future of Terror, Crime and Militancy (Santa Monica, 2001).

[14] A. Politi, European security: the New transnational risks (Paris; 1997), p. 1-2, 17; F. Pastore, Reconciling the Prince's Two "Arms". Internal-external security policy coordination in the European Union (Paris, 2001), p. 1-2.

[15] P. Zelikow, The Transformation of National Security. Five Redefinitions, The National Interest (2003) No. 71, p. 19-20. This is best illustrated by the example of the terrorist attacks on New York and Washington of September 11, 2001, organized and carried out by Al Qaeda, that is a foreign group from the perspective of the US, although entirely on the United States territory.

[16] See more in L. Freedman (ed.), Strategic Coercion (London, 1998); C. Gray, Maintaining Effective Deterrence (Carlisle, 2003).

[17] R. de Wijk, The Limits of Military Power, The Washington Quarterly 25 (2002), p. 82-85.

[18] Because even in the case where it is possible to determine a geographical "centre of gravity" of sorts for the deterred non-state actor, an attack

launched on such "centre" would necessarily involve infringement on the sovereignty of the state where the threatening entity operates, and this entails the risk of losses among the civilian population (i.e. the population that does not participate in the activities of the threatener). See M. V. Rasmussen, A New Kind of War: Strategic Culture and the War on Terrorism (Copenhagen, 2003), p. 13; R. de Wijk 2002 (En. 17), p. 80-81.

[19] It is assumed that deterrence is effective and credible if it is the deterring entity that shows more determination rather than the deterred one. And in the context of the confrontation between a state and a non-state actor (the latter being motivated both politically, as terrorists are, or economically – criminal organizations), it is usually the other way round, as the actions taken by the latter is often their only option. The effect is that the tolerance level of such entities to potential losses resulting from a retaliatory attack is very high. See more in J. Lepgold 1998 (En. 10), p. 131-150; P. K. Davis and B. M. Jenkins, Deterrence & Influence in Counterterrorism (Santa Monica, 2003).

[20] C. Gray 2002 (En. 2), p. 8-9, 12-13; R. Jervis, An Interim Assessment of September 11: What Has Changed and What Has Not?, Political Science Quarterly 117 (2002), p. 39.

[21] K. Waltz, The Continuity of International Politics, in K. Booth and T. Dunne (eds.), World in Collision: Terror and the Future of Global Order (New York, 2002), p. 353.

[22] F. Osinga, Security, War and Strategy after 9-11, in P. van Ham et. al., Terrorism and Counterterrorism. Insights and Perspectives after September 11 (The Hague, 2001), p. 28.

[23] K. Ifantis, Understanding International Politics After the 11 September Terrorist Attacks: A Note on the New Security Paradigm, Perceptions 7 (2002), p. 114-115; R. L. Kugler, National Security in a Globalizing World of Chaos: The US and European Response, in P. van Ham and R. L. Kugler, Western Unity and the Transatlantic Security Challenge (Garmisch-Partenkirchen, 2002), p. 42-43.

[24] This is well illustrated by the case of Columbia, where stability and security are extremely adversely affected by the fighting between left-wing and right-wing terrorist organizations. One of the consequences of the fighting is reduced central government's ability to control their own territory and ensure public order there. See M. G. Manwaring, Nonstate Actors in Colombia: Threat and Response (Carlisle, 2002), p. 3-12.

[25] This largely results from the fact that in the case of states that belong to the Western civilization (also countries of the former Eastern block, "restored to the West"), the intensity of traditional threats to security has dropped decisively, that is the risk of military aggression directed against them. This, in turn, translated into a relative (not necessarily objective) rise in importance of new, "non-conventional" threats to security, including asymmetrical ones.

[26] More on the influence of media on the perceptions of security and importance of individual threats in: D. Owen, Transnational Mass Media Organizations and Security, in M. E. Brown (ed.), Grave New World: Security Challenges in the 21st Century, Georgetown University Press (Washington, 2003); P. Seib, The News Media and the "Clash of Civilizations", Parameters (2004-2005).

[27] Explicit statements about combating and preventing asymmetric threats are made in, e. g. latest security strategies for Poland, Czech Republic and Romania, as well as documents that specify military strategies and tasks of the armed forces of the United Kingdom (Strategic Defense Review: A New Charter, July 2002), Germany (White Paper 2006 on German Security Policy and the Future of the Bundeswehr), USA (Quadrennial Defense Review Report, February 6, 2006), as well as the NATO-aspiring states, such as Croatia (Strategic Defense Review, 2005) and Macedonia (Strategic Defense Review 2003).

[28] The Comprehensive Political Guidance, announced at the last NATO summit in Riga, being a peculiar substitute for the new Alliance's strategic concept, considers the preparation of the allied forces to combat asymmetric threats as the most important task within the next 10 to 15 years. The importance of threats considered asymmetric (even if the term itself is not used explicitly), is also underscored by the final declarations of the last three summits of the organization in Prague, Istanbul and Riga, see <http://www.nato.int/docu/basics.htm> (28 February 2007). The European Security Strategy of 12 December 2003 lists among the most important threats to security of the EU terrorism, organized crime and the proliferation of weapons of mass destruction to non-state actors, see: A secure Europe in a better world, European Security Strategy <Hhttp://ue.eu.int/uedocs/cmsUpload/ 78367.pdf> (28H February 2007).

[29] It should be added that following September 11, 2001, in the wake of a dramatic intensification of counterterrorism activities by the international community (notably the US), the pace of development of terrorist groups' capabilities in their organizational and operational aspects (capabilities to launch attacks, but also the "supporting activity" – logistics, communication, propaganda and recruitment of new members, funding, etc.) decelerated, although it does not have to be a lasting trend. See D. Benjamin and S. Simon, The Next Attack. The Globalization of Jihad (2005), p. 17-31.

[30] According to many researchers, the terrorist attacks, which were in the past (for instance at the time of domination of left and ethno-nationalistic groups, that is in the 1970s and 1980s) more of form of a "brutal political discourse", now are turning into "war substitute" and a manifestation of "total" confrontation (from the perspective of perpetrators), that is one intended

to defeat or destroy the opponent (state and its residents), rather than to convince him. See B. Hoffman, Terrorism Trends and Prospects, in I. O. Lesser (ed.), Countering the New Terrorism (Santa Monica, 1999), p. 9-10, 15-18; W. Laquer, No End to War. Terrorism in the Twenty-First Century (London-New-York, 2003), p. 209-231.

[31] From the viewpoint of criminal groups, the attractiveness of the white-collar crime results from the usually relatively high profitability of such actions, low risk of getting caught, and in most cases relatively low risk of serving a long sentence if the perpetrators are arrested. The factor that reduces their attractiveness, however, is the requirement to have appropriate, often extremely specialized, skills and, in some situations (e. g. document forging) also technical means and equipment. See more in M. Castle Transnational Organized Crime and International Security (Vancouver, 1997); V. Sokolov, From Guns to Briefcases. The Evolution of Russian Organized Crime, World Policy Journal 31 (2004).

[32] M. Conway, What is Cyberterrorism?, Current History 101 (2002); C. Ferguson et al., The Four Faces of Nuclear Terrorism (Monterey, 2004).

[33] Terrorists and other non-state actors, owing to their transnational status, are able to get access to this type of vulnerable spots more easily than traditional armies, which increases their chances for an effective attack. See more in T. Homer-Dixon, The Rise of Complex Terrorism, Foreign Policy 128 (2002), p. 52-62.

[34] J. Record, Force-Protection Fetishism. Sources, Consequences and (?) Solutions, Aerospace Power Journal XIV (2000); E. Luttwak, Towards Post-Heroic Warfare, Foreign Affairs, 74 (1995). However, as pointed out by the already mentioned Swiss researcher H. Braun, although the relative salience of a threat from non-state actors is higher for Western states, at the same time the absolute vulnerability to the negative impact of their actions is markedly higher in developing (non-Western) countries. In other words, although the actions by non-state actors that pose asymmetric threats might be targeted mostly at the security of developed countries (of the West), their real impact on the state structure may prove more significant for less stable and less developed states outside the West. See H. Braun 2003 (En. 6), p. 33.

[35] A similar picture is presented by Terrorism Knowledge Base, drafted by the Memorial Institute for the Prevention of Terrorism, Oklahoma (MIPT). According to the data in the database, in 2002 303 acts of international terrorism were perpetrated, in 2003 276, in 2004 399, in 2005 311 and in 2006 216 (which accounted for a mere 3.3 % of all acts of terrorism worldwide, including domestic incidents), see <http://Hwww.tkb.orgH> (28 February 2007).

[36] Although in 1991-2006 as many as 3,500 terrorist incidents were recorded in Europe, the number of fatalities was only 504, while less than 2,500 were injured. In the same period in North America 3,179 people died

and 3,960 were injured in 139 terrorist attacks (2,982 died on September 11, 2001), see <Hhttp://www.tkb.orgH> (28 February 2007).

[37] In the light of the data collected by Monterrey Institute of International Affairs, Center for Nonproliferation Studies (MIIS CNS), there were 475 documented incidents of this type in the entire 20th century, yet these were not only cases of using chemical, biological and radioactive substances (so far, nuclear weapons have not been used for such attacks), but also attempts to use. See G. Cameron, Multi-track Microproliferation: Lessons from Aum Shinrikyo and Al Qaida, Studies in Conflict & Terrorism 22 (1999), p. 278.

[38] Perpetrators of actually launched attacks of this type were usually using a badly prepared or harmless substance (e. g. impermanent, hardly absorbable or not enough virulent pathogens) or were using an ineffective method for carrying the destructive means (e. g. trying to spray in the air particles that are too big and too heavy leads to their speedy fall and limited effect). Most frequently, however, the quantities of the destructive substance they were using were simply too small, see: J. Parachini, Putting WMD Terrorism into Perspective, The Washington Quarterly 26 (2003); N. Gurr and B. Cole, The New Face of Terrorism: Threats from Weapons of Mass Destruction (New York, 2001).

[39] Although the number of terrorism's (both international and internal) casualties has dramatically risen in recent years (8,197 deaths in 2005, 11,894 in 2006), similarly to the frequency of the attacks themselves (4,878 attacks in 2005, 6,435 in 2006), this has been mainly the result of intensified terrorist activity in the Middle East (3,056 attacks and 6,477 fatalities in 2005, 4,500 attacks and 9,560 fatalities in 2006) and South Asia (884 incidents and 1,012 fatalities in 2005; 1,196 attacks and 1,843 fatalities in 2006). In 2005, 259 attacks (56 fatalities) were jointly launched in Europe and North America, while only 40 took place in 2006 (7 fatalities). Data from MIPT Terrorism Knowledge Base <http://www.tkb.org> (28 February 2007).

[40] See B. Hoffman, Terrorism by Weapons of Mass Destruction: A Reassessment of the Threat, in C. W. Pumphrey (ed.) 2000 (En. 7), p. 92-93; In total, only 103 persons died in over 101 terrorist (i.e. politically motivated) attacks in the 20th century where all types of non-conventional means were used (mainly dangerous chemicals and biological substances, which produce the average lower than with conventional terrorist attacks, see B. Tucker, Chemical and Biological Terrorism: How Real a Threat?, Current History 99 (2000), p. 148.

[41] J. Lewis, Cyber Terrorism: Missing in Action, Knowledge, Technology & Policy 16 (2003); M. Conway, What is Cyberterrorism?, Current History (2002), p. 436; Since no single, successful act of cyberterrorism has been launched, this is in serious opposition to the acts of cyberspace security infringement, recorded at the same time. Considering the statistics of the

American Research Centre Computer Emergency Response Team Coordination Center (CERT/CC), in 2003 alone (this was the last year covered, CERT/CC stopped recording them owing to an excessively high growth in the number of incidents), there were almost 140,000 cases of that (for the purpose of this summary, cases of simultaneous damage to multiple computers with the same malicious software, e. g. a virus, were recorded as one incident), see: <http:// www.cert.org/stats/cert_stats.html>.

[42] Even the organizations that have exceptional human and financial capabilities among all terrorist organizations, i.e. Al Qaeda and the Japanese cult Supreme Truth, have achieved limited success, despite undeniable determination and many years of efforts (especially in the latter's case). A dozen or so attacks by the Supreme Truth using a biological weapon (anthrax) did not generate any losses, and initially even failed to be recorded by the Japanese security forces. Their actions with chemical weapons (nerve gas Sarin) have led to only 19 fatalities in only two incidents (attacks in Matsumoto in 1994 and Tokyo in 1995). Al Qaeda's biological and chemical armaments have never reached beyond the conceptual stage, and all efforts in recent years to use such substances by groups openly admitting, or suspected of, links with the organization stood no real chance of success. See more in G. Cameron 1999 (En. 37); J. Spyer, The Al-Qa'ida Network and Weapons of Mass Destruction, Middle Eastern Review of International Affairs 8 (2004).

[43] More in J. Lewis, Assessing the Risks of Cyber Terrorism, Cyber War and Other Cyber Threats, see: <Hhttp://www.shaneland.co.uk/ewar/docs/dissertationsources/institutionalsource1.pdf> (28H February 2007).

5

Working on the Ground – The Way to achieve the Transatlantic Compromise

Beata Górka-Winter

Even a casual observer of transatlantic relations can easily compile a long list of problems that hamper the harmonious development of those relations. The philosophy of waging war on terror (in particular in terms of the tools used), ignoring international organizations that restrict the pursuit by the United Sates of their policy objectives, such as the United Nations or the International Criminal Court, the US rejection of some agreements in the area of arms control and disarmament, and finally pushing through the controversial (not only for Europeans) anti-missile shield project – these are just excerpts from a longer list of charges brought against G. W. Bush's administration. Unconcealed aversion, or even hostility, against US-designed concepts for international order escalated among European societies in particular following the US intervention in Iraq in 2003, and the developments in the country, leaving the nation on the brink of civil war, rather than ensuring stabilization, render America no longer a desired leader in the international arena for Europeans. The Transatlantic Trends survey of 2006 shows that a mere 37 % of European citizens like the US as the leader. What is more, supporting the US and their vision of security policy may even cost the European governments public confidence drop in their own societies. The proposal to send additional forces to Afghanistan almost ended with Jan Peter Balkenende's government resignation in the Netherlands, more recently leading to a government crisis in Italy.

Worst-case scenarios for the development of transatlantic relations appear to prevail among experts, too. Many expect a lasting loosening of the ties within this community, or even their break-up, in particular that even new, historically pro-American members of NATO (Poland, Czech Republic, Hungary, but not Romania) are increasingly more reluctant towards American ideas. This is related not only to their accession to the European Union and the need to find a compromise among 27 members, but also to a growing sense that the US do not support them in achieving their foreign policy objectives.[1] Poland, for instance, represents a steep decline in this respect. Positive attitudes about the role of the United States dropped by 24 %(from 62 % a year ago to the present 38 %).[2]

All the opinions presented above go on to prove that the image of the United States as viewed by Europeans has been seriously tarnished. On the other hand, the same poll shows that there are certain similarities in identifying threats for international security on both shores of the Atlantic. Both the US and Europe are afraid of terrorism, growth of Islamic fundamentalism, nuclear ambitions of Iran, fiasco of the stabilization process in Iraq, etc.[3] Next to it, in particular among political decision makers, awareness lingers, even if not voiced *expressis verbis,* that neither Europe nor the United States are able to face those threats alone, and the need to resolve burning issues renders this cooperation nearly obligatory. The problem is that this awareness always shows up late in the day, initially dominated by rivalry and distrust.

This paper argues that the most conducive ground for the re-creation of proper transatlantic relations will primarily be those areas where the image of the United States and Europe is at stake. This condition is, first and foremost, met by the operation in Afghanistan. All NATO countries have their military contingents with ISAF and both parties are aware that they are doomed to effective cooperation. A lost battle against the Taliban movement, reviving across the country, will undermine the confidence in the North Atlantic Alliance and adversely impact its deterrence capabilities, which does not lie in the best interest of either Europe, or even the US. Even if the importance of NATO for the US security policy dwindled significantly in the post-cold war period, the Afghan operation has demonstrated that the Alliance still remains one of the crucial tools to advance the American interests.

Failed Strategy for a Failed State

One of the biggest blunders of the administration headed by G. W. Bush, was the rejection of the offer of help from the North Atlantic Alliance in forming the anti-terrorist coalition, and the subsequent slow inclusion of the European allies in the state re-establishment process. In the campaign against the Taliban in 2001, the US utilized military assistance of a handful of allies only (mainly the UK, Canada, France), while NATO's contribution to the action against the Taliban and Al Qaeda was marginal. Already after the commencement of stabilization actions, the United States were initially unwilling to see the European share in the establishment of subsequent Provincial Reconstruction Teams, and neglected the most important aspect of the process, which is an immediate launch of state-building actions. The Pentagon's plans, eventually prevailing over proposals from other departments (notably the Department of State and its subordinate USAID agency), focused primarily on military elimination of the enemy, and provided only for a limited presence of aid other than humanitarian.[4] The Department of Defense, in an attempt to guarantee for the US the freedom of actions in the territory of Afghanistan, also blocked, despite the arrangements from Bonn, 2001, the deployment of a greater number of international forces.[5] Instead, local military groups were supported (e. g. the Northern Alliance) to get them to help with the Taliban (which proved a fairly short-sighted strategy, as it was later difficult to convince them to acknowledge the authority of Karzai's central government). As late as in mid-2003, the United States changed their strategy and became involved in larger reconstruction projects, as well as allowed greater ISAF's responsibility in the Afghan operation.

Not without its significance for this change was the intervention in Iraq, launched in March 2003, and the need to deploy massive resources and military force there. Since that time, the United States have gradually been more and more avidly seeking European support for the Afghan mission. However, while it was not difficult to get the support for the intervention in Afghanistan shortly after the September 11th attacks (as demonstrated by invoking by the North Atlantic Council of art. V of the Washington Treaty), subsequent disenchantment of the European NATO members with American behavior put a question mark over whether they would be willing at all (with a few exceptions) to generate a greater military force and assume greater responsibility for Afghanistan's reconstruction. Bearing in mind the Americans' reserve towards Europe's participation in this operation (even in the ad hoc-formed coalition, not all officers from the allied states were admitted to operational planning) and their being increasingly inclined to act unilaterally, the governments of European states decided to remain reserved in relation to the new proposals from the US.

It is worth noting here, taking an objective look at the issue, that it is an ambiguous case and it is hard to say who is right and who is wrong. The American reluctance to involve NATO structures in military operations of key importance for their security policy objectives has its roots in the Kosovo campaign, which revealed large shortcomings in terms of capabilities to carry out operations of this type (problems with interoperability, strategic transport, etc.). There has been some improvement here since that time – armed forces in Europe are upgrading their potential, becoming more professional, filling in gaps in strategic equipment (e. g. Poland bought F-16 fighters and CASA transport aircrafts), yet the gap in technology is continuously widening, and in recent years the difference in defense spending between the European states and the US has grown dramatically. In addition, most European governments are still unwilling to deploy their soldiers for strictly combat missions and their participation in the operations is conditional on compliance with the national caveats. Political factors play a role here, too. To agree on some solutions among 26 states is time-consuming and, as argued by American politicians, unnecessarily ties their hands in a situation where the national security of the United States requires serious action.

European arguments are equally justified. They accuse Americans of excessive use of military tools where the situation requires a wider array of measures.[6] Only when the military strategy fails, or turns out to be insufficient, the United States look for allies (with Afghanistan and, to a certain extent, Iraq serving as the most distinct cases for this argument), who, excluded from drafting strategies for involvement in the region, must still face all the negative ramifications.

NATO – Unloved Wife or a Necessary Partner?

An example of facing the consequences of the shortage of good strategies is Afghanistan. It is not an exaggeration that towards the end of 2006 the entire Afghan operation had to be started almost from the scratch, as stabilization and reconstruction actions had been neglected altogether. Although it was an *ad hoc*-formed coalition that was carrying out the intervention in the region, gradually, the responsibility for the success of the state reconstruction, or even fighting the Taliban and other, constantly reinforcing illegal militants, was in practice handed over to NATO. The Alliance took command of ISAF operations in August 2003. The task of the multinational force at that time was to help the Interim Administration to ensure security in Kabul and around (including security of the airport), as well as to protect the personnel of the UN mission to Afghanistan (UNAMA). In addition, ISAF was to support the Interim Administration in establishing and training the Afghan armed forces, as well as carry out basic infrastructure projects. Only in October 2003 the allies agreed (mainly at the request of the Afghan themselves, and the UN Secretary General) to accept more responsibilities, first of all to expand the scope of the mission to reach beyond the Kabul area. At the request of President Hamid Karzai, the ISAF mandate included assistance with the presidential (2004) and parliamentary elections (2005).

Gradual expansion of the presence of NATO troops in the territory of Afghanistan began in 2004 with the formation of the so-called Provincial Reconstruction Teams (PRT)[7]. By October 2004, NATO took five PRTs in the north of the country. Since the beginning of 2005, NATO continued to expand, this time to the west, and from 2006 to the south and east.

From 2003, NATO has also been involved in the security sector reform in Afghanistan. Forces of the Alliance are assisting the Afghan government in establishing the national armed forces, the police, as well as take part in the process of disarmament, demobilization and reintegration (DDR) of parties to the conflict and, to a limited extent, combat drug production and trafficking. NATO is the key stakeholder in effective support to the DDR process started in October 2003. It centers around demobilization and disarmament of all (legal and illegal) armed groups operating so far in Afghanistan, as well as ensuring that former militants have alternative ways to generate income. So far, owing to ISAF support, approximately 200,000 people have been disarmed. NATO also supports the Afghan government in reclaiming and securing stores of weapons, which came into possession of individual groups, and are now to be used by the Afghani National Army (one of the largest illegal weapons stashes was found in Sheberghan in the north of Afghanistan, where approximately 80 tons of explosives and some 150,000 infantry mines were confiscated).

ISAF forces also support the establishment and training of ANA (next to the United States, France, Germany and the UK are particularly active in this respect). Equipment and uniforms were also provided to the Afghan army. Until today, some 30,000 soldiers have been trained and armed (according to the assumptions of the Bonn agreement, by 2009 the Afghan army headcount will have reached 70,000 soldiers), the Training Centre was established in Kabul, along with the Afghan National Defense Academy. ANA soldiers are already capable of executing important security missions: they fight the Taliban in the south of Afghanistan (e. g. the "Warrior Sweep" operation in July 2003, "Mountain Resolve" in November 2003 or "Achilles" in 2007), perform combined patrols with ISAF forces, prevent fighting among local commanders' groups, collect the reclaimed military equipment, protect government facilities, etc. NATO's role in ANA training is to grow even more, with NATO liaison missions (Operational Mentor Liaison Teams) being established at the different levels within ANA. The alliance is also involved in training and logistics assistance for the Afghan police (e. g. due to disastrous road conditions in the country, the police have to use air transport, provided by the allies). NATO is also providing ANA with equipment – Hungary and Slovenia alone jointly offered some 30,000 submachine guns to ANA.

Even though there has been undeniable success in these areas – the present tasks of NATO are far from being easy. The state re-establishment process, neglected for the first two years of American involvement, is now at the stage where drug traffickers and the Taliban militants, two key players to be defeated if lasting stabilization is to prevail in Afghanistan, are not getting weaker at all. No consistent program for the economic reconstruction of the country, notably for fighting opium plantations (also here, the US chiefly opted for military tools, that is physical destruction of opium plantations), helps such negative phenomena grow, rather than diminish, escalate and provide the financial powerbase to illegal militants. This very issue of fighting opium fields still arouses controversies among the allies. The proposal for a more active NATO's involvement in this area, supported by the US and the UK, was opposed by e. g. France. It was argued that destroying poppy plantations, machinery used to process it or penalizing those who sell it by ISAF could antagonize local communities (especially that for many it is the main source of income), and expose ISAF force to attacks from local drug barons. At present, NATO's role in this area will be limited to "backstage" actions (collecting intelligence, logistics support, securing convoys with confiscated drugs and help with their destruction), and all actions that could lead to open confrontation are still with the Afghan services.[8] On the other hand, the United States still advocate radical actions. A recent appointment of the former US ambassador to Columbia, William Wood, as the ambassador to Afghanistan, is treated by some as a proof of that. Experts are concerned that Wood will attempt to implement in Afghanistan action plans intended to fight the drug business, similar to those that failed in Columbia (destruction of plantations with herbicides).[9]

The present situation in Afghanistan should make the United States more prone to co-operation with their European allies. Notwithstanding their reservations as to the way the Afghan campaign is run by the US, they finally decided to essentially take over the responsibility for the operation. Many governments (already mentioned Dutch and Italian authorities) put their political future at risk, but still agree to send sizeable military contingents to the region. In total, Europe (including European allies from outside NATO) has deployed nearly 22,000 soldiers[10] for ISAF, and a number of states decided to authorize them to engage in combat operations.[11] Poland, a country that has significant responsibilities in Iraq, is among them, and in 2007 will provide ISAF with one thousand-strong contingent, including maneuver battalion of some 500 soldiers, to protect a road section between Kabul and Kandahar. Since autumn 2006, NATO forces, together with the coalition forces and the Afghan army, have been involved in high-intensity actions (e. g. operation Medusa). Also, at the beginning of 2007, NATO ministers for foreign affairs decided to increase civilian and military aid for Afghanistan.

Combined effort of NATO and the United States is also necessary to exert pressure on Pakistan, as this state's attitude will be crucial for solving the problem of the Pakistani and Afghan frontier, where Pashtun tribes reside, who offer shelter to the Taliban and re-emerging Al Qaeda network. A poorly protected and easy-to-cross border between Pakistan and Afghanistan makes smuggling much easier, which thwarts NATO efforts as regards disarmament of illegal groups and arms confiscation. In exchange for making sure that private armies operating there do not penetrate into Afghanistan to fight, Pakistan promised to the Waziristan council members that the Pakistani army would not invade their territory. The agreement turned out to be unilateral, and the intelligence gathered indicates that it is the very area where main recruiting centers for volunteers to fight in Afghanistan are located. Truly, it is up to the US to exert political pressure on President Musharaff[12], but NATO could invest in practical cooperation. Recently, a joint, Afghan-Pakistani-NATO intelligence centre has been opened, and Pakistani officers are attending military training offered by NATO.

It is beyond any doubt that the complexity of the problems that Afghanistan is facing surpasses NATO's operational potential, and even the planned southbound expansion and extension of the mandate are not going to change the situation materially. Many tasks that the success of the Afghan operation depends on are not performed by NATO at all. This applies to the already mentioned problems with Pakistan. Ambitious NATO plans on the Afghan mission undeniably require deeper reflection among the allies, which should lead to a consistent and politically acceptable strategy of further involvement for both parties (the United States and Europe). For obvious reasons, the Alliance should strive to ultimately become the primary forum for discussions and coordination (at least in some areas) of security actions in Afghanistan. This primarily applies to the security sector reform. The duration of the operation will primarily depend on the health of the Afghan law enforcement agencies, currently being formed, and their ability to ensure security for their own citizens. Thus far, NATO's role in reforming the security sector in Afghanistan has been limited to supporting the process only, while it should be much more extensive. Responsibility for the speed of the process in specific areas is with the leading states that cooperate with the Afghan authorities. Decisions on the design and funding of the reforms are made outside NATO, notably at subsequent conferences of donor states. The Alliance's efficiency is thus limited by factors NATO cannot directly affect. Therefore, the organization should strive to become the forum for political discussions and centre for coordinating efforts related to SSR.[13]

The European Union – Any Role in Afghanistan?

The long-term concept of involvement of the allies in Afghanistan should also consider the absolute requirement to cooperate more closely with other players in the process of re-establishment of the Afghan state.[14] At an early stage of the United States and NATO involvement, security considerations required the military to take actions beyond their proper competence. In the longer run, this does not appear the proper way to do it, and many allies do not agree with NATO's involvement in reconstruction actions. That is why, for obvious reasons, a natural partner in Afghanistan for the US and NATO, primarily in terms of implementing civilian projects, should be the European Union, which has the necessary tools, complementary to those in NATO's possession. Not without its significance is the colonial past of many of its members and historical experience in the regions where operations are in progress at the moment. Although the Alliance does deal with civilian aspects of post-war reconstruction, it is not its primary task, no planning procedures in this respect have been worked out, and, despite a sizeable body of experience gathered since the beginning of the Balkan crisis, the options in this area are fairly limited.[15] Outstanding success may result from the cooperation in terms of security sector reforms. The European Union should (perhaps as part of a separate mission) take over the bulk of efforts related to the formation of the Afghan police and border guard, including the design of funding mechanisms for those units. EU's experience may also come in useful for the re-establishment of administrative state structures or judicial system reforms (in the latter case, it actually is establishment rather than reform). Subsequent EU missions should also embrace the judiciary: training of the Afghan court clerks, judges and prosecutors. In the future, the EU should also launch a program for Afghan farmers, which is already at the planning stage.

Thus far, the European Union has been rather unwilling to become involved in Afghanistan's reconstruction, partly for the same reasons NATO was. No real influence on the involvement strategy (the EU Special Representative is not even a member of the Executive Steering Committee for PRT) is the reason behind EU's reserve when discussing their potential presence in the region. The cooperation between NATO and EU in this respect has been very disappointing (yet it must be admitted that the NATO Senior Civilian Representative holds meetings with the EU Special Representative in Afghanistan).[16] The topic of Afghanistan is not even tackled at joint meetings of the North Atlantic Council and the Political and Security Committee, which is even more telling, given that the membership in the two organizations overlaps almost entirely, and the EU members that remain outside NATO (Sweden, Finland) collaborate with the Alliance on numerous missions. Many experts link the present state of affairs with the attitude of the French, who, worried that the United States could interfere too much with the emerging EU's European Security and Defense Policy, does not want the two organizations to cooperate too closely (or, more precisely, the US and EU).[17] There are also voices that closer cooperation between the European Union and NATO would finally weaken the Alliance.[18] Formal discussion on some topics within the organization is thwarted by the dispute between Turkey and Cyprus (Turkey does not want Cyprus to receive the Alliance's classified information).

Only in recent months has the situation slightly improved. In May 2007, the European Union is going to launch its own mission to Afghanistan. The objective for some two hundred instructors is to train the Afghan police. The project, implemented so far by a small German mission (approximately 40 trainers) almost completely failed, and the Afghan police are still corrupt and incapable of taking responsibility for the country's security. On the other hand, the planned financial involvement of EU in Afghanistan appears to be rather poor. In 2007-

2010, the European Commission is planning to spend only 600 Million Euros in aid (in 2002-2006, over three billion Euros were offered for the reconstruction in Afghanistan). It is true that these funds will be used exclusively by civilian projects: judicial reform, development of the agricultural sector (including programs for ensuring alternative sources of income for poppy farmers), improved medical care, which means that the investment funds are intended for the sectors that have suffered underfunding. It is also worth noting that, despite vehement protests from some NATO and EU members about the American intervention in Iraq, both organizations finally decided to launch their own missions in the country, and become involved, even if to a marginal extent at the moment, in some areas of the country's reconstruction process. The Alliance has launched a training mission for the Iraqi Army (NATO Training Mission), and the European Union is running the Rule of Law mission (EUJUST LEX), intended to train 700 persons from the legal sectors (judges, prosecutors, police officers, etc.).

Prospects

The recent crisis in transatlantic relations has led many commentators of political life to believe that partners from both shores of the Atlantic should establish a new platform for cooperation, a new institutional formula for strategic partnership building. However, it is difficult to agree with the above concepts. If the allies fail to put more effort in working out a joint vision on how to combat contemporary threats for security, the new institution will be merely yet another, bureaucratic substitute for genuine cooperation. Obviously, there are no perfect solutions, so it is worthwhile to focus on improving those tools that, performing better or worse, already exist. Closer cooperation between NATO and the European Union should certainly be sought. New concepts have emerged in this respect, namely that the Alliance can use the EU's mechanisms for civilian crisis response in the same manner that EU is using the tools and resources of NATO under Berlin Plus agreement.[19] At present, this concept still has numerous opponents, but we cannot rule out the possibility that the necessary involvement of both organizations in a host of new, increasingly more complex operations, does ultimately necessitate closer cooperation between them. The cost of establishing large-scale civilian and military tools by both organizations may in practice prove to be too high for them to replicate each other's efforts. In this context, it is important to ensure that EU and NATO actions for the establishment of the Battle-groups and the NATO Response Force respectively are compatible and do not duplicate. Both forces should be capable of cooperation, which entails the need to work on e. g. organization of joint training, joint standards for certification of units and agreeing rotation plans for individual units.

It also appears that the United States ultimately have done their homework on the failure of both the Afghan and Iraqi mission. The new security strategy for the US of March 2006 focuses more on non-military tools for solving conflicts, and on effective multilateralism and conflict prevention. The importance of post-conflict stabilization and reconstruction, American foreign aid (including development aid), improved aid distribution and democracy promotion are also underscored. In November 2005, a Department of Defense Directive was issued on the Military Support for Stability, Security, Transition, and Reconstruction, which deals with the military participation in stabilization and reconstruction projects, while in December 2005 the Office of the Coordinator for Reconstruction and Stabilization was also formed under the auspices of the Secretary of State, integrating actions of all governmental agencies in this respect.[20] It would be good to see those institutions' contribution to improved cooperation between the US and their European partners.

Endnotes

[1] See e. g. J. Bugajski, Iwona Teleki, America's New Allies, Central-Eastern Europe and the Transatlantic Link, CSIS 2006.

[2]   Detailed   BBC   Worlds   Service   survey   results   at <Hhttp://www.globescan.com/news_archives/bbcusop/bbcusop.pdfH>.

[3] See Transatlantic Trends, Key Findings 2006, p.7-9. Also E.Lamo de Espinoza, Differences that make a difference, in S. Serfaty (ed.), Visions of the Atlantic Alliance, The United States, the European Union, and NATO (Washington D.C.: Center for Strategic and International Studies, 2005), p. 40-44.

[4] More on this M. G. Weinbaum, Rebuilding Afghanistan, Impediments, Lessons, and Prospects, in F. Fukuyama (ed.), Nation-building, Beyond Afghanistan and Iraq (Baltimore: The Johns Hopkins University Press, 2006), p. 136-141. On political inside stories around the decision of the European allies to support the United States, more in, e. g.: European forces in Afghanistan: learning lessons, Document A/1930, Assembly of WEU, 20 June 2006.

[5] Towards the end of December 2001, ISAF force totaled 5,000 soldiers and was based in Kabul and vicinity only.

[6] More on the American attitude to post-war re-establishment of states in e. g. J. G. McGinn, J. Dobbins, K. Crane, S. G. Jones, R. Lal, A. Rathmell, R. Swanger, and A. Timilsina, America's Role in Nation-Building: From Germany to Iraq (Santa Monica, CA: RAND, 2004).

[7] It is worth noting that PRT is also an American idea, dating back to the Vietnam war. In Afghanistan, first PRTs were set up shortly after the coalition forces' intervention and were managed by the United States.

[8] More on this topic in the interview with Gen. James L. Jones, „DOD news briefing with Gen. James L. Jones" at <Hhttp://www.nato.int/shape/news/2006/03/060307b.htmH>.

[9] See: Plan Afghanistan: Another Colombia mistake, Commentary by Sam Logan for ISN Security Watch (20/02/2006), at <Hhttp://www.isn.ethz.ch/news/sw/details.cfm?id=17270H>.

[10] As at the beginning of January 2007.

[11] Despite so much contribution of the Europeans to the Afghan operation, it is commanded, as a result of the composite command mode adopted, by an American general.

[12] An example of such pressure is the last visit by Vice President Dick Cheney to Pakistan (February 2007). He threatened that the Congress, where Democrats are currently in majority, would block aid for Pakistan (some 800 million Dollars), should Musharaff fail to take determined actions to eliminate Al Qaeda hideouts at the Afghan-Pakistani frontier.

[13] For a more detailed picture of NATO engagement in Afghanistan see: B. Górka-Winter, Operacja stabilizacyjna NATO w Afganistanie, Sprawy Międzynarodowe, no. 3/2006.

[14] See: J. Dobbins, NATO Peacekeepers Need a Partner, International Herald Tribune, September 30, 2005.

[15] More on this topic in e.g. J. Dobbins, What the wise men might say, in S. Serfaty (ed.), Visions of the Atlantic Alliance, The United States, the European Union and NATO (Washington D.C.: CSIS, 2005), p. 241-244. See also: Mihai Carp, NATO Policy and Perspectives on Reconstruction Operations and NATO-EU Cooperation, in NATO-EU Cooperation in post-conflict reconstruction, NATO Defense College, May 2006, p. 38-41.

[16] As admitted even by the NATO Secretary General Jaap de Hoop Scheffer, see: Jaap de Hoop Scheffer, NATO's Political and Military Transformation: Two Sides of the Same Coin, speech at NATO Annual Conference, Brussels, 14 April 2005.

[17] See e.g. D. Keohane, Unblocking Eu-Nato Co-Operation, CER Bulletin, Issue 48, June/July 2006.

[18] See R. Asmus, Rethinkink the European Union: Why Washington Needs to support European Integration, in S. Serfaty (ed.), Visions of the Atlantic Alliance, The United States, the European Union and NATO (Washington D.C.: CSIS, 2005), p. 28-29.

[19] D. S. Yost, Introduction: Key issues in post-conflict reconstruction for NATO and the European Union, in NATO-EU Cooperation in post-conflict reconstruction, NATO Defense College, May 2006, p. 9.

[20] More on the subject in B. Carreau, U.S. Perspectives on Stabilization and Reconstruction, in NATO-EU Cooperation in post-conflict reconstruction, NATO Defense College, May 2006, p. 52-57.

6

Integration and Security in Europe: The Strategic Dimension of EU Enlargement

Dietmar Herz

The year 2004 marked the beginning of a new chapter in the history of the European Union. The enlargement of the Union and the deepening of European integration – long deemed incompatible goals – were implemented in quick succession: On May 1, ten new member states joined the European Union. On June 18, 2004, the European Council adopted the text of the Constitutional Treaty for the European Union.

These major steps in European integration are accompanied by both hopes and fears. Following Eastern enlargement, older member states are increasingly worried as to whether they will be able to cope with the competitive conditions of the larger Union. On the other hand, new EU members fear a potential sell-out to "affluent Old Europeans". Moreover, the elation over the agreement of the Heads of State and Government on the EU Constitutional Treaty has been dampened by rejection of the Constitution in national referendums in France and the Netherlands 2005.

These sentiments obscure the fact that directly after World War II, the vision of a united Europe was not yet more than a vision. But from today's perspective, the process of European unification must be recognized as the decisive force for the banishment of war from Europe.

European Integration – A Peace Project Initial Situation and Beginning

Through the creation of the United Nations, the victorious powers of World War II established an institution that embodied the hopes for a new world order. The conferences at Yalta and Potsdam focused on how to deal with defeated Germany. It remained undetermined, however, what kind of order should be created in Europe, a continent devastated by total war.

A revival of the old Westphalian order in Europe hardly seemed advisable. The war had exposed the danger inherent in a system of European states that was based on rivalry and the balance of power. The sovereign nation-state no longer appeared to be the unchallenged model of political and social order. The rivalry of European nation-states was one of the causes of World War I. And since no European peace order had been established during the years between the wars, nothing could counter the national-socialist drive for expansion and destruction.

After World War II, the crisis of the nation-state was accompanied by a serious loss of the European countries' influence on international politics. This new weakness was neither temporary nor could it be remedied by the successful reconstruction of cities and industries. As a result of the altered international constellations, Europe had to abdicate from being the center of world politics. In this context, two aspects should be especially emphasized:

–   The European powers, notably France, the United Kingdom, the Netherlands and Belgium, were no longer able to maintain their colonial empires. Deprived of their colonial properties and positions, they also lost their roles as global players.

–   The two new "superpowers" – the US and the USSR – divided the world among themselves into two separate spheres of influence, the border of which ran through divided Germany. No region could escape the vortex of East-West confrontation. The structure of the international system was bipolar.[1]

Initially, many actors did not acknowledge the consequences of World War II, for the inexorability of the (European) bipolarity of the Cold War unveiled itself only gradually. Those states that had emerged victoriously from the war were reluctant to accept their relative loss of power. This became manifest in light of the considerable losses in the wars waged by the departing colonial powers.

Despite the apparent obsoleteness of the European nation-state, early reflections on the (new) shape of Europe tied in with old traditions to create a balance of power. Accordingly, precautions had to be taken against the resurgence of German ambitions for hegemony. The foundation of a democratic and federal West German state seemed to be the first – though insufficient – guarantee against German revisionism. At the same time, it was not an option for the United States and Great Britain to hold Germany down in a weak position. They increasingly realized that they needed it as an ally in the Cold War.[2]

But if the Federal Republic was remilitarized as a member of the "anticommunist alliance", the intricate problem of French-German rivalry would resurface. The French-German "inherited hostility" and the duality of Germany and France, which had shaped the continent since the French Revolution, had been the root of permanent conflict throughout the 19th and 20th centuries. Hence, in the early days of the post-war era, France initially attempted to keep Germany in check by the use of a policy of dominance and impairment. But this could not be brought in line with British and US American intentions to build Germany up as an economic, political, and military counterbalance to Soviet expansionism. This dilemma following from the old notion of balance could only be resolved by a forward-looking approach.

On May 9, 1950, the French Foreign Minister Robert Schuman announced a compelling vision that was to become the starting point of the endeavor of European integration. It is worthwhile to recall the central statements of the *Schuman Plan*:

> World peace cannot be safeguarded without making creative efforts proportionate to the dangers which threaten it. The contribution which an organized and living Europe can bring to civilization is indispensable to the maintenance of peaceful relations. […] A united Europe was not achieved and we had war. [… The French government] proposes that Franco-German production of coal and steel as a whole be placed under a common High Authority, within the framework of an organization open to the participation of the other countries of Europe. The pooling of coal and steel production should immediately provide for the setting up of common foundations for economic development as a first step in the federation of Europe, and will change the destinies of those regions which have

long been devoted to the manufacture of munitions of war, of which they have been the most constant victims. The solidarity in production thus established will make it plain that any war between France and Germany will be not merely unthinkable, but materially impossible.[3]

Embodied by the Schuman Plan, the turn-about in French foreign policy was a courageous one. And it was well received. The initiative was accepted by German Federal Chancellor Konrad Adenauer and it was endorsed by other European states and the USA.[4]

In April of 1951, Germany and France as well as Italy, Belgium, the Netherlands and Luxemburg concluded negotiations on the Treaty on the Foundation of the *European Coal and Steel Community (ECSC)*, which took effect in July of 1952. By means of the ECSC, the steel and coal production of these six states became subject to a supranational "High Authority". Thus, France's and Germany's "arms factories" were deprived of national control. It was this strategic consideration – to make war impossible through economic integration and interdependence – that was at the core of the notion of European unification. The cornerstone of a new European peace order had been laid.

The founding of the ECSC implied the realization of European integration according to the "Monnet method".[5] The French top official Jean Monnet, after whom the method was named, had designed the Schuman Plan. He assumed that economic interdependence caused by the integration of carefully selected sectors (like coal and steel) would result in the integration of even more sectors. Finally, the process of integration would spill over to the fields of "high politics", leading to political union. From 1952 to 1954, Jean Monnet, the mastermind of early European integration, was the first President of the High Authority of the ECSC.

The High Authority was assigned the task of initiating European legislation and policies. These were discussed and decided upon by a Council of Ministers composed of representatives of the member states. Essentially, the "Community Method" has been retained until today, with only two major differences: First, the High Authority evolved into the "European Commission". Second, the rather unimportant Parliamentary Assembly became the European Parliament, which now co-decides on European legislation with the Council of Ministers.

The Treaties of Rome

Integration according to the "Monnet method" was not the only conceivable path towards the unification of Europe. The major political alternative was the immediate creation of a European federal state as demanded by the European movement in the post-war period. The federalists were not satisfied with overcoming the nation-state through technocratic steps of successive sectoral integration. The sovereign nation-state should, according to their theory, be directly abolished through a European federation, making war impossible forever. Many considered this federalist idea to be too radical. Consequently, even the most promising undertaking – the creation of a *European Political Community (EPC)*, initiated by Italian Minister President Alcide de Gasperi in 1952 – was doomed to failure. A high-profile commission had drafted a constitution designing a federal order by 1953. The project, however, disappeared from the political agenda after plans for setting up a supranational European army – the European Defense Community which had been under discussion since 1950 – were turned down by the French National Assembly.

Further steps of integration were less ambitious but in accordance with the Monnet method, politically achievable. On March 25, 1957, after two years of negotiation, the heads of the French, German, Italian, Belgian, Dutch and Luxemburgian governments signed the *"Treaties of Rome"*. The first of these, the "Treaty establishing the *European Economic Community*" (EEC Treaty), stipulated the creation of a "common market" with "four market freedoms", the free movement of goods, persons, services, and capital. This appeared to be particularly favorable for Germany since the internal market was deemed a great opportunity for the increasingly competitive German industrial sector. Complying with France's request, the agrarian sector was included in the common market, too. Also originating from French demands, the "Euratom Treaty" created the *"European Atomic Energy Community"*. This treaty called for the establishment of a common market for nuclear energy and for further research in the area of civil uses of nuclear energy under the supervision of a supranational authority.

Agreement on the Treaties of Rome was possible because all participating states expected economic advantages.[6] Still, all negotiators were conscious of the fact that more was at stake than simple trade agreements. According to the preamble, the treaty "determined to lay the foundations of an ever closer union among the peoples of Europe". Their goal was "to preserve and strengthen peace and liberty by thus pooling their resources".

The Europeans had made the first of many steps towards integration. Periods of stagnation notwithstanding, the integrationist approach of the Treaties of Rome paved the way for extinguishing the fear of wars in Western Europe through the progressive interweaving of the European economies. It is an achievement of European integration that a Franco-German war is impossible today.

European Integration (1957 through 1992)

The implementation of the Treaties of Rome proved to be a great challenge. The creation of the common European agricultural market quickly exposed the exhausting nature of European integration. On January 14, 1962, the first common organization of the agricultural markets was adopted. But as the deadline was actually December 31, 1961, the clock in the conference room was stopped and the resolution was dated back in order to give the impression the decision was made on time. The first President of the EEC Commission, Walter Hallstein, characterized those agricultural negotiations with the following catch phrases: "137 hours of discussion, 214 hours in the subcommittee, 582,000 pages of documents, three heart attacks".[7]

The agreement fixed price floors for agricultural commodities and insulated the EU agricultural market from the pricing pressures imposed by world trade. Incidentally, widely held convictions that the German agrarian sector had been sacrificed to French interests are incorrect. The system of price guarantees was geared to the high German prices. Hence, German farmers were not at a disadvantage. On the other hand, the Common Agricultural Policy (CAP) resulted in higher prices for EU consumers and it complicated the market access conditions for producers residing outside the Union. That system – which is currently being fundamentally reformed – also provided false economic incentives and caused overproduction.[8]

One of the main intentions had been to guarantee the employees in the shrinking and crisis-prone agrarian sector a stable and adequate level of income. The common European agricultural policy particularly succeeded in cushioning and shaping the structural changes which affected the large French agrarian sector. Although the economic irrationality of the first common organizations for agricultural markets is undeniable, one major success of the common European agricultural policy should be recognized: by being guaranteed a stable source of income, the people dependent on agriculture became incorporated into the democratic welfare state.[9]

By comparison, the realization of the internal market initially flowed more smoothly. As was the case with the agrarian market, painstaking and detailed negotiations on directives, regulations, and decisions were necessary. But the late 1950s and the 1960s saw rapid advancements: By July 1, 1968, all national tariffs and quotas were abolished and replaced by a common tariff. Trade between the member states of the Community was strongly on the rise.

Because of the world economic crisis of 1973, circumstances worsened, causing stagnation in people's ambitions for integration during the second half of the 1970s. The deteriorating economic situation made it more difficult to reach compromises. And the Council of Ministers' principle of unanimity – which was retained due to pressure from France – inhibited the adoption of many measures. While the costs of the CAP exploded, British claims for reduced payments of contribution had been putting a strain on the climate of the Community since the accession of the United Kingdom. The notion of "eurosclerosis" spread.

Not until the beginning of the 1980s did European integration gain new momentum: in order to stimulate economic growth and to prevent the worsening of the EC's position in world trade. The *Single European Act* of 1986 revised the EEC Treaty and laid the cornerstone for the completion of the internal market. The European Commission proposed a complementary package of 300 single measures. By December 31, 1992, the internal market was to be completed.[10] Internal European trade indeed experienced another boom.

Since its foundation, the EC has not only reached a higher level of integration but as an economically successful project, it also had great appeal to other states. Between 1957 and 1995, the number of members grew from six to 15 countries (the accessions included the United Kingdom, Denmark, and Ireland in 1973; Greece in 1981; Spain and

Portugal in 1986; Sweden, Austria, and Finland in 1995). However, in the process of European integration – the enlargement and the deepening of the integration project – the perspective that political stability in Europe was the crucial impetus for European integration was lost. That aspect was obscured by never-ending discussions about milk quotas and non-tariff trade distortions. A turnabout occurred after the German reunification refocused the role of European integration on stability.

German Reunification and European Integration

In light of the big accession rounds, a "small" enlargement is often forgotten: When the German Democratic Republic joined the Federal Republic of Germany on October 3, 1990, it simultaneously acceded to the European Community. But the German reunification raised fundamental questions about Europe's security architecture. Other European states were worried about a possible resurgence of German nationalism and feared that the bigger Germany would endanger the balance in Western Europe. In an article that received much attention, US political scientist John Mearsheimer forecast the collapse of European integration, the revival of rivalry among nation-states and even the proliferation of nuclear weapons.[11] Though some of this scenario's aspects seem exaggerated:[12] German reunification – rendered possible by the end of the East-West confrontation – put questions of security and stability back on top of the agenda of European politics.

From the point of view of French President François Mitterand and German Federal Chancellor Helmut Kohl, it was a historic endeavor to anchor the reunited Germany within the political system of the European Community. Plans for the launch of a common European currency had been discussed even prior to the end of the Cold War and German reunification. The necessity of a common European foreign policy had already been acknowledged in the 1980s. But that both were adopted in the *Treaty of Maastricht* in 1992 essentially owes to the "German question" and related concerns about the balance in Europe. Particularly the creation of the Economic and Monetary Union and the decision in favor of the Euro – which, by the way, was indeed in Germany's economic interest – signified that there was no perspective for Germany outside the European Union. An autarkic and incalculable Germany was thus ruled out. And as was the case after World War II, European integration was the solution to the German question.

Uncertainties after the End of the East-West Confrontation

The deepening of European integration through the Single European Act of 1986 and the Treaty of Maastricht of 1992 took place against the background of epochal changes in Central and Eastern Europe (CEE). Under Mikhail Gorbachev, who had been the Secretary-General of the Communist Party since 1985, the Soviet Union granted the CEE states unprecedented freedoms to govern their politics and economies. While there had been calls for more freedom and democracy before – especially in Poland where the Solidarność movement fought for liberty – all communist regimes in Central and Eastern Europe were overturned after 1989. The wave of democratization that swept the region was accompanied by fundamental economical reorientation: Regarded as the cause of economic stagnation, planned economies were replaced by market economies in a very short amount of time.

Instability in Central and Eastern Europe

Euphoria about the transformation of dictatorial planned economies into democratic market economies did not remain unchallenged. It was soon joined by concerns about the international stability of the region as well as about the internal stability of the CEE states. Apart from the fundamental necessity to consolidate democracy and market economy, there were mainly two factors of uncertainty.

When the hegemonial order of the Warsaw Pact imposed by the Soviet Union collapsed, the question was raised as to how the power vacuum was to be filled. More than anything else, the states of Central and Eastern Europe – the region from which the Soviet Union withdrew – were afraid that Russian revisionism might put their newly gained independence into question through new hegemonial aspirations. These questions of security policy required an answer even more pressingly for the CEE states than for Western Europe.

Excitement about the newly gained sovereignty and freedom was dampened by the apparition of nationalism. In a region where the "homogenous" nation-state is an exception and ethnic diversity is the rule, nationalism constitutes a crucial test of internal stability. Tension between Czechs and Slovaks within Czechoslovakia were eased by the division into the Czech Republic and Slovakia, whereas in other multi-ethnic countries nationalistic tendencies and minority conflicts persisted. There are large minorities in almost all Central and Eastern European states. In the Baltic republics of Estonia and Latvia the Russian minority accounts for 28 and 30 % of the population respectively. In Slovakia, one in ten belongs to the Hungarian minority. Hungarians (7 %) also live in Romania, as well as the Sinti and Roma (2 %). The Turkish minority in Bulgaria accounts for 10 % of the population. In all these cases, there are many other small groups.

To face the risks of rising nationalism and to implement a new security architecture for Central and Eastern Europe, three options seemed conceivable. The first project was the European Union, which essentially aims at overcoming the nation-state. Another idea was to further develop the Organization for Security and Cooperation in Europe (OSCE) – a forum for the settlement of international disputes – into a regional security system. Last but not least, NATO could affiliate new members and issue security guarantees.[13]

The Return of War to Europe

While plans for the shape of a security architecture for Europe were still under discussion, western Southeast Europe was swept by a wave of violence. The brutality of the ethno-nationalistically motivated wars and civil wars that were waged on the Western Balkans put Europe into a state of shock. It foiled the hopes for an epoch of peace after the end of the Cold War. In the light of the sprees of violence, mass-rapes and ethnic cleansing the necessity for immediate action was obvious.

The breaking apart of Yugoslavia was already foreshadowed by electoral victories of nationalistic parties in 1990. After the declarations of independence of Slovenia and Croatia on June 25, 1991, the dynamic events could hardly be contained. The Yugoslav Federal Army attacked Slovenia and Croatia. While the war between Yugoslavia and Slovenia was put to an end after ten days and resulted in relatively minor casualties, the war against Croatia rapidly escalated in the summer of 1991. After civil war broke out in Bosnia and Herzegovina in 1992, the return of war to Europe was definite.

Luxemburg's Foreign Minister Jacques Poos, whose country held the Presidency of the European Community at that time, proclaimed that the "hour of Europe" had come. The US primarily regarded the crisis in the Balkans as a European problem. But the European Community failed to take a coherent stance, even in the month of the signing of the Treaty on the European Union which included a Common Foreign and Security Policy. Initially, the EC was undecided as to how to respond to the several declarations of independence of 1991. Later, it resolved to link the diplomatic recognition of the new Balkan states to compliance with certain conditions such as the respect for human rights and the introduction of democratic structures. Irritating its European partners, however, Germany recognized Croatia and Slovenia on December 19, 1992, without either consulting other member states or reviewing the adherence to the elaborated criteria. Even after this public disagreement, the major European actors did not manage to develop a common strategy for the Balkans. Whereas Germany took a rather pro-Croatian stance, France and the United Kingdom tended to support the Serbian side and the preservation of the Yugoslavian multi-ethnic state.

The European Union's lack of concepts and political disunity became evident when, in the summer of 1995, Bosnian-Serbian troops attacked the UN-protected zones in the Muslim enclaves Srebrenica and Zepa in Bosnia, and a Dutch UN battalion did not intervene while at least 7,500 people were deported and executed. Only the US with its military capacities was capable to put an end to the hostilities in the Balkans and to coerce all conflicting parties to take a seat at the negotiation table. On December, 14, 1995, the Dayton agreement was finally signed. Even in implementing the agreement Europe was reliant on NATO's indispensable assistance.

The European and American crisis management in South-East Europe, "the greatest collective security failure of the West since the

1930s", as Richard Holbrooke put it,[14] revealed the strengths and weaknesses of all actors involved. The US realized too late that Europe was not able to maintain order in the Balkans. But it deserves credit for finally assuming leadership and for enforcing peace. In contrast, the Europeans' weakness was of both diplomatic and military nature. Still, the debacle in the Balkans taught a lasting lesson.

Enlargement and Stability

The disaster in the Balkans showed the European Union quite plainly what could happen in Central and Eastern Europe if the region was not successfully stabilized and offered perspectives. If the developmental prospects remained indistinct, the "buffer states" between the EU and the Commonwealth of Independent States (CIS) would be menaced by social and political disruptions; distorted perceptions of threats would slow the pace of the transformation process. Germany and Austria would be the first to be affected by security-related imponderabilities. Therefore, it was in the vital interest of these two countries in particular to offer a clear perspective to Central and Eastern Europe.[15]

To offer accession to the CEE nations was the obvious next step for the European Union. The EU had already gained experience with the stabilizing effects of a promise of accession. When Spain and Portugal joined in 1986, one of the major strategic goals was to consolidate democracy and the market economy, thereby expanding the range of democratic stability. It is generally acknowledged that the positive political and economic development in Portugal and Spain can substantially be attributed to the promise and success of European integration. Similarly, the offer of accession could also be strategically used as an instrument to foster stability in Central and Eastern Europe.

Eastern Enlargement

As of 1989/90 most CEE states wanted to join the European Union.[16] But until the conclusion of the Maastricht Treaty in 1992, the predominant question was how to deepen European integration in order to accommodate reunited Germany. This superceded the development of a genuine strategy for the equally important question of how to treat the CEE states striving for accession at first. But the possibility to reunite the European continent was compelling. German foreign policy in particular had worked towards overcoming East-West-confrontation by way of a spirit of cooperation and dialogue: The socialist-liberal Brandt/Scheel-government, upon assuming office in 1969, began to develop relations with Central and Eastern Europe. Bringing East and West together again – not keeping it apart – was a natural outflow of the spirit of the tradition of the so-called "Ostpolitik". Germany concentrated on its own reunification at first, but subsequently it was to become a driving force behind the EU Eastern enlargement.

During this hesitant phase, beginning in 1991, the European Community drew up so-called "Europe Agreements" with a total of ten CEE countries. They were designed as free-trade agreements and were accompanied by political dialogue as well as technical and financial assistance. Yet, they did not include a clear perspective for accession. Moreover, the details of the regulation of market access were hardly munificent, especially with regard to the access to the EU agrarian market. Accordingly, the Europe Agreements were deemed insufficient. The CEE states did not want to accept anything but full membership.

Against the background of the incidents in the Balkans, the European Council of Copenhagen in June 1993 brought about the decisive reversal. The Heads of State and Government finally formulated a clear offer to the CEE countries to become members of the European Union. The accession was conditional on the compliance with what became known as the "Copenhagen criteria" and has since then been applied for all states resolved to join:

- "Political criteria": Accession candidates are required to display institutional stability, including a consolidated democratic system based on the rule of law, as well as respect for and the protection of human rights and minorities.
- "Economic criteria": Candidates must have a functioning market economy. They have to prove their capacity to cope with market forces and competitive pressures within the Union.
- Adoption of the *acquis communautaire*: In the EU, the French term *acquis communautaire* refers to the totality of EU law. The

adoption of the *acquis* was compulsory in earlier enlargement rounds, too. Accession candidates are required to prove their ability to take on the obligations of membership, including economic and monetary union.[17]

Further important components of the EU's Eastern enlargement policy were formulated in 1994 and 1995. To some extent, they made new demands on candidates. But essentially they fleshed out a "pre-accession strategy" leading the newcomers up to the EU. Financial aid in the amount of € 6.7 billion was provided between 1995 and 1999.

The CEE states did not hesitate to accept the European Union's offer. In 1994, Hungary and Poland applied for membership in the European Union, as did Bulgaria, Romania, Slovakia, Estonia, Latvia, and Lithuania in 1995, and the Czech Republic and Slovenia followed in 1996.

The prospect of accession did not fail to make an impact. The conditions, along with the attraction of EU membership, demanded enormous efforts in the applicant states to realize reforms. The European Commission published regular reports on the extent to which the Copenhagen criteria were already fulfilled. These reports served as a basis for the decision of the European Council to enter into negotiations with accession candidates.

Based on the Commission's recommendations, the European Council in Luxemburg resolved to negotiate the EU accessionwith five CEE states (Czech Republic, Estonia, Hungary, Poland and Slovenia) in December 1997, and, with Cyprus in March 1998. Soon it became apparent that creating two classes of CEE states was not advisable as other countries had also made progress towards accession. Hence, in December 1999, the European Council in Helsinki decided that, as of February 2000, there would also be negotiations with Bulgaria, Latvia, Lithuania, Romania and Slovakia. The new German socialist-green government of Gerhard Schröder, which had assumed office in 1998, was committed to that policy in particular.

The negotiations focused on details of the adoption of the *acquis* by the accession candidates. On behalf of the EU, and based on positions adopted by the Council of Ministers, the European Commission conducted the negotiations with each country. 700 officials of the European Commission negotiated altogether 9,000 pages of the *acquis* in 200 bargaining groups. Every single area of EU policy was dealt with, resulting in some easy solutions and some complicated ones. At times negotiations were severely strained by issues such as the Austrian-Czech quarrel on the Czech nuclear plant Temelin which was said to be unsafe. Nevertheless negotiations with eight CEE states (Estonia, Latvia, Lithuania, Poland, Czech Republic, Slovakia, Hungary and Slovenia) as well as with Malta and Cyprus were finalized, by December 2000. In order to give applicants enough time for democratic "technicalities" in 2003, but also in view of the upcoming elections for the European Parliament on June 13, 2004, the date of enlargement was fixed for May 1, 2004. Throughout the CEE states overwhelming majorities approved the accession to the EU in respective national referenda.

This is especially remarkable since some results of the negotiations were not undisputed. To name four of the most controversial:

- Under certain conditions, the freedom of movement of persons, i.e. an EU citizen's right to live and work in other EU member states, may be restricted during a transitional period of up to seven years. This regulation originated from older members' worries about extensive labor migration from East to West which was feared to put even more pressure on already strained labor markets.
- During a transitional period of seven years – twelve in the case of Poland – CEE states are still permitted to nationally regulate, i.e. restrict, the acquisition of properties by foreigners. Apart from that, EU prohibits such "discrimination" between nationals and EU foreigners. At the root of these exceptions are fears of a possible sell-out of land to "affluent Old Europeans".
- Accession countries will benefit from EU agrarian subsidies only gradually. In 2004, 2005 and 2006, they were eligible for 25 %, 30 % and 35 % respectively of the existing system's regular subsidies. Not until 2013 will they be able to fully benefit from the payments. The delayed integration into the EU agrarian market stems from the problem that the immediate inclusion of the newcomers' big agrarian sectors into the system of agrarian funds would disrupt the entire EU budget.
- From the moment of membership, funds of the EU regional policy are at the accession countries' disposal. Many regions of the EU-15 consider this a problem. Since the entitlement for regional

funding is measured according to the average income within the EU, and since this average is lowered by the accession of economically weak states, poorer regions of the "old EU" are likely to be excluded from regional policy. In particular, some regions of Eastern Germany are affected.

The results of the accession negotiations were not ideal for any participant. Transitional arrangements and restrictions concerning agricultural subsidies and the free movement of workers in particular caused a great deal of discontent in Central and Eastern Europe.[18]

Certainly, the eastward EU enlargement might have been accomplished earlier, more quickly and more boldly. But critics often overlook that this enlargement had to be asserted against manifold objections. It should be emphasized that prior to the enlargement, a deepening and a fundamental reform of the EU had to take place. Of course it still remains uncertain as to how efficient the institutions of the EU will operate with 25 members and whether the Treaties of Amsterdam (1997) and Nice (2000) sufficiently reformed the institutional make-up and the decision-making procedures. But would it not have been irresponsible to continue to leave the CEE nations striving for accession in uncertainty?

By opting for Eastern enlargement the European Union gave the countries of Central and Eastern Europe a clear perspective that helped them to obtain economic and political stability. This is not to deny that NATO's Eastern enlargement was a substantial contribution to the stabilization of the region, too. In February 1995, former Czech President Václav Havel underlined its relevance in an interview with the German newsmagazine "Der Spiegel":

> For safety reasons the accession to NATO is indeed more important for us than to the European Union. No one knows what developments lie ahead of us or whether we are taken by an unpleasant surprise. Now time is really ripe for serious negotiations on our NATO membership – it alone provides a security guarantee. The integration in the EU remains a long-term process.

Other politicians from Central and Eastern Europeans argued similarly.

The downside of NATO enlargement was that it fed the impression that Russia was deliberately excluded from Europe. Indeed the option of making the Organization for Security and Cooperation in Europe (OSCE) – the successor of the Conference for Security and Cooperation in Europe (CSCE) – the core of a European security system which would be based on dialogue and cooperation, played a less important role as NATO was enlarged. But in order to avoid alienate Russia, NATO availed itself of instruments known from the CSCE/OSCE process: a couple of institutionalized for a Russia-NATO dialogue were created. Although the OSCE is not the central institution to bring together NATO and Russia, it is playing an important role in recognizing and managing crises at the peripheries of Europe today.

At present, both EU and NATO, after their respective Eastern enlargements – and to a certain extent the OSCE – are designing a common security architecture for Central and Eastern Europe. Whereas NATO responds to the question of security, the EU provides a point of reference for politics, the economy and society by inviting European integration. This orientation contributes to the stabilization in several ways. The economical and political Copenhagen criteria effected enormous reforms efforts and prevented a backslide to dictatorship and command economy. Trade within the internal market generates growing wealth and thus creates a basis for the lasting stability of democracy. The inclusion into the "European project" that aims at overcoming the nation-state helps to alleviate nationalism which threatens international relations and gives rise to minority conflicts. With the strategic decision in favor of enlargement, the European Union found its own approach to secure peace and stability in an ever growing area.

The Perspective of the Balkans

Like the preceding wars in the Balkans, the Kosovo conflict (1998/99) proved that the European Union did not dispose of sufficient military capacities for the pacification of conflicts. It did, however, play a significant role in the reconstruction and stabilization of the Balkans. In June 1999, the EU initiated the Stability Pact for Southeast Europe. Forty states and international organizations joined forces to encourage cooperation in the region as a means to safeguard democracy, minorities, economic stability as well as military and internal security. The Stability Pact is composed of all states from the Balkans, all EU member states, international organizations (NATO, OSCE, Council of Europe etc.) and other important international actors (the US, the Russian Federation). Headed by a special coordinator in Brussels (Erhard Busek since January 1, 2002) the stability pact is endowed with six billion Euros.

In order to develop a future-oriented vision for the Balkans, the EU again has availed itself of the instrument of accession pledge since 1999/2000. "Stabilization and Accession Agreements" are to be concluded with five states of the Western Balkans – Croatia, Serbia, Bosnia and Herzegovina, Macedonia and Kosovo. Pending fulfillment of certain political and economic criteria, participants shall be provided with generous financial aid.

The Stabilization and Accession Agreements aim for the promotion of democracy, the rule of law, economic development, administrative structures, and regional cooperation. Moreover, they establish a formal framework for political dialogue and contain measures for the improvement of economic and trade relations between the EU and the respective state. But above all, they give the long-term prospect of an accession to the EU, thus exceeding the otherwise similar "Europe Agreements".

So far, the offer of Stabilization and Accession Agreement (SAA) has made impacts to varying degrees. The conclusion of the negotiations with Serbia as well as with Bosnia and Herzegovina hinged on their insufficient cooperation with the International Tribunal in The Hague. After the EU saw progress in the set goals, negotiations with Bosnia and Herzegovina were started in November 2005. On April 9, 2001, Macedonia was the first country to sign the Stabilization Agreement. Macedonia applied for accession to the EU in March 2004 and it was granted candidate status in December 2005. Negotiations with Albania about a stabilization agreement were commenced in 2003 and in June 2006 the agreement was signed. Croatia became the forerunner in the process of accession of the Western Balkan states. A stabilization agreement was signed in October 2001. In February 2003, Croatia applied for EU membership, too. In June 2004 Croatia was confirmed a candidate state and after its full cooperation with the International Criminal Tribunal for the former Yugoslavia negotiations were taken up.

These remarks shall not obscure the fact that stability in the Balkans is still very fragile. But the positive development shows that the EU's offers are received well and set off positive dynamics.

Turkey

In this context, some remarks should be made on the discussion about a possible accession of Turkey to the EU. Turkey was already given a perspective for such an accession with an association agreement of 1963. On April 14, 1987, Turkey formally applied for membership in what was then the European Community. The European Commission rejected this application due to Turkey's economic and political situation and to the unresolved Cyprus conflict. Since Turkey's accession to the EU was not considered a serious option, efforts were focused on the progressive establishment of a common free-trade zone.

The situation changed with the European Council of Helsinki in 1999. At that time, the Heads of State and Government stated: "Turkey is a candidate state destined to join the Union on the basis of the same criteria as applied to the other candidate states."[19] Since then, based on the Copenhagen criteria, the European Union has published an annual report on Turkey's progress in view of a possible accession to the EU. In December 2004, the European Council decided to engage in accession negotiations based on the Commission's recommendation. Negotiations were started in October 2005 and since then have caused controversies among and within the member states.

Like in the states of Central and Eastern Europe, the prospect of a possible accession to the EU has set off an enormous reform-oriented dynamic in Turkey. The preconditions formulated by the EU helped strengthen democracy and human rights as well as improve the critical treatment of minorities. Thus, once again the enlargement strategy is a powerful instrument of the EU to exercise positive influence on regional security.

The "Strategic Dimension"

The European Union has a vital interest in a stable geographic environment. But in order to remain effective, the instrument of enlargement must be linked to stringent conditions. It cannot be applied without any geographic reasoning. Hence, the "European Neighborhood Policy" shapes the relations to all those regions for which there can be no accession perspective within the next decades. As a privileged partnership, the Neighborhood Policy maps out a closer political, security-related, economic, and cultural cooperation, including financial aid. This is conditional to the rule of law, responsible government, respect for human and minority rights as well as the promotion of neighborly relations. The Neighborhood Policy aims at strengthening stability, security and prosperity. Since 1995 it has been developed for Southern and Eastern Mediterranean regions within the framework of the Barcelona process. It was France that initiated this course of action parallel to Germany's promotion of the Eastern enlargement. Special importance is attached to the peace process in the Middle East, too. The European Union developed a Neighborhood Policy for its (new) Eastern neighbors (Ukraine, Belarus and Moldavia) and the Caucasus states in May 2004.

These forms of dialogue and cooperation are essential components of the European Union's Common Foreign and Security Policy. Without a continuous Neighborhood Policy shaping the geographic environment, all other progressive efforts dedicated to the establishment of the EU as an international actor would constitute a misguided set of priorities. But the European Union must expand its capacities in terms of foreign and security policy by exceeding the operating range of its Neighborhood Policy.

This necessity arises from the analysis of the international environment. According to the European Security Strategy (ESS) – which was adopted by the European Council of Brussels in December 2003 – Europe has to face the following threats: terrorism, proliferation of weapons of mass destruction, regional conflicts, failed states, and organized crime.[20] In addition, underdevelopment – caused and aggravated by conflicts – and the dependence on energy resources are referred to as global challenges.

The European Security Strategy makes it clear that both outside and inside the Union ever greater expectations are targeted at the EU as an actor in foreign and security policy who finally needs to live up to its size and economic strength and take international responsibility.

However, the deficits of the current Common Foreign and Security Policy are obvious. The EU still lacks, first, adequate military capacities, second, a coherent institutional make-up with clear competences, and third, a sufficient convergence of the EU member states' foreign policies. The common international stance is threatened by the divergence of interests.

The Build-up of Military Capacities

The concurrence of the lack of European military capacities and the European Union's claim for an international role evokes an "expectation-capabilities gap", as it was famously called by Christopher Hill.[21] During the Kosovo war, that problem was exposed to the European Union in a more dramatic nature than ever before. Facing the technological superiority of the Americans and forced to concede that Europe had only marginally contributed to the success of NATO's aerial warfare, the Europeans were embarrassed. They awakened to the urgent necessity to supplement the Common Foreign and Security Policy with massively expanded military capabilities, i.e. a European Security and Defense Policy (ESDP).

The British-French meeting at St. Malo in December 1998 provided the decisive impetus for further developments. In 1999, the initiative was taken up by the European Council of Cologne. The Council decided that, by 2003, the EU should be able to deploy 50,000 to 60,000 troops in two months' notice, as a "Rapid Reaction Force", and keep them in operation for at least one year. The missions should serve to carry out the "Petersberg tasks": humanitarian and rescue tasks, peace-keeping tasks and tasks of combat forces in crisis management, including peace-making.

Since then, first missions of that kind have been realized:
-   The NATO summit in Istanbul decided in June 2004 that the Stabilization Force in Bosnia and Herzegovina (SFOR) – so far led by NATO – will be finished by the end of 2004 and be replaced by a

respective EU force. This mission – the EUFOR-Althea – started in December 2004.

- From March 31 until December 15, 2003, the European Union carried out its first joint military mission. Operation "Concordia" continued a number of NATO-led operations in Macedonia that had been carried out since August 2001 to implement the Framework Agreement of Ohrid of August 13, 2001.
- On December 15, 2003, the European police mission "Proxima" assumed certain tasks in Macedonia. 200 uniformed police officers and international civil personnel from all 15 EU member states and some other states supervised the training of Macedonian police until December 14, 2005. This mission was followed by EUPAT with 30 police advisors.
- On June 12, 2003, the UN Security Council mandated EU combat troops under the command of France (as a so-called "Framework Nation") to carry out the operation "Artemis" in the Democratic Republic of Congo until September 1, 2003. Artemis replaced a transitional multinational force that tried to stabilize the situation in the civil war-torn region. Since April 2006 the EUFOR RD Congo military operation supports the MONUC during the period of the democratic elections.
- Since June 2005, the EU has been supporting AMIS II in Darfur with military and civilian aid.

These police and military operations provide first experiences as to how CFSP could rely on ESDP resources. In this context, it is a crucial question where the headquarters of each operation should be located. In April 2003, France, Germany, Belgium and Luxemburg proposed to erect a new EU headquarters for the ESDP in the small Brussels suburb of Tervuren, to be independent from NATO. As the US regarded this as a (hopeless) attempt to create the core of a rivaling military power, it strongly resisted "Project Tervuren". Some EU members considered the project a superfluous duplication of existing NATO structures. Furthermore, it was questionable as to whether the "small European" initiative would ever be able to set up the necessary reconnaissance and transport capacities that were already available at NATO.

At present, the EU is still experimenting with different headquarters locations for its missions. The headquarters of "Artemis" was situated in France, the "Framework Nation". "Concordia" was conducted from the NATO headquarters in Mons. The headquarters of the EUFOR RD Congo mission is situated at Potsdam in Germany. The trend is that in the medium- and long-term a "European Security and Defense Identity" will be developed within the framework of NATO and that EU missions will be able to access NATO's infrastructure ("Berlin plus"). This makes sense for reasons of efficiency. Along these lines, the EU states as well as the US should focus on building a strong European pillar of NATO that is capable of independent action.

The Institutional Structure

Through the Treaty of Maastricht, the Common Foreign and Security Policy was institutionally constituted as an area of intergovernmental cooperation. The Presidency of the Council which rotates every six months is responsible for the representation of the European Union in external affairs and for carrying out some tasks of coordination. This was soon deemed insufficient. In order to improve the "visibility" of European foreign policy, the Treaty of Amsterdam contained the establishment of the position of the High Representative for the Common Foreign and Security Policy of the European Union ("Mr. CFSP"). Amsterdam achieved a valorization of the CFSP but it also resulted in an unclear distribution of competences between the High Representative and the Commission because all the various Commissions' positions responsible for different aspects of foreign relations (e. g. foreign relations, enlargement, trade, and development) persisted, including those of the respective Directorates-General.

The Constitutional Treaty streamlines the institutional structure of the CFSP in very important aspects.[22] The current institutional division between the Secretary-General and High Representative for the CFSP and the Commission will be overcome by way of the creation of the position of a "European foreign minister". According to the so-called "double hat" model, he or she will represent the Union in external affairs, preside over meetings of national foreign ministers, be a member of the European Commission, and be the head of a European diplomatic service at the same time. A couple of years ago, Henry Kissinger said that he did not know which telephone number he should dial if he wanted to speak with "Europe". Once the European Constitution is ratified, he will know whom to call.

The Constitution extends the possibility of qualified majority votes in the areas of European foreign and security policy. This may enable the EU to act even if no consensus can be reached. But the possibility of a qualified majority vote should not be overemphasized. There should never be a situation in which one or more EU members are outvoted routinely or in questions of critical interest. This would put the acceptance of the CFSP in question. The institutional reform creates a strong foreign minister who can align the positions of the EU members through negotiations and persuasion. Without fundamental foreign policy convergence, however, even new robust institutional mechanisms will reach their limits.

A Convergence of Foreign Policies

On January 30, 2003, several newspapers published an advertisement entitled "Europe and America must stand united", the "Letter of Eight" from the Heads of State of Government of the United Kingdom, Italy, Spain, Portugal, Hungary, Poland, the Czech Republic, and Denmark. The signatories expressed solidarity with the Bush administration, which at that time was preparing for the invasion of Iraq. They emphatically supported the US administration's undertaking to topple Saddam Hussein – with force if necessary – and to stop the (assumed) possession of weapons of mass destruction. The letter's wording suggested that the authors (Blair, Berlusconi, Aznar, Barroso, Medgyessy, Miller, Havel, and Rasmussen) spoke for all of Europe.[23]

In fact, the signatories did not consult with the other EU states and penned a letter that was incompatible with the following passage from the EU Treaty: "The member states shall support the Union's external and security policy actively and unreservedly in a spirit of loyalty and mutual solidarity. They shall refrain from any action which is contrary to the interests of the Union or likely to impair its effectiveness as a cohesive force in international relations" (Art. J.1 EU Treaty).

Prior to this, the coherence of the EU foreign policy had already been damaged by the opponents of the war in Iraq. In summer 2002, without any discussion with its EU partners, Germany dedicated itself to not supporting a war in any case. The use of this position in the campaigns for federal election eliminated any and all leeway for the development of a common European stance. The lack of a spirit of togetherness – which shaped all European reactions on the preparations for war – finally also characterized French President Jacques Chirac's harsh criticism of the accession candidates among the signatories:

> They have missed a great opportunity to shut up. At the same time, these countries are, let me say that, not very well-educated and somewhat ignorant concerning the dangers that are inherent in aligning too quickly with the American position.

The dramatic failure of the Common Foreign and Security Policy of the European Union during the Iraq crisis was not only a matter of partnership and diplomacy. The fundamental problem was Europe's division into two camps, i.e. the lack of convergence of the European nations' foreign policy objectives. The Common Foreign and Security Policy was designed as a tool of intergovernmental cooperation and is determined by Heads of State and Government in the European Council and the foreign ministers in the Foreign Council of the EU. There is no superior authority that can define European foreign policy in a hierarchical manner. The Presidency of the Council can exercise substantial influence on the formulation of compromises through diplomacy and skillful negotiations. In case of fundamental dissent, however, the requirement of unanimity effectively paralyzes the European Union's foreign policy. Even a successful ratification of the Constitution would not resolve that problem. The Iraq crisis constitutes the most extreme example for the failure of CFSP. It demonstrates that CFSP requires the convergence – not the identity – of the member states' foreign policy orientations.

In view of the fact that every EU member state has pursued a distinctive foreign policy for several centuries, it would be a surprise if CFSP worked smoothly right from the beginning. The French African policy may serve as an example for both the deep national roots as well as the process of "Europeanization" of certain foreign policy traditions. Even after the French colonies had gained independence, it was still a major goal of France's foreign policy to maintain its sphere of influence in Africa. But after facing immense difficulties – for example because of France's intervention in Rwanda –, French foreign policy is being Europeanized and multilateralized.[24] Since what France can achieve with current resources is now at its very limit, the country is seeking cooperation with its European partners. This becomes manifest in the EU operation "Artemis" in the summer of 2003 which was given the task of stabilizing Eastern Congo's civil war-torn region of Bunia and improving the humanitarian situation there. In this case, the Europeanization of foreign policy does not remove specific interests – France claims a leading role in Europe's African policy – but this change of perspective requires that the concerns of other EU states are considered to an increasing extent (for instance, the consideration of human rights and democracy).

Every single member state of the European Union has comparable long-lasting foreign policy traditions. Think of the United Kingdom's relations to the Commonwealth and its special relationship with the US. These traditions do not easily lose their effectiveness, but they can be integrated into the EU context. The process of "salvaging" now unachievable national foreign policy objectives through Europeanization is characteristic, though not the only process of convergence of foreign policies in the EU. Two others factors are: First, it will be increasingly relevant that the interdependence of European economies and the openness of inner-European borders will establish common economic and security policy interests, conceived in the context of a Common Foreign and Security Policy. Second, the continuous cooperation in the European institutions of the Common Foreign and Security Policy also affects the formulation of national policies. The permanent cooperation results in the development of "shared identities" which in turn influence the reflection on aims and options. The effects of economic interdependence and the European socialization of the foreign policy personnel will give rise to a European orientation, particularly in the new EU member states which were recently affected by this process.

It is not to be expected, however, that this will override fundamental security policy considerations of the new EU states of Central and Eastern Europe. After the end of the Cold War, these states were very quickly assured of NATO membership. This solution to the question of security policy created strong transatlantic loyalties that will persist as long as the CEE states do not alter the definition of their security situation needs which currently is not seriously considered. Poland, Hungary, and the Czech Republic's support for the US war in Iraq originates from basic security policy considerations not from the desire for prestige (as it was the case with Spain and Italy). These appraisals will not be altered by changes of government (as in Spain). In light of Germany's dependence on US security guarantees during the Cold War, this should be met with understanding.

The idea of a multipolar world order in which the power of the United States of America is balanced by the counterbalancing power of the European Union cannot be realized. In the enlarged Union, every policy undermining NATO and directed against the US would lead to the paralysis of the European Union's foreign policy. The European Union has to rely on a productive partnership with the US if it wants to grow as an international actor. A policy aimed against NATO and to compete with the US does not take into account the US-oriented security needs of the CEE states and would cause substantial harm to a possible future convergence of EU member states' foreign policies.

Outlook

After the EU Eastern enlargement, it is neither possible nor reasonable for the EU to seek a larger international role in opposition to the US. A prudent German foreign policy should therefore try to influence the EU's foreign policy in such a way that the new EU member states are not forced to choose between the EU and NATO. Consulting with the US cannot always succeed, of course. It requires a deeper insight on the part of the United States that a Europe capable of a Common Foreign and Security Policy actually promotes the transatlantic partnership.

As for the US, attempts to discriminate between "old" and "new" Europe (Donald Rumsfeld) are short-sighted, and for many reasons are not compatible with traditional US policies toward Europe. From the very beginning, the US has supported and promoted European integration as a contribution to the lasting pacification of Europe. In order to prioritize stability, the US even accepted short-term economic disadvantages. The US consciously accepted that regional integration in Europe might hamper access to European markets. In the US the strategic dimension of European integration is seen more clearly. In the beginning of European integration, security issues were at the center. They were crucial for the decision in favor of Eastern enlargement, and they are an essential element of the European Union's enlargement policy towards the countries in the Western Balkans. When the US demands Turkey's accession to the EU, it recognizes that the European Union's enlargement policy creates an expanding zone of stability.

For the purpose of the transatlantic partnership, the European Union should take greater responsibility as an international actor. For the time being, the strengths of a Common Foreign and Security Policy – gaining operative capabilities through an evolved European Security and Defense Policy – will be peace-keeping, humanitarian tasks, and crisis management. A European intervention army is not in sight. Thus, the US should take opportunities for cooperation seriously and put projected European-American conflict scenarios aside. A strong European pillar of NATO is advantageous to both sides of the Atlantic Ocean.

Certainly the interaction of many foreign policy actors is necessary to create a more productive relationship between European Union and NATO. With respect to that, the European Union and the US in particular must review their foreign policies. But the opportunity must now be seized for the enlarged European Union to become a global factor for stability, above and beyond the original goal of the stabilization of the European continent.

Endnotes

[1] John Lewis Gaddis, The Cold War (London: Allen Lane, 2006); Richard Ned Lebow and Janice Gross Stein, We all lost the Cold War (Princeton, NJ: Princeton University Press, 1994).

[2] As an account of US foreign policy towards Europe in the post-WW II period cp. Beate Neuss, Geburtshelfer Europas? Die Rolle der Vereinigten Staaten im europäischen Integrationsprozess 1945 - 1958 (Baden-Baden: Nomos-Verlag, 2000).

[3] Brent F. Nelsen, The European Union: Readings on the theory and practice of European integration (Boulder, Col.: Lynne Rienner Publ., 2003), pp. 13 f.

[4] As general accounts of European integration cp. Desmond Dinan, Origins and evolution of the European Union (Oxford: Oxford University Press, 2006); Neill Nugent, The government and politics of the European Union (Basingstoke, Hampshire: Palgrave Macmillan, 2006).

[5] Integration theory reflects upon and tries to generalize Jean Monnet's approach, cp. Ernst B. Haas, The Uniting of Europe: Political, social, and economic forces 1950 – 1957 (London: Stevens, 1958); Leon N. Lindberg, The political dynamics of European economic integration (Stanford, Cal.: Stanford University Press, 1963); Leon N. Lindberg, Regional integration: Theory and research (Cambridge, Mass.: Harvard University Press, 1971). As a general overview on integration theory see Ben Rosamond, Theories of European integration (Basingstoke, Hampshire: Palgrave, 2002).

[6] Andrew M. Moravcsik, The choice for Europe: Social purpose and state power from Messina to Maastricht (Ithaca, NY: Cornell University Press, 1998).

[7] A. M. Moravcsik (En. 6), p. 212.

[8] Cp. Wyn Grant, The common agricultural policy (Basingstoke: Palgrave, 2003).

[9] Alan S. Milward, The European rescue of the nation-state (Berkeley, Calif.: Univ. of California Press, 1992).

[10] The project „1992" inspired an intense theoretical debate between "intergovernmental" and "neofunctional" integration theory. Starting points were Andrew Moravcsik, Negotiating the Single European Act: National interests and conventional statecraft in the European Community, International Organization 45, no. 1 (1991), pp. 19-56, and Wayne Sandholtz and John Zysman, 1992: Recasting the European bargain, World Politics 42, no. 1 (1989), pp. 95-128.

[11] John J. Mearsheimer, Back to the future: Instability in Europe after the Cold War, International Security 15, no. 1 (1990), pp. 5-56.

[12] Cp. Stanley Hoffmann, Robert O. Keohane and John J. Mearsheimer, Back to the future, part II: International relations theory and post-cold war Europe, International Security 15, no. 2 (1990), pp. 191-199; Bruce M. Russett, Thomas Risse-Kappen and John J. Mearsheimer, Back to the future, part III: Realism and the realities of European Security, International Security 15 (1990), pp. 216-222.

[13] Andrew J. Williams, Reorganizing Eastern Europe: European institutions and the refashioning of Europe's security architecture (Aldershot, Hants, England, Brookfield, Vermont: Dartmouth Pub. Co, 1993).

[14] Cp. Richard C. Holbrooke, To end a war (New York, NY: Modern Library, 1999).

[15] Beate Neuss, No business as usual: Die Osterweiterung der EU als Herausforderung eigener Art, in K. Schubert and G. Müller-Brandeck-Bocquet (eds.), Die Europäische Union als Akteur der Weltpolitik (Opladen: Leske + Budrich), pp. 45-63.

[16] Ulrich Sedelmeier and Helen Wallace, Eastern Enlargement, in: H. Wallace, W. Wallace and M. A. Pollack, Policy-making in the European Union (Oxford: Oxford Univ. Press, 2005).

[17] European Council, Conclusions of the Presidency – Copenhagen, June 21-22 1993.

[18] Cp. John Gillingham, European integration, 1950 - 2003: Superstate or new market economy? (Cambridge: Cambridge Univ. Press, 2003), esp. pp. 410-411.

[19] European Council, Conclusions of the Presidency – Helsinki, October 10-11, 1993.

[20] A Secure Europe in a better world. European security strategy, Brussels, 12 December 2003.

[21] Christopher Hill, The capability-expectations gap, or conceptualizing Europe's international role, Journal of Common Market Studies 31, no. 3 (1993), pp. 305-328.

[22] Co. Treaty establishing a constitution for Europe, Article I-28 (The Union Minister for Foreign Affairs).

[23] The letter was published in various European newspapers on January 30, 2003. Cp. Daniel Brössler , Offener Brief – heimlich ausgearbeitet; Die Initiative zur Irak-Erklärung der Acht ging vom Briten Blair und dem Spanier Aznar aus, Süddeutsche Zeitung, January 31, 2003, p. 2; Elizabeth Pond, Friendly fire: The near-death of the transatlantic alliance (Pittsburgh, Pa.: European Union Studies Association, 2004).

[24] Francois Gouttebrune, La France et l'Afrique: Le crepuscule d'une ambition stratégique?, Politique Étrangère 4 (2002), pp. 1033-1047.

7

To Understand the Understated

Ryszard Stemplowski

The European Union is changing and the security outlook is changing. The NATO future role requires a better transatlantic understanding of the issues involved, and a lot more.

One way of thinking about the future is to begin by defining a desired effect in a given moment in the future, and then looking for and identifying the actual forces and/or processes which might lead to its attainment. One would design a role for NATO, and would identify the forces and processes that lead to its fulfillment. My way is different: I shall point to some understated problems related to NATO, following with the repetition of my views in question.[1] T

Parallelism of the European integration: Except for a very few and diminishing number of countries, the Western and Central European states achieve the growing number of their vital goals by participating in two institutions: the European Union and NATO. The states are fulfilling more and more of their functions through the two integrating institutions. The scopes of the two institutions are increasingly overlapping, owing largely to the EU evolution and the spill-over effects in the two institutions. It is a source of tensions, domestically and internationally, including the transatlantic relations.

The new security outlook consists in the adjustment to the new dimension of the transnational terrorism, proliferation and the existence of the failed states. This implies the new threat assessment and type of reaction. There are differences between the European members of NATO and the US with respect to both the threat assessment and the means to be applied in reaction to the threat. The Europeans hesitate to recognize that the threat is worldwide and the means may include preemption, and there are differences among the Europeans on top of that.

There is vast asymmetry in military power. It hangs over the transatlantic dialog and complicates the parallelism of European integration mentioned above.

Provided the EU develops its common foreign, defense and security policies, and adopts its Constitution, one way to remove the increasingly troublesome parallelism would be to reconstitute NATO into a transatlantic triad or a tri-partite alliance, composed of the EU, USA and Canada. It would help, if the EU substitutes for the UK and France in the UN Security Council, and for the UK, France and Italy in the future G-??.

Changing hegemony in the world system: The USA will not be able to remain a hegemon forever. The system needs a hegemon, nonetheless, as any such system does. Some European reservations with respect to the US hegemony notwithstanding, there is no candidate to this position which would suit the EU better than the USA. One way to solve the problem, for some time, would be to join forces in a hegemonic tandem: US-EU (or a hegemonic triangle: Canada-EU-USA?). A lot is going on in the economy to this effect.

Development of the transatlantic identity: The spontaneous growth of the collective identity, visible as it is, does not keep up with the growing challenges we face together (tell me what threats you fear and I will know who you are). The development of the collective identity is, to an extent, a function of the external threats, and of the transatlantic ability to cooperate in facing them. There is a need for some concerted actions in the EU and USA/Canada public diplomacies to enhance the identity.

International security and development: NATO as a military actor will be successful worldwide, if the NATO member countries manage to make use of the parallel system of EU-USA-Canada economic cooperation. The better harmonization of the NATO out-of–area operations and the NATO members' policies of aid for, and development support in the underdeveloped countries, the higher is the countries' acceptance of such operations in the vast territories of the underdeveloped parts of the world.

International security and sovereignty (the case of Middle East): The Middle Eastern nations are unable to resolve the conflict on their own. One is able to envisage that the conflicts might be pacified and eradicated before its metamorphosis into a very major war. However, such a prospect assumes the extraordinary (unthinkable?) solution of an interim, albeit long-term, internationally-organized limitation of sovereignty of several states in the region, including Israel and the emerging Palestinian state, with the NATO peace enforcement/peace-keeping forces, many hundred thousand strong, and thousands of civil volunteers from the EU countries, participating in the undertaking for several decades, possibly based on UN approval.

In conclusion:

(a)   If the aforementioned issues are not investigated systematically, and the governments concerned do not face them in a more serious way, and the public debate is not developed, the role of NATO may not be designed adequately by the decision-makers and accepted by the polities concerned.

(b)   I certainly believe the investigation, government dialog, and public debate in question are not adequate and, alas, will not be significantly improved.

(c)   NATO is going global nonetheless, and we should begin bracing ourselves for further complications that could be appeased, if not prevented altogether.

Vision is needed, and the present-day utopians may turn out to be the realists of tomorrow. The West is for democracy and for freedom and yet it is uncertain about almost everything. If we are to work for progress in transatlantic relations, we have to set a target we have not yet attained. If we are to keep aspiring to progress in transatlantic relations incessantly, we have to aim at the impossible that can never be attained and that is an absolute unity. However, the connection between a practical target and the impossible one – or the ostensibly impossible - can be aimed at in a practical way. It can be institutionalized by creating a Transatlantic Confederate Union (TCU). I mean union, not unity. It is less than the Americans and Canadians practice in their countries, and it is a characteristic the European Union is taking on step by step. Only an idea great enough may mobilize people for greater things in one or two generations, provided they understand what is at stake. (Speaking from the experience of my nation: Had the Poles not fought to bring about the allegedly impossible, no free Poland would have materialized to become a NATO member and join in the development of the EU.) Can we – the rationally and realistically thinking people of the West – commit such a recklessness as to dream about the impossible? And yet it may result from the intertwined processes in progress: The relative decline of US economic power, the federalization of the EU, the growing community of values and interests in the EU and North America, and – the decisive stimulus – increasing international insecurity (especially given the proliferation of WMD, the second holocaust looming over the Middle East, and a creeping Great Depression Two). NATO may fulfill a twofold function of a bridge to the TCU, and a worldwide organization including the strategic partners like Australia, Brazil, Japan, India, South Africa, Ukraine, and, hopefully, the would-be democratic Russia.

Endnotes

[1] For my printed and electronic publications on the topic, see <http://www.stemplowski.pl>

8

The Future Role of NATO:
Some Themes of the Debate

Helen R. Desfosses

The debate over the future role of NATO has many themes. This paper is meant to be a brief introduction to some of the key ideas in a vast analytical literature. Several of these themes, and others, have been tackled in greater detail by other contributors to this volume.

NATO's Adaptive Potential

One of the main questions is whether NATO remains the political-strategic bedrock of the Transatlantic Community, or has the world moved on? NATO has worked mightily to establish its new relevance in the post-Cold War world, but some scholars, such as Sean Kay, have asked whether it has reached "the limits of its adaptive potential." His view is that NATO has experienced both "continued survival and simultaneous decline"[1]. On a more positive note, scholars such as Celeste A. Wallander explain that while in some areas, "NATO's aspirations still exceed its achievements", "NATO's persistence through its adaptation to new conditions", as well as its development of "new assets", are significant and warrant further study[2].

This question of whether NATO has reached the limits of its adaptive potential is especially meaningful and timely given the development of the European Union. Will the European Union take on more responsibilities for Europe's security[3], and how will this affect the original goal and unfinished mission of the organization which was to help create an environment in which Europe could assume an equal responsibility for its own security? A related issue is whether "an emerging set of EU security capacities" will affect NATO's role, and the importance that the United States attaches to it. Finally, there is the gripping question of whether Europe is as strategically important to the United States as it once was[4].

And what is NATO's relevance to fighting the war on terror, which has become such a major preoccupation of the United States?[5] Roles for NATO include prevention, intelligence sharing, and helping to deny terrorists weapons of mass destruction. The range of opinion here varies from the skepticism of Sean Kay to many more positive assessments[6]. For example, Christian Tuschoff argues that "contrary to the often-heard argument that the September 11 terrorist attacks marginalized NATO…the Alliance proved its purpose and functioning"[7].

Factors explaining NATO's Survival

Exploring the factors behind NATO's survival is also important. The scholarly literature on this issue emphasizes several issues. The first is the considerable accomplishments of NATO since its founding. It is clear that NATO is "linked to an idea of a transatlantic community based on a sense of common history" and achievement. Many scholars argue that "the alliance is taken for granted as a 'common good', proceeding from that premise to discuss the adjustments each party should make in order to safeguard this common good"[8].

Also, NATO's accomplishments have been numerous since the collapse of the Soviet Bloc. These accomplishments include helping to navigate the transition from the old order to the new; working to end the fighting in the Balkans; furthering the political integration of Central and Eastern Europe, and reaching out to the Russians, to name just a few[9]. NATO has also made many organizational adjustments, engaging in multiple membership expansions and deliberations regarding additional ones. Then there are the many challenges that NATO has taken on in new areas, such as Afghanistan, where the United Nations is calling on NATO to expand its functions to include such roles as helping to stop the drug traffic on which the Taliban draws heavily for funding and support.

NATO is also taking on new roles in the Middle East. The New York Times columnist, Thomas Friedman, has discussed the participation of NATO in the multinational force designed to keep the peace between Israel and Hezbollah after their war in summer 2006. He quoted a top diplomat as saying that "the UN/European force evolving in Lebanon may offer a new model....The fact that it has a heavy European/NATO component makes it credible to Israel, and the fact that it has a UN umbrella makes it acceptable to the Arab world"[10].

Another factor explaining NATO's survival is sheer persistence and tradition. Kay worries that "alliance rules and decision-making procedures have made the costs of working through NATO too high for the United States", he argues strenuously that "fundamental reform, particularly of its decision-making procedures, [is critical] to the survival of NATO". He points out how detrimental the current situation is, where one or two dissenting countries can block the entire institution from acting "when its capacities are needed"[11]. Nevertheless, Sjursen reminds us that the "marginal costs of maintaining [NATO] outweigh the considerable costs of creating an entirely new set of norms, rules and procedures"[12]. This is a particularly relevant concern to current United States policymakers, whose support for NATO sometimes wavers or seems less than that of the Europeans. However, analysts have pointed out that NATO "gives the United States a seat at the table in Europe, which it gets no other way"[13].

Factors affecting NATO's Future

The first factor to explore here is the impact of the war in Iraq and the methods that the United States used to develop a coalition. Analysts have asked whether the extent to which the United States broke with the principles of multilateralism around Iraq, showing a preference for new partnerships, new staffs and new steps, had long-standing implications for the future of NATO[14]. The way that the US dealt with NATO in deciding to go ahead with the war challenged "the NATO value consensus", increasingly focusing on "coalitions of the willing", with an emphasis on the view that "the mission defines the coalition". This emphasis provided further evidence of moves away from the "multilateral principle of the indivisibility of security within NATO".[15]

A second factor is divergence of opinion between American re-spondents and Europeans about the continuing significance of NATO, and such issues as American domination. The most recent survey re-garding views of NATO among American and European respondents provide important data.[16]

A third factor is a generational problem. As Kay put it, "Sadly, a new generation of leaders emerging on both sides of the Atlantic does not share the same drive to keep the alliance viable".[17] As Professor Renée de Nevers of Syracuse University pointed out in her remarks that it does not help that "two-thirds of the members of Congress came to office after the end of the Cold War, nor that many staffers have left as well"[18]. She went on to point out that the recent White House report on "The National Security Strategy of the United States of America" mentions NATO less than a dozen times, compared to almost three dozen times in the 1960s.[19]

Scenarios for NATO's Future

There are many scenarios for NATO's future discussed by analysts in their writings and at this conference. These include the following: First, NATO becomes more of a political framework than an alliance; second, there develops a global NATO; third, NATO develops differ-ent relationships with its partners; fourth, a tripartite NATO emerges, focusing on the United States, the EU and Canada, as Ryszard Stem-plowski has argued in this volume[20]; fifth, a new hegemon is created; sixth, the US moves on. Finally, it remains to be seen whether elites on both sides of the Atlantic will not only acknowledge NATO's con-tinued significance, but also work to burnish its reputation in the minds of the younger generation.

Endnotes

[1] S. Kay, What Went Wrong with NATO, Cambridge Review of International Affairs, (2005)18, 1, pp. 69, 78.

[2] C. Wallander, Institutional Assets and Adaptability: NATO after the Cold War, International Organization, 2000, 54, 4, pp. 731-733.

[3] P. Gordon, Their Own Army, Foreign Affairs, 79, 4 (July/August, 2000), pp. 12-17.

[4] S. Kay 2005 (En. 1), pp. 79-81.

[5] R. Lugar, Sen. NATO's Role in the War on Terrorism, US-NATO Missions Annual Conference, Brussels, Belgium, 2002, January 19.

[6] S. Kay 2005 (En. 1), pp. 74-78.

[7] Ch. Tuschoff, Why NATO is Still Relevant, International Politics, 2003, 40, pp. 101-120.

[8] H. Sjursen, On the Identity of NATO, International Affairs, 2004, 80, pp. 688, 701.

[9] S. Kay 2005 (En. 1), p. 82.

[10] T. Friedman, Land for NATO, New York Times, September 13, 2006.

[11] S. Kay, 2005 (En. 1), p. 80.

[12] H. Sjursen 2004 (En. 8), p. 701.

[13] J. Walker, Keeping America in Europe, Foreign Policy, 1991, 83, pp. 128-142.

[14] S. Kay 2005 (En. 1), p. 75.

[15] H. Sjursen 2004 (En. 8), p. 702; D. Porch, Europe, America, and the "War on Terror", Strategic Insights, 2004, III, p. 4; Center for Contemporary Conflict, Naval Postgraduate School Electronic Journal available at <Hhttp://www.ccc.nps.navy.mil/si/2004/apr/porchApr04.aspH.>; S. Kay 2005 (En. 1), p. 75.

[16] TransatlanticTrends, 2005, <Transatlantictrends.org/doc/TTToplineData2005.pdf>.

[17] S. Kay2005 (En. 1), p. 82.

[18] See p. 7 ff. in this volume.

[19] Whitehouse.gov/nsc/nss.html.

[20] See p. 113 ff. in this volume.

Transatlantic Community and Challenges
of the Broader Middle East

9

The Iranian Nuclear Crisis – A Test for the New Transatlantic Partnership

Lukasz Kulesa

In spite of Iran's assurances that its nuclear program is to serve solely civil purposes, the scale and advancement of work on it give risc to anxieties that the true reason is to secure the Islamic Republic with the capability to construct a nuclear weapon. Whether Tehran can be stopped depends on close cooperation of the key members of the international community and – first of all – on cooperation between the United States and European states. Hitherto attempts, undertaken by EU countries, at solving the crisis on their own through negotiations with Iran proved to be as ineffective as the isolation policy and tough rhetoric of the United States. Though in 2006 the transatlantic partners joined forces with the aim of putting sanctions on Iran through the UN Security Council, deep discrepancies still exist between them as to the policy vis-à-vis Tehran. This might upset the recently achieved transatlantic concord.

Although reports of advancements in the implementation of the Iranian nuclear program began to appear as early as the 1990s, it was only in 2002, when information indicating its advancement was disclosed, that the international community began to pay increased attention to Iran. The escalating confrontation not only aggravated the situation in the Middle East but also took on a global character – as it concerned problems of vital importance for the modern international system as such. Its direct cause was the issue of non-proliferation of nuclear weapons. In the broader context it was a conflict between states with different political systems, also presented either as a clash between the developing and developed states concerning access to technology or as the next confrontation between Islam and the West. The Iranian crisis has had its impact on the global economy as well (an increase in oil prices) and on relations between the major global power centers – the United States, the EU, China, India and Russia.

The Iranian issue has proved to be of key significance for the condition of the transatlantic partnership. The early stage of the Iranian crisis coincided with a deep crisis in transatlantic cooperation following the Iraq intervention. The attitude of some European states and the US to Iran and its nuclear program differed as well. It seemed that the Iranian crisis might only serve to deepen the gap between the states on the two sides of the Atlantic and confirm the thesis, propagated by Robert Kagan, on fundamental differences between the US and Europe.[1] This is why the issue of the Iranian nuclear program was a test: how the transatlantic partnership would work in new conditions?

The Decline of the Transatlantic Partnership

The transatlantic partnership might be understood as a particular relationship in the area of security between the US and Europe based on common values.[2] Thanks to a developed system of mutual contacts; bilateral and multilateral, informal and institutionalized (e. g. through NATO), it allows close cooperation in internal problem solving, as well as seeking agreement on and implementation of cohesive policy concerning external issues. In this perspective, the transatlantic security partnership means, first of all, the existence of a common identity: a set of beliefs, shared by each of the parties, as to the organization of social life and the domestic and international policy. The parts of this identity are the belief, that the use of force in dispute-solving inside the partnership is unacceptable, and the observation of the rules of loyalty, negotiation and search for compromise.[3]

The beginnings of the transatlantic community can be traced back to the policy of President Wilson and the engagement of the US in Europe during World War II.[4] There is no doubt that the decisive role in the emergence of the common identity was played by the threat from the Soviet Union and communist ideology after 1945. A necessity emerged to bind the states on the two sides of the Atlantic as closely as possible, to maintain the support of their societies for this relationship and to find a way of managing crises within the community in such a way that they could not be used by the Communist camp. The North Atlantic Alliance proved to be a tool that allowed achieving those goals.

The end of the Cold War forced the transformation process of the transatlantic partnership and the search for a new *raison d'être* in the area of security. The 1990s were marked by the Balkan conflict and NATO enlargement. The new enemy that united the partners was the instability in Europe, both in the form of local conflicts and ethnic cleansing and the maintenance of a security vacuum in Eastern Europe. Similarly to the Cold War period, the role of the leader and initiator was played by the US. However, other states assessed the threats in the same way and had an important influence on the dynamics of the development of events, if not on its direction.

The year 1999 seems to be the zenith of the development of the transatlantic partnership after the Cold War. Three Eastern European states: Poland, Hungary and the Czech Republic joined NATO. The preservation of the unity of allies in the air campaign against Yugoslavia was managed successfully, as was the introduction of NATO troops to Kosovo. In spite of the fact that the North Atlantic Alliance was faced with further enlargement, and bringing the situation on the Balkans back to normal remained far from being complete, security of Europe was ensured. Thus, instability ceased to be a sufficient threat to make a basis for this particular common identity that the transatlantic relationship was based on.

After the Al Qaeda attacks on September 11, 2001 it could have been thought that terrorism would become a new factor binding the transatlantic partnership. The US, however, expected all of its partners to subordinate totally to the US "war on terror" strategy which gave priority to military action and perceived effectiveness to be the basic premise of policy. Such an approach meant that – if needed – the US could both resign from the use of NATO forces and to look for states that share its point of view outside the transatlantic community. In the beginning, all the partners gave their support to US activities, including the independent US operation in Afghanistan. The extension of the strategy to the preventive attack doctrine, however, and the selection of Iraq as its target have given rise to a sudden crisis within the partnership. Though the partners shared the perception of the terrorist threat, the interpretations of the character of threat from Iraq and its scale differed sharply. This time, the authority of the United States and its arguments were not enough to force the partners to adopt the American point of view. What lacked was the common belief that the threat is comparable to the one from the communist danger or the threat of destabilization in Europe, which could have convinced other states to "close ranks" in the superior aim of preserving the transatlantic unity.

The transatlantic conflict, arising out of the Iraqi issue, was interpreted in two ways. According to the first interpretation, it meant the end of the transatlantic partnership as a particular community of values stemming from the identical perception of threats. It was to be replaced with the system of the so-called coalitions of the willing, pragmatic configurations changing with circumstances. There could also take place a faster emancipation of the European Union in the area of security and the roll-out of its own independent strategy with the use of methods differing from those of the US. According to the second interpretation, the result of the crisis was to be a strengthening of the transatlantic partnership. The real perspective of its fall should force the states on the two sides of the Atlantic to reflect on what a vital role close relations between them play in their foreign and security policies. It could enable them to return to closer cooperation. The Iranian crisis proved to be the first serious verification of the two hypotheses.[5]

The Iranian Crisis and the Initiative of European States

In September 2002, the National Council of Resistance of Iran, an opposition organization with links to an armed group called People's Mujahedin, began to disseminate detailed information concerning Iranian nuclear installations and the advancement of the Iranian nuclear program.[6] The construction of uranium enrichment plant in Natanz has been revealed, as well as heavy water production plant in Arak and the existence of workshops in Tehran manufacturing centrifuges for uranium enrichment.

At the same time, the Iraqi crisis, related to the issue of possession of weapons of mass destruction by the Saddam Hussein regime, was aggravating. The Iranian authorities did not want its nuclear program to be treated in a similar way as Iraqi programs of weapons of mass destruction. As a response to the charges, they decided to cooperate with the International Atomic Energy Agency (IAEA) as well as to disclose information on its program. This was supposed to make the international community focus its attention on Iraq.

The investigation by IAEA inspectors confirmed that Iran was developing an extensive nuclear program and that among other things was preparing to commence the production of enriched uranium in a plant in Natanz (this way can be obtained either fuel for nuclear power plants or highly enriched uranium, a component of nuclear explosives). In May 2003, Iran confirmed its intent to build a research reactor with power output of 40 MWt cooled with heavy water. Reactors of this type use natural uranium and they can be relatively easily adjusted to produce large quantities of plutonium necessary to build an atomic bomb.

No direct evidence was found, however, that Iran was intending to build an atomic bomb and that its nuclear program is of a military nature. The forum on which the reaction of the international community for the Iranian crisis depended in the first place was the Board of Governors (the executive authority of IAEA), composed of 35 members. The United States were making attempts to convince it to hand the case over to the UN Security Council.[7] Other states, however, feared that after a rapid overthrow of the Iraqi regime, the United States would seek an armed confrontation with Iran. Because of this, the Board of Governors limited itself to issuing a statement, in which it expressed its concern at the fact that Iran violated the obligations it had taken and urged the state to cooperate.[8]

In summer 2003, three EU states (France, Germany and the UK) put forward a proposition to begin negotiations with Iran. This initiative was related to previous contacts of the European Union with the

Islamic Republic. After the election of Mohammad Khatami for President of Iran in 1997 initiated changes in the internal and foreign policy of Teheran, the EU decided to hold "a constructive dialogue" with Iran.[9] As part of this strategy, progress was to be achieved simultaneously in the realms of political contacts, development of economic relations and the observation of human rights. The European states considered the gradual extension of contacts with the Islamic Republic as a more effective strategy than the policy of isolation pursued by the United States.

The three largest EU states (the so-called E-3 group) were in a good position for beginning direct talks with Iran. They had a common belief that the issue of the Iranian nuclear program could be solved through negotiations. This also provided an opportunity to demonstrate that European states, divided on the issue of Iraq, are capable of cooperating in order to solve another crisis related to nonproliferation of weapons of mass destruction. Moreover, it made it possible to prove to the US that the "European" way of crisis-solving through negotiations (as opposed to threats or use of force) could be effective. In August 2003, the Foreign Ministers of France, Germany and the UK sent a letter to the Foreign Minister of Iran, Kamal Kharrazi, in which they proposed an opening of talks.

Meanwhile, more and more evidence was emerging proving that Iran had supplied IAEA with false information on its nuclear program. The most important finding of IAEA inspectors were the traces of highly enriched uranium in samples taken in the Natanz plant.[10] For fear of other states giving their support to the tough US position, the Islamic Republic decided to open talks with the E-3. Foreign Ministers of the three European states paid a visit to Iran in October 2003 for a meeting with Hassan Rohani, the Secretary of the Iranian Supreme National Security Council, who was appointed to hold talks concerning the nuclear program.

On October 21, 2003 a joint statement was issued.[11] Iran emphasized that it would fully cooperate with the IAEA and would suspend works on uranium enrichment and processing. It also announced that it would sign The Additional Protocol to the Nuclear Safeguards Agreement with the IAEA (which took place on December 18, 2003), and that until its ratification by Parliament it would voluntarily abide by its provisions. E-3 ministers announced that they acknowledged the rights of Iran to peaceful use of atomic energy and believed that the crisis might be solved at the level of the Board of Governors of IAEA. For Iran, this meant keeping at bay the threat of handing the case over to the Security Council. The United States, still calling for a tougher position from the international community as regards Iran, was isolated.

Negotiations with Iran

The first success of European diplomacy seemed to confirm the virtue of the negotiations policy. The United States, however, was expressing serious doubt as to whether an agreement could be reached that would guarantee that Iran would not achieve capabilities for the production of nuclear weapons.[12] It was suspected that the European states, driven by their own economic interests, would agree to a compromise that would allow further development of the Iranian program. It would mean that in a dozen or so years a strategic adversary of the US and its allies in the Middle East would be an Iran as a nuclear power.

In 2004 – 2005, the attention of the United States was focused, however, on Iraq. Forecasts of quick stabilization of the situation in this country and of establishing a model Islamic democracy in the Middle East, did not come true. Americans and their allies engaged themselves in a long process of rebuilding the political system and structures of the Iraqi state, realized in the conditions of terrorist attacks as well as ethnic and religious conflicts. In these circumstances, it was vital that Iran would not act against American interests in Iraq. The influence of Iran on the situation in the neighboring country stemmed not only from religious factors[13], but also from close ties with the Shiite political groups, the role of which was increasing together with the progress of political transformation.

Military and political involvement in the stabilization of Iraq and economic costs related to it, as well as the burden it posed for the American administration meant that in this period the US had limited options to take the initiative in solving the dispute over the Iranian nuclear program. The European negotiations, from which the United

States officially distanced themselves, were thus de facto favorable to the American policy in the Middle East.

The talks between the European states and Iran were complicated, marked with many tensions and crises. Iran made attempts to impose its own interpretation of the scope of the program suspension, for example it considered that the suspension of works on centrifuges involves only new agreements signed for their manufacture. This would mean that it could continue the production of equipment on the basis of previous orders. In August 2004, Iran announced that it intended to begin processing of a large quantity of uranium concentrate in Isfahan, as its obligations supposedly encompassed exclusively refrain from using the processed uranium in centrifuges.

Thus, it has become necessary to conclude a new agreement that would establish more precisely the conditions and objectives of the European-Iranian negotiations. In order to secure the support of other EU states and not to make the impression of a "directorate" being established to conduct EU's foreign policy, the largest EU countries included the High Representative for the Common Foreign and Security Policy, Javier Solana, in the talks. The new agreement with Iran was signed in Paris on November 15, 2004.[14] This time the scope of suspension of the Iranian nuclear program was outlined in detail. It was also agreed that it remained in force until an agreement is concluded that would provide "objective guarantees that Iran's nuclear program is exclusively for peaceful purposes" and would "provide firm guarantees on nuclear, technological and economic cooperation and firm commitments on security issues".

During the visit of the US President G. W. Bush to Europe in February 2005, the results of talks with Iran were presented. The European states assured that they did not intend to give in on the most vital issue – the verifiable limitation of the nuclear program by Iran. They tried to convince the President to send Iran a visible signal that the United States support their activities. On March 11, 2005 Secretary of State Condoleezza Rice announced a new American position on Iran. The United States gave its official support to the E-3 states and decided not to object to opening of talks on Iran's WTO membership and to consider the issue of exports of spare parts for airliners to this country.[15]

It might seem that there was a possibility of bringing the crisis to an end. Two problems, however, made the final agreement difficult. Firstly, the US rejected to directly join the negotiation process, in spite of the fact that it was the only state that could present important additional proposals to Iran. First of all, they would need to concern security guarantees, and also concessions in particular issues – in giving consent to deliveries of spare parts to aircrafts and to handing over to the Islamic Republic the assets frozen in the US after the fall of the Iranian monarchy.

Secondly, the key significance to the success of negotiations was in agreeing upon measures to guarantee that the Iranian nuclear program would be implemented for peace purposes only. The E-3 states, supported by the US, took the position that the only guarantee could be Iran's total resignation from those elements of the program that could enable manufacturing of fissile materials for nuclear explosives: uranium enrichment, operating a heavy-water reactor and the construction of an installation for re-processing used fuel and plutonium retrieval. Iran agreed to temporary and voluntary (which it emphasized many times) suspension of these elements of the program. It stressed, however, that the possession of technologies related to all stages of the fuel cycle is an inalienable right of any state. Although it could agree to concessions on particular issues, it ruled out permanent resignation from its rights.

In spite of the fact that during negotiations the positions were not brought any closer, the E-3 group decided to draw up an agreement proposal and to submit it to Iran in early August 2005. It was assumed that until that time the new president of Iran, elected in June, could obtain influence over how the policy was shaped. Most Western commentators forecasted the victory of an experienced politician, a former president in 1989 – 1997, Ali Akbar Hashemi Rafsanjani. It was foreseen that he might be ready for a compromise ending the crisis and for a "new opening" in foreign policy. The victory of the former mayor of Tehran, Mahmoud Ahmadinejad, in the second stage of elections on June 25, 2005, was a big surprise. In his election campaign, Ahmadinejad emphasized that Iran must maintain dignity in its contacts with the West and could not resign from its rights.[16] The scope of the future involvement of the new president of Iran in foreign policy and the influence he could have on it remained unknown.

Failure of the European Concept

In late July 2005, Iran notified the E-3 group that it considered August 1 as a final date for the proposal of the European states to be submitted. The group decided to put forward its offer in the first week of August. Iran, expecting that it would not contain the most important issue – the European consent to uranium enrichment, notified IAEA on August 1 that it would commence uranium processing in the Isfahan plants. In response, the E-3 states filed a motion for an extraordinary meeting of the Board of Governors and at the same time sent their proposal to Iran.

The document entitled "Framework for a Long-Term Agreement between the Islamic Republic of Iran and France, Germany and the United Kingdom, with the Support of the High Representative of the European Union" was handed to Iran on August 5, 2005.[17] Its most important elements were: European security guarantees, a proposal of deepening political cooperation, acknowledgement of Iran's rights to develop a peaceful program of nuclear energy and granting of limited support (including joint development of additional guarantees of deliveries of nuclear fuel for Iranian reactors and the location of supplementary nuclear fuel stock outside Iran), establishment of cooperation in economic matters and scientific research as well as giving support for Iran's application for WTO membership.

In exchange, Iran was to limit its nuclear program to operating energy reactors, to discontinue work on full fuel cycle and to interrupt work on the research reactor in Arak, as well as to obligate itself not to withdraw from the Non-Proliferation Treaty and to ratify the Additional Protocol as early as in 2005. The EU offer did not anticipate permanent limitation of the Iranian nuclear program – a modification of Iranian obligations could take place during a Ministry-level conference in 10 years.

Already on the day it received the document, Iran described it as unacceptable. It officially rejected the proposal on August 8, 2005 and at the same day it began processing the first portion of uranium in Isfahan. It was the best proof that the European negotiations policy had failed. The E-3 states moved closer to the American position and decided to toughen the policy towards Iran and to hand the Iranian crisis case over to the Security Council. However, when the US refused to rule out an attack on Iranian nuclear installations[18], the European states began to express their concern, fearing the loss of control over the situation.

At the meeting of the Board of Governors of IAEA in September, it became clear that the proposal of handing over the case to the UN Security Council did not find broader support. Of key significance was the position of Russia, which openly expressed its opposition.[19] The European states were forced to present a modified project of a resolution that did not anticipate the handover of the case to the Security Council. The resolution was adopted with the majority of the votes of 22 countries on September 24, 2005. Venezuela was the only country to vote against, but as many as 12 states (including China and Russia) abstained from voting. It proved that the international community lacked unanimity as to its response to the Iranian crisis.

In early November, Russia presented its concept of a compromise solution to the crisis: the nuclear material produced in Iran was to be enriched in Russia and then sent back to Iran in the form of fuel sets for reactors. The European states and the US supported the Russian proposal. Iran initially rejected it, gradually, however, it began to demonstrate growing interest in it, trying to keep the intervention of the UN Security Council at bay.

Aggressive statements by President Ahmadinejad, and especially his negation of the Holocaust and his references to the statement by Imam Khomeini that "Israel must be wiped off the map"[20], had its impact on the development of the situation. This strengthened the belief of the European states and the US, that Iran in possession of nuclear weapon production capabilities and weapons deliveries systems constitutes a major threat to international security.

The Iranian Issue in the UN Security Council

The agreement within the transatlantic partnership that Iran should feel the negative impact of its conduct made it easier to cooperate on directing the issue to the Security Council. A common position, consistently promoted by the US and European partners, allowed to overcome the resistance of Russia and China. The direct reason was the decision of Iran, which informed the IAEA on January 3 that it had decided to resume research "related to a peaceful nuclear energy program".[21]

Before the extraordinary meeting of the Board of Governors in February 2006, the change in the positions of Russia and China became visible. The two states had to make a choice: either to give support to the European Union and the United States or to continue to support the Islamic Republic. The choice was difficult, concerning their political and economic interests in Iran. At the request of Russia, a compromising solution was agreed upon. The Board of Governors announced that it would hand over the Iranian *dossier* in March. An additional month was supposed to give Iran some more time to correct its policy. Iran reacted to the resolution by withdrawing from voluntary compliance with the provisions of the Additional protocol and informing on commencement of preparations for the launch of uranium enrichment process in the Natanz plant.[22]

In early 2006, a new form of policy cooperation in the Iranian issue emerged – these were the meetings of representatives of the US, the UK, France, Germany, Russia and China. What led to the formation of this informal group (called P5+1, as it was composed of five permanent members of the Security Council and Germany) were both political factors (awareness of the significance of the crisis, agreement as to the fact that Iran should not possess nuclear weapons) and practical ones (the need for better coordination of activities and improved communication). There is no doubt, however, that such a dialogue was established under pressure from the US and the European states.

In the works of the Security Council on the Iranian issue, the key significance lied in finding a compromise between the position of the US, the UK and France, in favor of gradual increase of pressures from the Security Council over Iran, and the position of Russia and China. Possible sanctions of the Council could involve nuclear cooperation with Iran and supplies of armaments to this country, i.e. areas which brought particular benefits to Russia.[23] Chinese contracts for energy resources deliveries from Iran would also be at risk. The two states feared that a process might start, which – in the situation of no concessions being made by Iran – would have to end with the introduction of sanctions, and even with the use of force against this country.

Predicting the resistance of Russia and China against commencement of discussions on the issue of Iran, France and the UK, supported by the US, presented in the first half of March a project of statement by the Security Council chairman concerning the issue. In practice, this type of document, adopted on the consensus basis by all Council members, contains unbinding recommendations. Negotiations over the text of the statement lasted till the end of March 2006. Under pressure from Russia and China, its content was eased. The Security Council called Iran to fulfill the recommendations of IAEA, and particularly the total and permanent discontinuation of any works on uranium enrichment.[24] In 30 days, a report on how the recommendations of the Council are fulfilled was to be issued by the Director General of IAEA. This meant that undertaking of any specific steps in order to solve the crisis was postponed to give Iran some time to change its policy.

Iran, however, did not intend to give in to pressures. On April 11, 2006, on a special conference, President Ahmadinejad announced that Iran had made a technological leap and produced in Natanz uranium enriched to 3,5 % level[25] and that the program would be further developed till industrial-scale uranium enrichment capabilities are achieved.

In late April, the Security Council received a report from Director General of IAEA, which stated that information possessed by the agency on the Iranian program of centrifuge production and the role of army in the nuclear program remain incomplete. In early May, France and the UK presented a project of a resolution. The project provided for that if Iran does not fulfill the requests of the Council, *inter alia* it does not discontinue uranium enrichment and does not suspend works on reactor in Arak, the Council „would consider such further measures as may be necessary to ensure compliance with this resolution".[26] What is important, the resolution would refer to competencies of the Council provided for in Chapter VII of the United Nations Charter, thus being of a binding nature and would free the way to the use of provisions on sanctions and use of force, contained in this chapter.

For Russia and China, however, the resolution project proved to be unacceptable. Thus, it was not voted in the Security Council. It was agreed upon instead that the E-3 group would submit a further proposal to Iran with a comprehensive solution to the crisis that would include both a list of benefits and possible sanctions. The European states and the US expected, in exchange for this concession, that Russia and China would support introduction of selective sanctions against Iran if it rejects this offer as well.

Apart from elements of the August 2005 proposal, rejected by Iran, the new one contained a promise of nuclear reactors to be constructed in Iran by European companies. Thus, the development of a nuclear energy system in the Islamic Republic would not exclusively depend on Russia. The most important element of the proposal was, however, the request of limiting the Iranian nuclear program. In response, President Ahmadinejad stated that the European states treat Iran as a child "telling him they will give him candies or walnuts and take gold from him in return".[27]

Iran began to seek establishing bilateral talks with the United States. On May 8, 2006 the Americans were delivered a letter of President Ahmadinejad, addressed to G. W. Bush. It was a surprising move of Ahmadinejad, who – a few months earlier – called Bush "a warmonger", whose place is before "people's tribunal".[28] In order to use the propaganda significance of the letter to the largest extent possible, Iran revealed its content after a few days. The letter did not contain any concrete proposals concerning the ending of the crisis. It was an emotional defense of the case of Iran, full of rhetorical questions and references to principles of religion and justice, as well as criticism towards Israel, the United States and the principles of Western democracy and liberalism.[29]

President Bush decided to ignore the letter of Ahmadinejad. Any polemic with the philosophical and religious theses contained therein would be perceived as considering Ahmadinejad a serious partner for discussion. There was no response, initially, to other offers from Iran of establishing direct negotiations. Such an approach was criticized, in the US as well, as no advantage was taken from the opportunity to take over the initiative in solving the crisis.[30] It had been reminded that the United States held talks earlier with such states as Libya or North Korea. The European states, and first of all Germany, advised the US to join the negotiations.

On May 31, 2005, Condoleezza Rice announced that the US is ready to join talks with Iran held by the E-3 group states, as soon as Iran will fully suspend uranium enrichment.[31] The Secretary of State emphasized that after this condition was fulfilled, multilateral talks on other topics and establishment of economic cooperation would be possible. This statement was, first, to prove the international community that the US was interested in peaceful solving of the crisis and, second, to strengthen the pressure on Iran to adhere to the talks on the conditions put forward by P5+1 group.

Ultimately, details of the European offering, supported by six states, were agreed upon in early June 2006. On June 6, Javier Solana delivered it to Tehran. The Iranian authorities promised to consider thoroughly the received proposals, many statements, however, including by the spiritual leader in Iran, Ali Khamenei and President Ahmadinejad, proved that the preliminary condition – suspension of the part of the nuclear program – is unacceptable for Iran. European states and the US expected that the official response of Iran would be known before the G-8 summit in St. Petersburg, held on July 15, 2006. Instead, Iran announced that it needed some more time in order to take a stance on the offer, and the answer would be given by August 22 (the end of the month of Mordad in the Iranian calendar). For fear of further delays, the Security Council adopted on July 31 the resolution no. 1696, that placed an obligation on Iran to suspend uranium enrichment by the end of August 2006 and that threatened with the use of "adequate measures" in the form of sanctions provided for in Article 41 of the United Nations Charter.[32]

Perspectives of Transatlantic Cooperation in the Issue of Iran

The Iranian crisis is, for one more time, in a turning point. If Iran accepts the offer and suspends a part of its nuclear program, putting the crisis to an end would become possible (in spite of continuing political confrontation between the US and Iran). If, on the other hand, Iran would reject the proposed conditions, a complex process of introducing sanctions against the Islamic Republic would commence. Possibly, in case of a veto by Russia and China in the Security Council, the EU states could introduce their own system of sanctions, similar to the American one.

The hitherto course of the Iranian crisis proved that a pragmatic cooperation between the US and Europe might be continued, also after the experience in Iraq. In the area of security, the transatlantic partnership underwent a transformation towards a more flexible community, where there is a place for periods of close cooperation as well as of differing policies. Certainly, in case of policy towards Iran, a loosening of transatlantic bonds could have been observed, however – contrary to the expectations of many experts – it did not automatically mean any severance of cooperation, or any strive for confrontation. Mutual loyalty of partners was visible both when the European states did not agree to a compromising solution to the crisis on Iranian terms and when the US curbed its criticism of European negotiations with Iran, and later proposed that it could join the talks. This allowed closer positions to be formed and joint activities in the period where the Iranian case was to be considered on the Security Council forum.

This does not mean, however, that there has ever existed an agreed division of roles between the American "bad cop" and the European "good cop", and that changes in the policy towards Iran were closely coordinated. On the strategic level, deep discrepancies between the US and Europe still exist. The United States invariably believes that the main problem lies in the Iranian power system and the ruling elites which only understand the language of force. The European states, on the other hand, continue to concentrate on the Iranian problem of the nuclear program and hope that a rational analysis of benefits and losses would convince the authorities in Tehran to compromise. The new transatlantic concord on the issue of Iran might thus prove temporary. If the United States propose the use of force against Iran or the European states begin to consider an independent agreement with the Islamic Republic, mutual grudges and accusations, known from the period of the Iraq intervention, might explode with twice as much force.

Endnotes

[1] R. Kagan, Potęga i raj. Ameryka i Europa w nowym porządku świata, (Warsaw: Studio Emka, 2003).

[2] Partnership in the area of security makes an element of transatlantic relations that also encompass a deepened cooperation in other areas: political, economic, social and cultural ones. See J. Gryz, Proces instytucjonalizacji stosunków transatlantyckich, Wydawnictwo Naukowe „Scholar", Warsaw 2004.

[3] The interpretation of the transatlantic partnership, presented above, is based of the „security community" notion introduced by K. Deutsch. K. W. Deutsch et al., Political Community and the North Atlantic Area: International Organization in the Light of Historical Experience (Princeton: Princeton University Press , 1957).

[4] A deepened analysis of the development of transatlantic cooperation can be found in D. Eggert, Transatlantycka wspólnota bezpieczeństwa, Żurawia Papers, vol. 5, Wydawnictwo Naukowe „Scholar", Warsaw 2005.

[5] For the chronology of the first stage of the Iranian crisis and its interpretation see for example P. Durys, Program nuklearny Iranu: implikacje dla bezpieczeństwa regionalnego i globalnego, Ministry of Defence, Defence Policy Department, Warsaw 2004; and Iran's Strategic Weapons Programs. A net assessment, IISS Strategic Dossier, International Institute for Strategic Studies, Routledge–Abingdon 2005.

[6] People's Mujahedin of Iran (MEK) have taken for its aim an overthrowing of the Iranian theocracy. They were given support by Saddam Hussein, who allowed MEK to operate from the Iraqi territory. See B. Bolechów, Terroryzm w świecie podwubiegunowym. Przewartościowania i kontynuacje, Wydawnictwo Adam Marszałek, Toruń 2002. After the intervention of coalition forces in Iraq in 2003, the fighters of MEK have been put in an internment camp.

[7] In line with Article III letter B point 4 of the Statute of IAEA: „[…] if in connection with the activities of the Agency there should arise questions that are within the competence of the Security Council, the Agency shall notify the Security Council, as the organ bearing the main responsibility for the maintenance of international peace and security […]".

[8] Statement by the Board, 19 June 2003, IAEA Media Advisory 2003/72 <http://www.iaea.org/NewsCenter/MediaAdvisory/2003/medadvise200372.html>.

[9] See W. Waszczykowski, Współczesne stosunki Iranu z Unią Europejską, „Zeszyty Akademii Dyplomatycznej" Warsaw 2003, No. 4, p. 20.

[10] Iran said that it had used second-hand equipment supplied by smuggling network run by a Pakistani scientist, A.Q. Khan.

[11] Agreed Statement at the End of a Visit to the Islamic Republic of Iran by the Foreign Ministers of Britain, France and Germany, Tehran, 21 October 2003, Iran's Strategic Weapons Programs (En. 5), p. 19.

[12] See R. J. Einhorn, A Transatlantic Strategy on Iran's Nuclear Program, The Washington Quarterly 2004, vol. 27, no. 4, p. 26.

[13] Around 60 % of Iraqi population are followers of the Shiite Islam – Iran's state religion. Major places of Shiite pilgrimages, Karbala and Najaf, are in the Iraqi territory. See Iran in Iraq: how much influence?, Middle East Report No. 38, 21 March 2005, International Crisis Group.

[14] Communication dated 26 November 2004, received from the Permanent Representatives of France, Germany, the Islamic Republic of Iran and the United Kingdom concerning the agreement signed in Paris on 15 November 2004, INFCIRC/637, IAEA <http://www.iaea.org/Publications/Documents/Infcircs/2004/infcirc637.pdf>.

[15] R. N. Burns, United States' Policy Toward Iran, Testimony before the Senate Foreign Relations Committee, May 19, 2005, p. 5 <http://foreign.senate.gov/testimony/2005/BurnsTestimony050519.pdf>.

[16] What does Ahmadi-Nejad's Victory Mean?, Middle East Update Briefing No. 18, 4 August 2005, International Crisis Group, p. 11.

[17] See Communication dated 8 August 2005 received from the Resident Representatives of France, Germany and the United Kingdom to the Agency, INFCIRC/651, IAEA <http://www.basicint.org/countries/iran/IranIAEA 20050808.pdf>.

[18] President G. W. Bush announced in his interview for the Israeli television on August 13, 2005, that where the stopping of Iran from acquiring nuclear weapon is concerned, all options are on the table. See Associated Press release: Bush: "All options are on the table" regarding Iran's nuclear aspirations, USA Today 13, 2005 <http://www.usatoday.com/news/washington/2005-08-13-bush-iran-nuclear_x.htm>.

[19] Reuters, Russian opposition threatens EU push on Iran, September 21, 2005.

[20] Ahmadinejad: Wipe Israel off map, Aljazeera.net, October 26, 2005 <http://english.aljazeera.net/NR/exeres/15E6BF77-6F91-46EE-A4B5-A3CE0E9957EA.htm>.

[21] Reuters, Iran to resume nuclear research, February 9, 2006.

[22] Reuters, Iran resumes uranium enrichment, ends UN check, February 6, 2006.

[23] In December 2005, Russia signed an agreement with Iran on delivery of 29 Tor-M1 missile systems for anti-aircraft and anti-missile defense of short- and medium-range. Its value was estimated at USD 700 million. See J.-Ch. Peuch, Russia: Moscow Confirms Missile-Systems Deal With Iran, Radio Free Europe/Radio Liberty, February 10, 2006 <http://www.rferl.org/featuresarticle/2006/02/f1477c44-4533-4436-b19d-1948ed806ce2.html>.

[24] Statement by the President of the Security Council, S/PRST/2006/15, UN Security Council, March 29, 2006 <http://www.globalsecurity.org/wmd/library/news/iran/2006/iran-060329-sprst2006-15.htm>.

[25] This is the level of concentration that allows use of this material as a fuel in nuclear reactors, but not as a nuclear weapon component. During the conference, a metal box was presented supposed to contain an uranium sample enriched in Natanzu plant.

[26] AFP, France, Britain propose binding UN resolution against Iran, The Tocqueville Conection, May 3, 2006 <http://www.adetocqueville.com/cgi-binloc/searchTTC.cgi?displayZop+30424>.

[27] Reuters, Iran scorns EU atomic incentives, Boston.com, May 17, 2006, <http://www.boston.com/news/world/middleeast/articles/2006/05/17/iranian_president_scorns_eu_atomic_incentives/>.

[28] AFP, Iran's Ahmadinejad says Bush should face people's tribunal, February 1, 2006, <http://www.theallineed.com/news/0602/01080946.htm>.

[29] The letter was broadly distributed by Iranian diplomatic posts, it was also translated into Polish: Tekst listu Prezydenta Islamskiej Republiki Iranu Dr. Mahmuda Ahmadineżada do Prezydenta Stanów Zjednoczonych Ameryki George'a W. Busha, document made available by the Embassy of the Islamic Republic of Iran in Poland.

[30] Among those who called for a commencement of talks with Iran were Chuck Hagel, an influential Republican senator, Madeleine K. Albright and a former national security advisor Samuel R. „Sandy" Berger. See G. Kessler, US under Pressure to Talk to Tehran, Washington Post, May 11, 2006, p. 20.

[31] Press Conference on Iran, May 31, 2006, US Department of State <http://www.state.gov/secretary/rm/2006/67103.htm>.

[32] Resolution 1696 (2006), S/RES/1696 (2006), UN Security Council, July 31, 2006 <http://daccessdds.un.org/doc/UNDOC/GEN/N06/465/03/PDF/N0646503.pdf?OpenElement>.

10

The Simple Numeration of the Israeli-Palestinian Conflict Resolution, 1967 – 2006

Rafael Reuveny and Jaclyn D. Streitfeld

The Jewish/Israeli-Palestinian interaction has generated one of the lengthiest and deepest conflicts in modern history. Since 1967, there have been many attempts to resolve the Israeli-Palestinian conflict, some coming from the actors themselves, and some coming from the outside. Yet all these attempts failed. Israeli, Palestinian and international leaders agree that the two state option is the only viable way out of the conundrum of ongoing conflict. Despite this understanding, the conflict has continued with no end in sight.

This simple truth immediately opens the door for a new question. Why have all these attempts failed? Perhaps their promoters have not worked hard enough? Perhaps the conflict is simply intractable? Or has there been something inherently faulty in these programs? Assuming we can answer these questions, and accepting the goal as the resolution of the conflict, can we use the insight gained from past experiences to say something about the way to attend this goal?

It is well known that some Israelis and Jews believe that the Palestinians ultimately want to destroy Israel, and some Palestinians believe Israel wants to dominate them. Others believe that Israeli and a Palestinian states simply cannot coexist between the Jordan River and the Mediterranean Sea. Taken together, these views imply indefinite conflict. Our premise is that Israeli-Palestinian peace is possible. Of course, peace can entail different levels of friendliness. Suffice it for us if this peace would denote the end of hostilities and the establishment of formal diplomatic relations. While deep Israeli-Palestinian friendliness may not come in the future, cold peace can also be stable. The peace Israel has with Egypt, for example, has been holding on for more than 25 years, despite its alleged coldness.

This essay argues that the positions and actions of the United States (US) inhibited the attempts to resolve the Israeli-Palestinian conflict since 1967 from succeeding. The scramble since 1967 has not been a bilateral relationship but rather a trilateral relationship. Our answer to the question of why have all the attempts to solve the dispute failed puts the blame squarely on the US policy: these attempts failed because the US ultimately did not actively support them and push them forward. In the past, when the US has put pressure on Israel to act on various diplomatic issues, even when Israel initially rejects the proposal it has eventually given in to US demands. Had the US wanted to actively support a resolution attempt, more pressure on the Israeli government was necessary, but in most cases the US abandons the plan without actively pushing the Israelis. In the remainder of this essay, we will first demonstrate the empirical validity of our observation on the US policy toward the attempts to resolve the conflict since 1967, and then go deeper into the way by which the US policy is the source of the repeated failures to resolve the conflict.

We must stress that this essay is neither anti-Israeli nor pro-Palestinian. We are not interested in polemics, and any attempt to restate our essay in this manner will misrepresent it. We are interested in an analysis of the way things are, not how they should be. We will demonstrate our thesis empirically by observing the behaviors of our actors over time, focusing on one type of event: formally stated conflict resolution plans. What were the positions of Israel, the Palestinians and the US on each of these plans? As we shall discuss, the triangle formed by the three positions has shaped each plan's fate.

The Essentials of the Israeli-Palestinian Conflict

The Israeli/Zionist conflict has lasted more than 100 years. Before 1947, the conflict was inter-communal, involving two young and evolving national political movements competing over the same land, which neither of them controlled (before 1918, the land was controlled by the Ottoman Empire, and in 1918-1948, the land was controlled by the British). The outcome of the 1967 war, in which Israel occupied the West Bank and Gaza Strip regions ("the territories"), fueled an already hostile debate and set the agenda for every conflict resolution attempt to follow. The essence of the conflict became one of mutual recognition: Until the late 1980s, Israel refused to recognize the Palestinian right for self-determination, and the Palestinians felt the same about Israel. In 1993, Israel and the Palestinian Liberation Organization (PLO) recognized one another, but on and off fighting has continued regarding the possession of territories and the nature of the Palestinian self-governance in the future.

Israelis and Palestinians are not isolated from the outside world. Various states and international organizations have proposed plans to resolve the conflict since 1967. This activity demonstrates that peace between Israel and Palestine is not strictly a regional, but rather an international concern and priority. Yet even international efforts which both Israel and Palestine agree to fall short of orchestrating the steps necessary to initiate and maintain a stable peace.

Today, most Israelis, Palestinians, and outside observers agree that the two-state solution is the most viable option available, but this opinion has not always been shared by the parties. The two-state solution was suggested by the United Nations in 1947. The Palestinians rejected it, while the Zionists accepted it. The idea was then removed from the table for the next 45 years. In 1949-1967, the two-state solution was not feasible as Jordan controlled the West Bank, Egypt controlled the Gaza Strip, and the Palestinians rejected the idea. The conflict continued to simmer. After Israel occupied the territories in the Six-Day War, the conflict changed its nature. In 1967-1992, Israel refused to deal with the Palestinians on a political basis, arguing they were not a people, and signaled its intent to annex the territories by building settlements all over the occupied land. The conflict exploded from time to time, only to be squashed by Israeli force. In 1987, the

Palestinians launched a full scale revolt against Israel, which has gradually changed the Israeli position in favor of a political solution to end the conflict.

After almost a century of conflict, in 1993 Israel and the PLO recognized each other and launched the Oslo process of conflict resolution. The architects of the process assumed that economic benefits would secure peace. Israel would gradually transfer land in the territories to a newly formed Palestinian governing body – the Palestinian Authority (PA). The PA would assist in guarding Israeli security, squelching Palestinian radicals who rejected the Oslo process. Over time, the economic gains would promote mutual trust. The political relations would improve, leading to a peace agreement.

Many academics and policymakers adopted this view. In the mid 1990s, Israeli Foreign Minister Shimon Peres talked about a new Middle East, Palestinian official Nabil Sha'th and Jordan's Prince Hassan called for the formation of a Middle Eastern economic community, and US Secretary of State Warren Christopher declared "the Middle East was again open for business". Scholars argued that the enmity was about to be transformed into friendship. It was assumed a peace agreement could be signed by October 1999, the date specified by the Oslo process.[1] This rosy scenario has not materialized.

In the 1990s, there were many violent Israeli-Palestinian confrontations. In late 1998, Israel decreed that it would not transfer more land to the Palestinians unless the PA cracked down on the Palestinian armed groups. The Oslo process remained frozen during the first half of 1999. In the summer of 1999, the Palestinian Chairman, Yasser Arafat, met with the new Israeli Prime Minister, Ehud Barak, and the two restarted the process. Soon after, there were more attacks and counter attacks and Israel accused the PA of not doing enough to fight terrorism. By November, Israel and the PA were disputing over Barak's comment that UN Resolution 242, which calls for Israeli withdrawal from the territories, did not apply to the Palestinians since they did not rule the area before 1967. Palestinian official Sa'eb Erikat said that Barak's comment killed the peace process and Arafat strongly condemned it. Tension rose as Israel and the PA disputed over the implementation of their late-1998 Wye-River agreement.[2]

Despite these setbacks, in July 2000 it again looked as if peace was feasible. Although the Camp David Summit did not lead to an agreement, talks continued. Then, on September 28, 2000, a visit by the then Israeli opposition leader Ariel Sharon to the site of the Al Aqsa Mosque in East Jerusalem provoked Palestinian protests that grew into a second full scale rebellion against Israel. The two sides continued to talk and in January 2001 progress apparently had been made. By then, the Barak government had lost the support of the Knesset. In March 2001, Ariel Sharon formed a new government, and rejected the evolving compromise. The conflict has escalated into a violent cycle of actions and reactions.

The June 5, 1967 Israeli Borders

If the actors in this conflict can agree that dividing the region into two separate states is the most logical solution, then why does the conflict remain in place? What force prevents any resolution that uses this premise as a basis from succeeding? One of the most persistent problems in this debate is the issue of borders; where does Israel end and Palestine begin?

The border dispute took center stage in the aftermath of the 1967 war. Israel had clearly defined borders in the 1949-1967 time period. After June 5, 1967, this changed quickly as a result of the Israeli victory in the war. Israel occupied the Gaza Strip and the West Bank, and many Israeli's sought to hold on to some portion, if not all, of the land taken during the war. Palestinians, most of whom remained on the land, clearly opposed this idea, and the international community supported this opposition. In November of 1967, the UN Security Council passed Resolution 242 in order to settle this issue.

Resolution 242 emphasized the inadmissibility of the attainment and occupation of land by war and called on Israel to surrender lands it occupied. All the states in the region were required to acknowledge the borders, sovereignty and territorial integrity of each other. Unlike Resolution 181 from 1947, which divided Palestine among Jews and Palestinians, Resolution 242 did not call for Palestinian statehood, but rather called for settling the Palestinian refugee problem. This language bears significance in the ongoing conflict because Israel chose to take a literal translation of Resolution 242. Israelis and Palestinians alike both saw this as a way of making the problem a humanitarian rather than political one. Israel used this point to argue against meeting the Palestinians at a Peace Conference since their leaders had no political clout, while the Palestinians used it to outright reject the Resolution and demand another that acknowledges their sovereignty.

While the Security Council viewed Resolution 242 as a demand for complete Israeli withdrawal from the territories, Israel interpreted it differently, stressing that the final submission of Resolution 242 omitted the article "the" before the word "territories." Thus the Resolution instructed Israel to withdraw from territories acquired in the 1967 war, not *the* territories. Israeli leaders argued that the Resolution therefore instructed them to withdraw from some *parts* of the territories not the *entire* territory. Israel ignored the reality that this interpretation contradicts the emphasis on the inadmissibility of territorial acquisition in war, and would only agree to a Resolution that called for partial withdrawal.

Security Council Resolution 242 set the tone for almost every conflict resolution attempt to follow. Throughout the 1990s, the attempts divided the territories into zones, granting some small portion of the territories to the PLO, and some larger portion to Israel. The PLO was also given certain aspects of self-government over local affairs (for example, education, services, civilian judicial affairs, cultural sovereignty), but not military and political sovereignty. The fighting intensified in the second half of the 1990s as the number of Israeli settlers in the territories continued to grow, more than doubling in 1993-2000 alone. It became apparent that this has been a political move for Israel, hoping to argue for the necessity of control over at least parts of the territories due to the large number of Israelis living there.

Disputes over the 1967 borders appear to be the stimulus for the sustained conflict in the region. Israel's two leading government parties have disagreed on how to treat the issue; Likud administrations supported keeping all of the territories and encouraged increased movement to the settlements while Labor administrations are willing to cede some land to the Palestinians or (before 1988) to Jordan in return for peace with the Arab countries in the region. Both the Labor and Likud parties have agreed, however, that at least some portion of the territories should remain in Israeli hands, and both have preferred a region with a Palestinian statehood that falls short of complete sovereignty.

The Palestinian side has refused to agree to any resolution that does not include recognition of Palestinian sovereignty in the territories and Israeli return to the 1967 border. Since the majority of resolution attempts use Resolution 242, and hence the 1967 border issue, as their basis, it seems this would be the cause of the deadlock since the resolution appealed to neither side.

The two sides, however, have not operated in a vacuum. As Israel's financial and military supporter, the United States (US) has maintained a critical position in all of the resolution attempts. Had it decided to impose a position on Israel regarding some attempt, Israel would have had no choice but comply. Let us proceed, if so, by describing the various attempts to resolve the conflict since 1967.

The Conflict Resolution Attempts

This section overviews the formal attempts to resolve the conflict, beginning with the UN Resolution 181, which proposed a division of Palestine between the parties in 1947, and culminating with the Israeli unilateral attempts to set Israeli border since 2003. We divide the time period to three segments: 1947-1992, 1993-January 2001, and February 2001-2006.

The 1947-1992 Period

In 1947, UN Resolution 181 officially partitioned the region into Israeli and Palestinian territories, granting 55% of Palestine to the Zionists and placed Jerusalem under international control. The Zionists accepted the resolution, while the Palestinians rejected it. In the 1948 war, the new state of Israel enlarged its share of Palestine to 78%. In 1949, Israel signed cease-fire agreements with the Arab countries it fought, but not with the Palestinians, who were not represented in the talks. In 1949-1967, the Israeli-Palestinian conflict simmered, turning violent along the border of Israel with the West Bank and the Gaza Strip from time to time. But in general, Israel accepted its 1949 borders as final.

The situation changed when hostilities ignited in the Six-Day War of 1967. In this brief war, Israel acquired the West Bank and Gaza

Strip and began devising plans to incorporate them within its borders. In the twenty-five years that followed the 1967 War, there was virtually no agreement between the parties, but there were many attempts to resolve the conflict. Table 1 displays these many attempts.

As shown in Table 1, two main themes contributed to perpetuating the conflict over this time period: recognition of the PLO and returning to the pre-1967 war borders. The large majority of resolution attempts in this period were based upon Israel returning to the 1967 borders, as prescribed in Resolution 242. The resolutions proposed by third parties often added recognition of the PLO to the parameters of the agreements. Since Israel's official stance during this time period was to disregard the PLO and to expand their borders into the acquired territories, it never backed down to accept any of the proposed resolutions.

A partial shift in policy took place during the 1980s, which involved proposals to incorporate the Palestinians into Jordan. The conflict resolutions attempts now accepted that the Palestinian problem was not only humanitarian. The plans offered assumed that the best solution would be to create some form of a Jordanian-Palestinian federation. Many Israelis still disagreed with this approach, since it included provisions for some of the territories to be turned over to Jordan. The goal of the PLO remained to break away from the Israeli control. Conflict resolution attempts that ignored the political nature of the Palestinian situation were deemed unacceptable. In contrast, the PLO seemed ready to talk over the Jordanian-Palestinian federation idea.

Table 1: Conflict Resolution Attempts in 1947-1992

Plan	Date	Issue	Propo-sing Actor	Final Position		
				US	Israel	Palesti-nians
Resolu-tion 181	Nov. 1947	Partition	UN	Accepted	Accepted	Rejected
Resolu-tion 242	Nov. 1967	1967 Borders	UN	Accepted	Accepted	Rejected
Rogers	Jun. 1970	Resolution 242	US	Abandoned	Rejected	Rejected
Yariv-Shemtov	Jul. 1974	Recognition of PLO	Israel	Ignored	Rejected	Considered
Ford's Reas-sessment	Mar. 1975	Resolution 242; Recog-nize PLO	US	Abandoned	Rejected	Condition-ally Ac-cepted*
Carter's Geneva Plan	Jul. 1977	Resolution 242; Recog-nize PLO	US	Abandoned	Rejected	Condition-ally Ac-cepted*
Carter's Auto-nomy	1978	Resolution 242; Palestin-ian Autonomy	US	Abandoned	Rejected	Rejected
Venice Declara-tion	Jun. 1980	Resolution 242; Recogni-tion of PLO	European Commu-nity	Rejected	Rejected	Accepted
Saudi-Arab League	Aug. 1981	Resolution 242; Implied recognition of Israel	Saudi Ara-bia	Rejected	Rejected	Accepted
Reagan	Sep. 1982	Resolution 242; Pales-tine-Jordan link	US	Abandoned	Rejected	Rejected
Hussein-Arafat Accord	Feb. 1985	Resolution 242; Pales-tine-Jordan link	Jordan	Ignored	Rejected	Rejected
London Agree-ment	Apr. 1987	Resolution 242; Pales-tine-Jordan link	Peres, Hussein	Ignored	Rejected	Rejected
PLO 1988 Overture	Nov. 1988	Peace; Rec-ognize PLO, state	PLO	Abandoned	Rejected	Accepted
Shamir's Plan	May 1989	Personal Pal-estinian Autonomy	Israel	Abandoned	Rejected	Rejected
Madrid Talks	Oct. 1991	Transition to final status	US	Abandoned	Abandoned	Abandoned

* PLO accepts if Israel returns to 1967 line.[3]

The 1993-2001 Period

A full-scale Palestinian revolt that broke out in December 1987 forced Israel to face the issue of Palestinian self determination. In 1993, the two parties agreed to recognize each other, and the issue of self-determination took center stage. The actors set the question of the border aside, to be discussed later, in order to gain ground on the issue of self-determination. The solution devised has created Palestinian autonomy in a series of non-contiguous areas where Palestinians live. As shown in Table 2, this strategy lead to several treaties.

Table 2: Conflict Resolution Attempts in 1993-2001

Plan	Date	Issue	Propo-sing Actor	Final Position		
				US	Israel	Palesti-nians
Oslo I*	Sep 1993	Transition	PLO	Accepted	Accepted	Accepted
Cairo Agree-ment**	May 1994	Transition	Israel	Accepted	Accepted	Accepted
Oslo II	Sep 1995	Transition	Israel and PLO	Accepted	Accepted	Accepted
Hebron Agree-ment	Jan. 1997	Transition	Israel and PLO	Accepted	Accepted	Accepted
Wye Agree-ment	Mar. 1997	Transition	US	Abandoned	Abandoned	Accepted
Sharm-el-Sheikh Memor.	Sep 1999	Transition	US	Abandoned	Abandoned	Rejected
Clinton's Camp David	Jul. 2000	Final Status	US	Ignored	Ignored	Rejected
Taba Talks	Dec. 2000	Final Status	Israel and PLO	Ignored	Ignored	Almost Ac-cepted***
Jorda-nian-Egyptian	Apr. 2001	Cease-fire and Return to Taba	Jordan and Egypt	Ignored	Rejected	Accepted
Mitchell Comm.	May 2001	Bilateral Cease-fire	US	Abandoned	Abandoned	Accepted
Tenet	Jun. 2001	Palestinian Non-violence	US	Abandoned	Abandoned	Accepted

*	Declaration of Principles on Interim Self-Government Arrangement
**	Gaza-Jericho Agreement Letters
***	The PLO accepts if it is granted sovereignty over territories, and Israel compensates Palestine on a 1:1 ratio, but Israel insisted on a 1:2 land swap ratio in its favor.[4]

In Table 2, the first four resolutions after the two parties recognized each other were also the first resolutions in which all three parties (i.e., Israel, the PLO and the US) agreed. The resolutions of the 1990s dealt mostly with creating a time-line for the transition to Palestinian statehood, and deferred discussion of contentious issues, particularly the borders of the Palestinian entity and the nature of its sovereignty, to the future.

The transition talks progressed with agreement on all sides. During the period, Israel was willing to discuss autonomy for the Palestinians, but refused to recognize actual statehood. The Israeli concessions involved areas that did not include Israeli settlements or army bases. Thus, the two were able to sign agreements for the short term. As the final status talks neared, Israel abandoned two interim agreements that called on it to transfer more land to the PA. In July 2000, Israel rejected a return to the 1967 line, and tension grew.

The final position column in Table 2 demonstrates this shift from consistent agreement to consistent disagreement. The time-line shows how quickly the violence was initiated after the failure of the final status talks of July 2000. By September 2000, the two parties were again in full scale fighting, and in January 2001 Israel abandoned the Taba talks, a last ditch to hammer a final status agreement. A few months later, Egypt and Jordan proposed a cease-fire agreement. Israel and the US ignored the attempt, and the fighting intensified.

The 2002-2006 Period

The final period in our analysis is marked by increased violence, often in the form of Palestinian guerrilla attacks and Israeli military movements and unilateral actions. Table 3 shows that the first three conflict resolution attempts proposed during this time period failed to stop the ongoing violence. When these resolutions failed, the Israeli government sought to end the conflict by unilaterally setting the Israeli borders; while these borders granted some new territory to Palestinians, they were still deemed unacceptable by the Palestinians.

Table 3: Conflict Resolution Attempts in 2002-2006

Plan	Date	Issue	Propo-sing Actor	Final Position		
				US	Israel	Palesti-nians
Saudi-Arab League	Feb. 2002	Arab-Israeli Peace	Saudi Arabia	Ignored	Rejected	Accepted
Zinni	Mar. 2002	Palestinian Non-violence	US	Abandoned	Abandoned	Accepted
Roadmap	Jul. 2002	If Palestinian non-violence, then negotiations	US	Abandoned	Conditionally Accepted	Accepted
Geneva Accord	Oct.-Dec. 2003	Final status agreement resolving all issues	Public figures in both societies	Ignored	Rejected	Implicitly accepted
The Fence	Nov. 2003	Unilateral Israeli move	Israel	Accepted	Accepted	Rejected
Disengagement	Dec. 2003	Unilateral Israeli move	Israel	Accepted	Accepted	Rejected, then accepted after the fact
Convergence	Jan. 2006	Unilateral Israeli move	Israeli Prime Minister Olmert	Considers	Considers	Rejected

* Israel conditioned its acceptance on 14 points.[5]

The cease-fire attempts demonstrate increased US support for Israel over the past decade. In Table 2, the Jordanian-Egyptian and Mitchell Commission cease fire attempts also imposed duties on Israel, requiring it to freeze the settlement expansion and remove its forces to their position on the eve of the Palestinian revolt in September 2000. Beginning with its Tenet Plan in June 2001 (Table 2), the US sought to achieve Palestinian non-violence first, which has been the Israeli position. This also has been the position of the Zinni and Roadmap plans. No final status talks would take place until the PA stopped all the attacks on Israelis. Both the PA and Israel accepted these plans. In contrast, the Saudi-Arab League and the Geneva Plans, which called for an immediate return to the negotiation table were accepted by the PA, but rejected by Israel.

In the period of 2003-2006, Israel sought to settle the conflict without a return to the 1967 borders. The initial plan to unilaterally set its own borders involves the creation of a fence separating the portions of the territories controlled by Israel and Israel, the rest of the West Bank. The disengagement from the Gaza Strip and Northern Samaria (Israeli army stayed in the latter area and has returned to the Gaza Strip in 2006), and the convergence plans are further Israeli attempts at resolving the conflict by unilaterally deciding which parts of the territories to leave. All these unilateral plans were rejected by the Palestinians.

The Empirics of the Conflict Resolution Attempts

The previous section demonstrated that different attitudes regarding the recognition of Israel and the PLO by the PLO or Israel, respectively, as well as different strategies for conflict resolution, have characterized each new phase of the conflict and the attempts to resolve it. This section will show that one unifying theme throughout the time period is the US' continued support for the Israeli position.

The final position results in Tables 1-3 empirically demonstrate that, more often than not, Israel and the US consistently agree on a position before the parties conclude the resolution attempts. In 32 resolution plans, the two parties have never formally disagreed on the outcome. The US has never accepted an agreement that Israel rejected and vice versa. Instead, when the actors diverge on an issue, the US abstains from formally stating a position and either abandons the plan mid-resolution, waiting for the attempt to run its course and die out as in the case of Carter's Geneva plan and Shamir's plan, or it never acknowledges the proposal and ignores its existence from the start, which is the approach taken with both the Saudi-Arab League and Jordanian-Egyptian peace plans.

Among the 32 plans, the US and Israel have only agreed with the Palestinians on four occasions. The only three-way acceptances of resolution attempts were the Oslo I Accord, Oslo II Accord, Hebron Agreement, and Cairo Agreement. In the case of the Madrid Talks, Israel and the PLO agreed by the virtue of abandoning the effort. The US, who initiated the effort with big fanfare and pressured Israel to come to Madrid under a threat of cutting financial aid, eventually also abandoned the effort. In six cases of mutual, Israeli-Palestinian rejection – the Rogers' Plan, Carter's Autonomy Plan, Reagan Plan, Hussein-Arafat Accord, London Agreement, and Shamir's Plan, the US did not provide an official stance, despite three of the plans (Rogers' Plan, Carter's Autonomy Plan, Reagan's Plan) being suggested by the US itself; the two sides never agreed on a plan without US support.

Since 1967, the US proposed 13 conflict resolutions plans, but either came to ignore these plans or abandoned them, essentially rejecting them. The US government ignores or abandons its own plans in all cases when Israel rejects them or when Israel does not fully accept all of their provisions, as occurred, for example, in the case of the American-nominated Mitchell Commission Report of 2001, which called on Israel to freeze the settlement activity. Israel rejected this provision. American silence and even angry responses and expressions toward Israel, while certainly not supporting the Israeli view, are also not open pressures on Israel to change its position, particularly when other forms of American types of supports, including economic, military, and shielding Israel from international criticisms continue.

Israel and the Palestinians reject or ignore proposals originating in their own courtyards with much lower frequency than the US does. Israel rejected two such plans. The Yariv-Shemtov Formula was rejected by Prime Minister Yitzhak Rabin. Prime Minister Shamir rejected his own plan, as he came to see it as granting too much autonomy to the Palestinians. In the Taba Talks, the PA and the government of Prime Minister Barak were very close to an agreement over the final status, but in the end adjourned without signing an accord. The following Israeli governments of Prime Minister Sharon and Prime Minister Olmert, and US President George W. Bush have ignored the Taba Talks as if they had never occurred. The Geneva Accord is the only case where Israelis and Palestinians were able to formulate a complete final status accord, dealing with all the contentious issues, but the signing parties, while salient public and even official figures, were not in a position of considerable power in either society. While the PA hinted willingness to discuss the Geneva accord, the Israeli government of Prime Minister Sharon, and especially Prime Minister Sharon himself, flatly rejected the accord.

The Empirics of the American and Israeli Policy Shifts

There are many times in these resolution attempts in which an American president's own policy is shifted by the nature of his country's relationship to Israel. President Carter openly expressed on several occasions that he felt the settlements were illegal and that the Palestinians deserved a homeland. To that effect, he sought to convene a conference in Geneva and resolve the conflict once and for all.[6] Israel rejected this initiative strongly, and Carter caved in. Another example of this is Resolution 242 itself. The Johnson administration notified Israel that it expected to see a complete withdrawal from the territories, but later defended Israel's interpretation of the 242 resolution.

Some American presidents seemed more neutral toward the issue than others. Some even took steps that brought them to head on collision with Israel, as President Carter did in the beginning of his presidency, and particularly as President George H. Bush did in 1991. The disputes, however, did not last for long. Eventually, the US position aligned with that of Israel. Pressured by the US, Israel agreed to participate in the Madrid Talks, but in the talks themselves implemented a stalling tactic. The following Clinton administration simply stood by and allowed the talks to die out.

Still, as the Madrid episode showed, the strong American pressure on Israel to come to Madrid was enough to cause an unwilling Prime Minister Shamir to change his policy of refusing to attend an international peace conference. Had the US really wanted to force Israel to take a certain policy then, it could have done it successfully. Madrid in fact, was not a unique incidence.

When the US insisted on some policy, which Israel has rejected, in the past Israel eventually bowed to the pressure. Examples include the eventual Israeli acceptance of the 242 resolution in response to pressure from President Nixon, the Israeli withdraw from the Sinai in response from pressure from presidents Nixon, Ford and Carter. Along similar lines, Reagan got Israel to let the PLO leave Beirut and retreat from the city, and President Clinton got Israel to accept the Hebron and Wye agreements and accept his own December 2000 plan. President George W. Bush successfully encouraged Israel to change the route of the separation fence, accept the idea of Palestinian statehood, and transfer control over the border crossing from the Gaza Strip to

Egypt to the PA (assisted by Europeans and monitored by Israeli cameras) following the disengagement.

Moreover, President George W. Bush got Israel to agree to allow the Palestinian residents of East Jerusalem to vote in the Palestinian elections of January 2006, and allow the Hamas party to run in the 2006 elections in the territories. When the Hamas party won the Palestinian elections (unexpectedly for the US and Israel) and formed a government, Israel decided to starve it financially, bringing it to either change its position toward Israel or fall down, the US at first went along, but then in May changed its mind and approved supplying funds together with the EU to the Palestinian Authority. Israel essentially gave its muted approval, and agreed to release moneys it owned to the Palestinians, which it collected in the form of taxes on goods the Palestinians import through Israel. This money, about US$ 55 million per month, is one of the most important components in the Palestinian budget.[7]

These American successes at pressuring Israelis to behave in a certain manner are not always part of formal resolution agreements. They are, however, informal means through which Israel can act to reduce, rather than increase, tension in the region. Positive diplomatic gestures, while not as binding as a formal resolution are still a step in the right direction, and are often a step which Israel would not take without prodding from the US. More importantly, they demonstrate that when Israel is pushed by the US to take a certain action, Israel does as she is told.

Thus, whenever the US put substantial pressure on Israel, Israel changed its policy. Any other policy outcome would have been utterly irrational on the part of Israel. For a country that receives lots of financial and military aid from another country is not entirely independent to make its own decisions.

The Evolving Big Picture

Tables 1-3 suggest that the Israeli, Palestinian and American positions evolved over time, but the evolution has varied among the actors. Israel has never fully given up on holding at least some part of the West Bank. The Palestinians came to accept an Israel confined to the June 5, 1967 borders. The US position has generally mimicked that of Israel. This section focuses on the three evolutions.

The primary issues since 1967 have been the formation of a Palestinian state and its territory. Israel has refused to return to the June 5, 1967 borders and before 1992 rejected Palestinian self-determination. Before 2003, it also rejected Palestinian statehood. Before the late 1980s, the Palestinian problem was said to be humanitarian and thus the solution required to incorporate them into the Arab states. Paradoxically, only in 1947 the Zionists had accepted Resolution 181, which called for Palestinian statehood. After 1967, Israel rejected this idea. The Labor governments sought to link the Palestinians to Jordan, keeping parts of the territories. The Likud governments sought to keep all of the territories. They encouraged Israelis to settle there, offering at most a personal autonomy to the Palestinians.

In the early 1990s, after several years of Palestinian revolt, Israel concluded that the Palestinian problem required a political solution. In 1994, Israel granted the Palestinians limited control over a small patch of land in the territories, yet still refused to accept the idea of forming an independent Palestinian state. In 2003, after three years of a second revolt, this one much more violent than the previous revolt, Israel accepted the idea of Palestinian statehood, under American pressure. But in effect, even now, Israel sought partial withdrawal, refusing to completely return to the border of 1967.

Moving to our second actor, the Palestinians rejected the 1947 partition plan offered by the UN under Resolution 181. In the following decades, they sought to regain control over all of Palestine and, in extreme versions, drive the Jews out. By the mid 1970s, the PLO was increasingly ready to accept a Palestinian state in the territories, side by side Israel proper. In 1988, PLO formalized this position, and in 1992 it began negotiations with Israel, assuming the process would lead to a Palestinian state. This hope did not materialize, and the fighting never really stopped. Still, our discussion suggests that since 1988 (and perhaps before) it has been possible to solve the conflict, provided that Israel would have left the territories and accepted a Palestinian state.

With this part of the big picture in mind, what does the diplomatic history reveal on the attempts to resolve the conflict and why have they all failed? The historical account of the attempts to resolve the conflict since 1967 indicates a pro-Israeli US bias. The US has played the role of a broker. Formally, it has served the go between the parties, providing facilities for negotiation and, at times, suggesting plans and texts. Yet the broker services provided were often biased, serving the interests of one party more than the other. Unlike brokers in the business world, which only seeks to help the parties to arrive at a deal, the American broker has basically taken the Israeli position.

As shown, in virtually all the resolution attempts since 1967, the US has supported the Israeli position. When Israel and the US disagreed, the US often has changed its view to match it to that of Israel, or simply has done nothing, letting the effort die out. During the Oslo process, in particular, the US brokering assisted Israel. The US, for example, did not push Israel to evacuate the territories once the PLO accepted Israel in 1988 and again in 1993. Nor did the US push Israel to accept Palestinian statehood. The Israeli settler project has continued to rely on land seizures and the US simply stood by, but even this was not the full story. The US pressured the Palestinians during the Oslo process to accept the Israeli actions by seemingly agreeing with Israel. The Palestinians were led to believe, or perhaps wanted to believe despite hints pointing to the other direction, that things would be resolved in the future. In the mean time, Israel stepped up the settlement project against the spirit of Oslo.

Since 1967, the US has supported Israel both materially and diplomatically. The US is Israel's predominant arms supplier, and provides Israel with billions of dollars in aid each year. From 1962 to 2004, Israel received from the US $ 143 billion in assistance.[8] Without the US support, the Israeli economy would have suffered greatly. This aid has been fungible – money, after all, is money – essentially financing the Israeli settlement project. Had this aid not been there, Israel would have had to finance this project alone, which would not have been easy or even possible.

The US also supports Israel ideologically and diplomatically in its refusal to return to the 1967 line. Paradoxically, this thesis has held true even when the US itself initiated a plan calling on Israel to pullout from the territories. Sooner or later, the US would abandon its own plan. Throughout the period, the US has vetoed UN resolutions condemning Israeli practice or seeking to sanction Israel.[9] The US also looked the other way when the settlements grew or did anything other than talk. When the Palestinians rejected the Israeli-US offer in Camp

David 2000, which would have left at least 10 % of the land in Israeli hands, the US blamed Arafat for reneging on a fantastic deal. By that time, however, the Palestinians understood the Israeli end-game. Shortly thereafter, their pent up anger exploded anew in an armed revolt. Going further than any other president, George W. Bush acknowledged in a 2004 letter to Israeli Prime Minister Sharon that the final border would have to take the large settlements into account. It is unrealistic, he writes, to expect Israel to return to the 1967 line.[10]

All that does not mean that the US has been a rubber stamp for Israel. As we saw, there are still cases in which pressure from the US forces Israel to take actions it initially rejects. Rather, the US has generally sided with Israel and shared its interpretations.[11] Even if the US may think of its policy toward the Israeli-Palestinian conflict as even-handed, it is essentially skewed in favor of Israel in the things that matter: providing military and financial aid, voting in patterns favoring Israel in the UN, pressuring the Palestinians to go along with the Israeli plans, and, most importantly, accepting the Israeli position on the 1967 border and the settlements.

If the US can in fact impose its will on Israel had it really wanted to do so, to what extent can it get the Palestinians follow its cues? The Palestinian leaders have accepted the Oslo and the Roadmap plans, but the Palestinian people have always contained elements rejecting these plans. This had to be expected, as these plans put the onus on the Palestinians. The US-brokered deals have called on the Palestinians to continue with business as usual until an undefined final status agreement would be concluded. In the mean time, Israel has declared its refusal to fully evacuate the territories and backed it by expanding settlements and bringing more settlers to the land. In retrospect, it had to be only a matter of time before the Palestinians would revolt again, and so it happened on September 28, 2000.

And so, in the absence of US focus on the substance of the conflict – the occupation and the settlements – the US mediation effort since the 1990s has focused on procedural matters. Much effort was put into setting the process that would lead to the final status, than on the final status itself. The US has attempted to appear as an honest broker, balancing the needs of both parties. In reality, this balancing act seems to have been more an act. For otherwise it is hard to understand why the US did not put its full gravity on Israel from the beginning, imposing the Clinton plan of December 2000 much earlier than when it was presented. It is also hard to understand why, after the two sides were so close in the Taba setup, the Bush administration simply ignored it and started fresh with a new balancing act.[12]

Resolving the Conflict

Facing the ongoing Israeli-Palestinian violence and the inability of the US and Israel to bring it to an end, it is beneficial to refer to the November 19, 2001 speech of US Foreign Secretary Powell, which defined the US position on peace the Middle East. "History, fate and success have combined to compel American leadership in the Middle East and around the globe," he said. "We welcome the opportunity to use our power and influence to make the world a better place for all of God's children." This promise can work only to the extent that others want to follow. The remaining options are coercion or getting rid of "obstructive" leaders. This was the essence of the US approach to Chairman Arafat since 2001. He refused to go along, so he had to go, politically that is. The US essentially supported Prime Minister Sharon's policy of making Arafat irrelevant. Of course, leaders may have to use coercion from time to time. But when the leadership is biased, it is no wonder that the other side rejects its cues.[13]

If the goal is to arrive to a stable and long-lasting Israeli-Palestinian peace, what then, are the policy implications of this analysis? This section does not seek to offer a detailed peace plan, but rather chart general ideas about what history suggests works, and about what is likely to fail. So far, the history of the attempts to resolve it tell us what has failed; all the attempts had failed. While history is not always the best predictor of the past, it is the only game in town when it comes to making such predictions.

In recent years, there have been three major peace efforts: the Israeli unilateralism (the fence, disengagement and convergence plans), the Oslo process, and the Roadmap plan. All of these plans have been formally supported by the US, except the convergence element of the Israeli unilateralism, which is still not formally declared. All of these plans failed to bring peace.

With regards to the Israeli unilateral attempts to set the tone of the final status by deciding on the border alone, there is no reason to believe that this approach will lead anywhere but failure. Pure logic and facts on the ground so far suggest that in the same way that it takes at least two parties to have a fight, it takes these two parties to arrive at peace. Ignoring the Palestinians side by arguing there is no partner to talk to, will not cause them to disappear. The Palestinians are in the West Bank and Gaza Strip to stay, much in the same way that Israelis are in Israel proper to stay. Any attempt to resolve the conflict by ignoring this simple fact is a non-starter.

With regards to the failure of the Oslo process, the US has ignored the Israeli settlement expansion, which went along in an accelerated rate while Israel and the Palestinians were talking peace in the 1990s. This expansion has been a double-edged sword: it has made the Palestinians angrier and less trustful of the Israeli intentions, and it has made the Israeli withdrawal more impossible, given the growing number of people that had to be relocated.[14] It is also clear that the US matched its position on the final status to the position of Israel. Thus Barak's offer in Camp David 2000 was described by US President Clinton as generous, while Arafat did not move as far as Barak did. But only a few months later, the US and Israel put forward a different offer, which called for almost a complete withdrawal. The problem was that it was already too late – the Palestinians were in the midst of a revolt, and Barak had lost the support of the Knesset.

With respect to the Roadmap and the American attempts to broker a deal under the George W. Bush Administration, it is apparent that this president has not been involved in the process to the degree that his predecessor was. Had Bush been more involved and willing to continue the process from where President Clinton left it, perhaps things would have unfolded differently. While the Palestinians did not move to disarm the armed groups, as the different US plans called on them since 2000, Israel has not stopped the settlement expansion (including in Greater Jerusalem) and had not removed the unlawful outposts, as called for by the Mitchell Report.

When all is said and done, once again, it takes at least two parties to have a conflict, and it takes at least these two parties to resolve it. Any conflict resolution plan that does treat Israelis and Palestinians as equal partners to the deal, and as equally responsible for the ongoing carnage, will most likely lead nowhere. The diplomatic history of the attempts to resolve the Israeli-Palestinian conflict suggest that the only resolution that can succeed is one that based on an Israeli return to the 1967 lines and the formation of a Palestinian state in the territories. The simple numeration of the recent decades demonstrates clearly that so far the US has not pushed for this type of a resolution. At the same time, the US is most likely the only force that can attempt to end the conflict along these lines.

Endnotes

[1] Open for Business, Peres, Sha'th, Hassan: R. Reuveny, Palestinian Islamism and Israeli Palestinian Peace, Research in Social Movements, Conflicts and Change 22 (2000), p. 219; Y. Elitzur, Economic Warfare: The hundred-year Economic Confrontation between Jews and Arabs (Tel Aviv: Cineret, 1997), p. 251; Haaretz, Israeli Daily Newspaper, (Tel Aviv, November 2, 1994). Optimistic assessments: S. Peres and A. Naor, The New Middle East (New York: Henry Holt, 1993); World Bank, Developing the Occupied Territories: An Investment in Peace (Washington, D.C.: World Bank, 1993); S. Fischer, L. Hausman, A. Karasik and T. Schelling (eds.), Securing Peace in the Middle East: Project on Economic Transition (Cambridge: MIT Press, 1994); G. Falah, Re-Envisioning Current Discourse: Alternative Territorial Configurations of Palestinian Statehood, The Canadian Geographer 41 (1997), p. 307-330; D. Newman and G. Falah, Bridging the Gap: Palestinian and Israeli Discourses on Autonomy and Statehood, Transactions of the Institute of British Geographers 22 (1997), p. 111-129.

[2] R. Reuveny 2000 (En. 1), p. 219-220; Haaretz, Israeli Daily Newspaper, (Tel Aviv, November 9-10, 1999); Yediot, Daily Newspaper, (Tel Aviv, August 13, September 24, October 10, 15, November 3, 10, 26, 1999.

[3] A. Gresh, The PLO, the Struggle Within: Towards an Independent Palestinian State (London: Palgrave-Macmillan, 1985); G. W. Ball and D. Ball, The Passionate Attachment (New York: W. W. Norton, 1992); G. Lanczowski, The Middle East in World Affairs (Ithaca: Cornel University Press, 1980); Y. Bar-Siman-Tov, The US and Israel since 1948: A "Special Relationship"?, Diplomatic History 22 (1998), p. 231-262; D. Shaham, Israel – 50 Years (Tel Aviv: Am Oved Publishers, 1998); A. Hareven, Wars and Peace: Israel and here Arab Neighbors. Continuity, Change, Issues and Documents (Jerusalem: Dvir, 1989); Y. Harkavi, The Bar Kokhba Syndrome: Risk and Realism in International Politics (Cappaqua, NY: Rossel Books, 1983); Y. Lukacs (ed.), The Israeli-Palestinian Conflict: A Documentary Re-

cord (New York: Cambridge University Press, 1992); W. B. Quandt, Decade of Decisions (Berkeley, CA: University of California Press, 1977); W. B. Quandt, Camp David: Peacemaking and Politics (Washington, D.C.: Brookings, 1986); Y. Sayigh, Armed Struggle and the Search for State: The Palestinian National Movement, 1949-1993, Institute for Palestine Studies, Washington, D. C. (New York: Oxford University Press, 1997); S. Spiegel, The Other Arab-Israeli Conflict: Making America's Middle East Policy, from Truman to Reagan (Chicago: Chicago University Press, 1985); Z. Schiff, A Formula Before its Time, Haaretz, Israeli Daily Newspaper, (Tel Aviv, June 14, 1994); T. G. Fraser, The Middle East, 1914-1979 (London: MacMillan, 1980).

[4] JPS, The PLO-Israeli Declaration of Principles Agreement (Oslo I), Journal of Palestinian Studies 23 (1993), p. 115-121; JPS, The Israeli-Palestinian Interim Agreement (Oslo II) on the West Bank and the Gaza Strip, September 28, 1995, Journal of Palestine Studies 25 (1996), p. 123-137; JPS, The Hebron Protocol, Journal of Palestine Studies 26 (1997), p. 131-138; JPS, Agreed Minute, Article 7: American Plan on al-Shuhada Street, Journal of Palestine Studies 26 (1997), p. 136-138; JPS, US special Middle East Coordinator Dennis Ross, Note for the Record, Jerusalem, 15 January 1997, Journal of Palestine Studies 26 (1997), p. 138-139; JPS, US Secretary of State Warren Christopher, US Letter of Assurance to Israel, Washington, 15 January 1997, Journal of Palestine Studies 26 (1997), p. 139; JPS, US State Department Spokesman Nicholas Burns, Statement on Further Redevelopments, Washington, 15 January 1997, Journal of Palestine Studies 26 (1997), p. 141; JPS, US Special Middle East Coordinator Dennis Ross, On-the-Record Briefing on the Hebron Agreement, Washington, 17 January 1997 (excerpts), Journal of Palestine Studies 26 (1997), p. 144; JPS, The Wye Memorandum, Journal of Palestine Studies 28 (1999), p. 135-146; JPS, The Hashemite Kingdom of Jordan and the Arab Republic of Egypt, Jordanian-Egypt Proposal for an Israeli-Palestinian Cease-Fire and Resumption of Negotiations, April 2001, Journal of Palestine Studies 30 (2001), p. 151-152; JPS, Secretary of State Colin Powell, Press Conference on the Mitchell Report, Washington, 21 May 2001 (excerpts), Journal of Palestine Studies 30 (2001), p. 169-171; Gaza-Jericho Agreement Letters, Cairo Agreement (Chevy Chase, MD: Jewish Virtual Library, 1994) <http://www.jewishvirtuallibrary.org/jsource/Peace/gjletter.html>; Y. Bar-Siman-Tov 1998 (En. 3); D. Shaham 1998 (En. 3); Z. Schiff 1994 (En. 3); H. Druks, The Uncertain Alliance: The US and Israel from Kennedy to the Peace Process (Westport, CT: Greenwood Press, 2001); D. Makovsky, Making Peace with the PLO: The Rabin Government's Road to the Oslo Road (Boulder, CO: Westview Press, 1996); B. Morris, Righteous Victims: A History of the Zionist-Arab Conflict, 1881-2001 (New York: Vintage Books, 2001); I. Bickerton and C. Klausner, A

concise History of the Arab-Israeli Conflict (Upper Saddle River, NJ: Prentice Hall, 2002); I. Bickerton and C. Klausner, History of the Arab-Israeli
Conflict (Upper Saddle River, NJ: Prentice Hall, 2006).

[5] I. Bickerton and C. Klausner 2002 (En. 4); I. Bickerton and C. Klausner
2006 (En. 4); S. Ben-Ami, A Front without a Rearguard: A Voyage to the
Boundaries of the Peace Process (Tel Aviv: Miskal-Yedioth Ahronoth Books
and Chemed Books, 2004); A. Harel and A. Isacharoff, The Seventh War
(Tel Aviv: Miskal-Yedioth Ahronoth Books and Chemed Books, 2005); G.
Baskin, No Palestinian Support for Israel's Convergence, Op-Ed/Articles,
Palestine Media Center, 10 May 2006 <http://www.palestine-
pmc.com/details.asp?cat=4&id=3081>; Y. Beilin, the Path to Geneva: The
Quest for Permanent Agreement, 1996-2004 (New York: RDV Books, 2004);
Geneva Accord, Geneva Initiative: A Model for an Israeli-Palestinian Perma-
nent Agreement (Tel Aviv: Geneva Initiative Headquarters, 2003)
<http://www.heskem.org.il/default.asp>; Zinni Proposal, Second US Joint
Goals Proposal (Jerusalem: Jerusalem Media and Communication Center,
2002); Roadmap, A Performance-Based Roadmap to a Permanent Two-State
Solution to the Israeli-Palestinian Conflict (US Department of State, 2003)
<http://www.state.gov/r/pa/prs/ps/2003/20062.htm>; Haaretz, Israeli Daily
Newspaper, US Response to the Geneva Accord (Tel Aviv, December 6,
2003).

[6] J. Boudreault, E. Naughton and Y. Salaam, US Official Statements: Israel
Settlements/The Fourth Geneva Conventions (Washington, D.C.: Institute for
Palestinian Studies, 1992).

[7] Hamas, elections: Haaretz, Israeli Daily Newspaper, (Tel Aviv, November 16, 2005). Border crossing: Israeli Daily Newspaper, (Tel Aviv, November 14, 15, 2005; Walla News, November 25, 2005; Washington Post, November 26, 2005. Transferring money to Hamas: NanaNews, May 11, 2006;
Associated Press, May 14, 2006. Voting in Jerusalem: Haaretz, Israeli Daily
Newspaper, (Tel Aviv, January 11, 2006).

[8] Up-to-date aid figures are provided in Greenbook, which is a publication
of the United State Agency for International Development (USAID), see:
Greenbook, Overseas Loans and Grants, US Agency for International Development (USAID) <http://www.qesdb.usaid.cdie.org/gbk/>.

[9] For a list of the American veto votes in the United Nations, see D. Neff,
An Updated List of Vetoes Cast by the United States to Shield Israel from
Criticism by the UN Security Council, Washington Report on Middle Ease
Affairs, Special Report (May/June 2005), p. 14-17.

[10] IMFA, Exchange of Letters Between PM Sharon and President Bush, Israeli Ministry of Foreign Affairs (Jerusalem/Israel, 14 April 2004)
<http://www.mfa.gov.il/MFA/Peace+Process/>.

[11] For example, in late 1997 the US sides with Israel in the disagreement between Israel and the PA on whether Israel alone (as Israel insisted) or Israel and the PA in cooperation (as the PA understood) will decide on the nature of the Israeli pullouts called for by the 1997 Hebron Protocol. For the formal exchanges and documents, see JPS 1997 (En. 4).

[12].Given that the US has chosen this approach position willingly, it must be the case that successive presidents concluded that it was in theirs or the US's best interest to do so. Further investigation of this important issue, however, would have to await for future research.

[13] Powell Speech: US Department of State, United States Position on Terrorists and Peace in the Middle East: Secretary Colin L. Powell Remarks at the McConnell Center for Political Leadership, University of Louisville, Kentucky (2001) <http://www.state.gov/secretary/former/powell/remarks/2001/6219.htm>.

[14] On the Israeli settlements in the territories and their adverse effect on the conflict, see R. Reuveny, Fundamentalist Colonialism: The Geopolitics of Israeli-Palestinian Conflict, Political Geography 22 (2003), p. 347-380.

11

Notes on the Perspectives of the US-EU Cooperation in the Broader Middle East and North Africa

Jan Bury

Both the US and the EU aim at spreading accountable and representative government, the rule of law and respect for human rights as enshrined in the Universal Declaration of Human Rights. These were named a strategic priority and moral necessity. The US and EU unite to push Middle East democracy. This was one of the key issues at the recent Davos summit.

Free and fair elections are considered central to democracy. But in fact this system worked in a wrong direction in the Broader Middle East recently. Radical parties won the elections in Iraq, Palestine and Egypt. So it seems this was a failure for the West. New constraints have been created. The reason for this situation is that the West employed the "double policy" standards while dealing with the Arab World. The oppressive regimes were supported for decades, while the West spread such slogans as democratization, separation of powers, human rights, rule of law, tolerance, good governance and justice. At present, the desire for reform in the Broader Middle East is stressed.

The highlights in the Broader Middle East and North Africa revolve around the following issues: the Israeli-Palestinian conflict, the ongoing Iraq war, the operation in Afghanistan, tensions between

Syria and Lebanon, the Sudanese conflict, strain between Pakistan and India and finally the Iranian Weapons of Mass Destruction (WMD) programs. Other important issues are counter-terrorism work and management of political transition in "Broader Middle East and North Africa" (BMENA) states. There are also issues specific to the Mediterranean like the future of Western Sahara, relations between Spain and Morocco (over enclaves, which is related to Moroccan nationalism), Morocco and Algeria, Libya and Tunisia, Egypt and Sudan, Israel and Syria, Greece and Turkey, Turkey and Syria. The NATO Mediterranean Dialogue can be identified within this framework as well.

It must be stressed that the help of the NATO is actually essential in BMENA projects, especially reflecting security issues, like WMD, terrorism, extremism, political instability.

The Bush Administration believes a deficit in political and economic freedom in the Muslim world is a key factor fuelling terrorism that poses the greatest security threat to the West. The Greater Middle East Initiative was a centerpiece of transatlantic diplomacy in 2006. This can also contribute to rebuilding frayed transatlantic relations, e. g. by engaging such countries as France and Germany in a multilateral front.

But the key issue is how to loosen authoritarian Middle East systems. The political, security and economic cooperation frameworks must therefore be established. The main constraint is that BMENA is too large for united cooperation – it is simply too diverse. Anyway, democracy must be brought first to Iraq, and this will be the test for the West.

Implementation

There were several significant international initiatives in the region in the past:
1. MEPI – Middle East Partnership Initiative (since 2002).
2. Euro-Mediterranean Partnership (EMP) a.k.a. the Barcelona Process.
3. BMENA Initiative, but this seems a secondary focus for both the US and the EU.

4. NATO Mediterranean Dialogue.
5. Middle East Peace Process (the Quartet process, the Roadmap process).

The Barcelona Process, present since 1995, was initiated by the European Union to encourage political and economic reform and to foster cultural and social dialogue from Morocco to Lebanon and Syria with moderate success.

The MEPI (Middle East Partnership Initiative), unveiled in December 2002, was a US Department of State program launched to support democratic reformers and to promote democratic reforms in the Muslim World. It was also committed to helping increase access and quality of education throughout the Middle East.

BMENA was launched in June 2004 at the G8 Summit with the Common Future (BMENA Initiative) as there was a consensus among Western states that continued political stagnation in the countries of the Middle East threatens the peace and stability in that region and the security of Western States.[1] One of the goals was to avoid the risk of radicalization and state failure in the region, as this threatens the rest of the World. Others were focusing on peace and stability through democracy, constant political adaptations and economic development. Javier Solana said that "BMENA was born of the tragedy of September 11".[2]

Therefore, promoting democracy in the region should be an area of the mutual US-EU cooperation. The areas of such a cooperation within BMENA are development assistance, technical counterterrorism cooperation and ultimately democracy promotion.

At the Istanbul Cooperation Initiative of 28 June 2004 the NATO offered practical security cooperation with BMENA, which stays alongside with the Mediterranean Dialogue and Partnership for Peace (PfP). The main fields of this cooperation are: counterterrorism, countering WMD, cooperation on border security to prevent illicit trafficking of drugs, weapons and people, disaster preparedness and civil emergency planning, training and education, participation in NATO exercises, advice on defense reform and civil-military relations, and promoting military interoperability.

It must be noted that the BMENA Forum is modeled on the APEC Forum and the Helsinki process. But while the Arab states show desire for the economic reforms, which they are being offered, they ignore Western rhetorical pressure for the political reforms they do not want. Then the main constraint is created. The economic reforms without political reforms can frustrate the Arabs and contribute to social instability.[3]

As far as the Middle East Peace Process is concerned, "the EU and the US are going to be very strong partners as we try and realize the opportunities before us in the Israeli-Palestinian issue", as stated by the Secretary of State Condoleezza Rice in Brussels on 9 February 2005.[4]

The US-EU commitment to the Roadmap for Peace in the Middle East through the Quartet Process (that is with Russia and the UN) shares the vision of two nations living side by side, in peace and security. However, the US have withdrawn the aid worth some US$ 350 million for the Palestinians to support political, economic and security reforms. The EU has withdrawn the aid, too, while there is an urgent need for aid to Palestine now. The Roadmap consisted of three phases:
1. ending terror and violence, normalizing Palestinian life and building Palestinian institutions,
2. transition (that is the creation of an independent Palestinian State),
3. Permanent Status Agreement and the end of the Israeli-Palestinian conflict.

Still, phase one's objectives have not been met and the future is questionable because of the Hamas-led government and the ongoing conflict with the Gaza militants. Furthermore, as US General William Ward commented on the assistance to the Palestinian security forces: "There must be effective action against terrorism, dismantling of terrorist infrastructure, but also a freeze on all settlement activity and dismantling of outpost".[5] The latter can be most difficult.

Constraints

The Arabs usually voice suspicion of attempts to impose democracy in the Middle East from outside, especially by the US. They name this in private conversations as *al mu'ammarah* (i.e. the conspiracy). They accuse the West of double standards and Western intentions in the Arab World are usually suspect.

Within this framework, the US support of Israel cannot be perceived as the root of the Arab hostility towards the US, but rather the employment of the "double policy standards" in the region by the US (and the West as well), matched together with the complex political, social and economic situation of the Middle East. This revolved around the backing of oppressive regimes in the Middle East and the stout position with respect to Iraq throughout the 1990s, in particular. Indeed the US military commitment in Iraq after the first Gulf War has damaged the image of the US among the Arab nations and inflamed the anger towards the West not only of the Iraqis but other Arabs as well. The March 2003 invasion merely deepened these sentiments. On the other hand, the US backing of oppressive Arab regimes placed this country in an unfavorable view among the helpless and oppressed. This can be viewed as a key factor fuelling anti-American terrorism.

In parallel, the existence of Israel is beneficial to the leaders of the region, as the vision of an external enemy is created, which diminishes the internal tensions and the citizens' dissatisfaction of the regimes. The bias and ill-fated knowledge of the West in the Arab World, particularly on the US and its political system, worsens the situation.

The solution to the deadlock seems the strengthening of activities within the confines of the BMENA Initiative, particularly in the field of education, poverty and unemployment control, as well as social protection.

Meanwhile the radical elements in the Middle East benefited from popular dissatisfaction with the political and economic order. This is also why Usama Bin Laden and Saddam Hussein were regarded as icons in the Moslem World.

However, the US seems to break with the previous policies of containment and security cooperation with repressive regimes and moves toward the promotion of democracy and development. Now the US applies a more assertive strategy of democratization in the Middle East.

But still there are differences in the approach on both sides of the Atlantic. The US tends to use force, while the European Union is more reluctant to threaten, mostly because it is in fact incapable to project power outside and even inside Europe.[6] The US seems impatient and eager to see the results, while Europe is keen on adopting the policy of "wait and see".

The common view in Europe is that the Bush administration is inclined toward unilateralism and largely uninterested in Europe. Many European governments were critical of the US decision e. g. to proceed with the missile defense. The US tends to use force, while Europe is keen on adopting the policy of "wait and see" for fears that the use of force may inflame the Arab street. Furthermore, Europe is more pro-Palestinian, which may be motivated by an underlying anti-Semitism.[7] Also, in many cases the US policies in the region were inclined toward containment and isolation, while the European Union's toward engagement, like as of Syria.

The US-EU Policies in the Greater Middle East: Cooperation or (Rather) Competition?

There is consensus over the need of democratization in the Middle East, but there are disagreements how this can be achieved. Firstly, there should be no "taboos" for the effective cooperation and reform.

The main issues in the reform are that liberal Arabs are not in majority, but they must be supported. On the other hand, the Western model of reforms did not integrate the Islamist political movements into the new vision of future. These movements have serious impact on people of the region. So, Western governments should concentrate now on the Islamist movements. The West should also make use of the Arab and Muslim diasporas in building democracy societies in the region.[8]

President Bush aimed at strengthening pluralistic civil societies and encouraging democratic and market reforms across the region, while offering aid and trade. But the US Greater Middle East Initiative (BMENA) is still considered a Trojan horse by the Arabs.[9] The problem is that the US maintains large military contingencies, especially in Iraq, which is seen as an "imperial presence", if not a "colonial" one by the Mid-Eastern society.

We also observe the economic competition in BMENA, not the cooperation of the West. Many US companies have European affiliates that are considered as EU companies. Also, European companies manufacture in the States. So, "when the US economy is thriving, Europe benefits, and vice versa", as noted by the US Ambassador to the European Union, Rockwell A. Schnabel.[10]

The enlargement of the EU saw a relocation of the funds to the new members at the expense of the Mediterranean Arab States. The new member states manufacture the same commodities, like agricultural ones, as the Mediterranean Arab states (except the "sweet" crude oil), so these Arab exports to the EU will be subject of great pressure (maybe except oil and certain agricultural products, like dates, olive oil, etc.). This situation has been used by the US.

Conclusions

To accomplish the successful reform of the Broader Middle East, as this essay has shown, several steps have to be made. First, the Arabs need an equivalent of the OSCE (Organization for Security and Cooperation in Europe) like the Organization for Security and Cooperation in the Middle East. The League of Arab States tended to fill the gap, but without a significant success in the past. This contributed to instability in the region.

Second, the European Union must play a major part in the reform process as it is closer to the Arab World than the US. Moreover, it has strong economic and trade relations. The Arabs believe the attitude of the European Union toward BMENA region is more balanced that that of the US. The EU has strong economic and security-related interests in the BMENA states. It is believed that the Western pressure for political reforms in the region is not taken seriously.

Third, the US BMENA Initiative, which can be considered a core component of the reforms package, is an attempt to expand political, economic and education opportunities throughout the region. Lack of reform is among the root causes of extremist violence. But we must acknowledge that the "plan" cannot be imposed from abroad: it must come from the people of the Greater Middle East.

Fourth, other areas of mutual US-EU cooperation in BMENA are to be: combating terrorism and the proliferation of WMD, promoting Middle East peace and stability, ensuring a reliable flow of oil and curtailing Islamic extremism. However, according to the European points of view, the Palestinian-Israeli conflict must be a priority, as it is a key driver of terrorism, Islamic extremism and political unrest among the European Muslims. And according to the US administration, terrorism and weapons proliferation comprise primary threats. Peace can prevail in the region only when these two threats are mitigated. This lack of common policy must be overcome. For example, Secretary Rice's direct involvement in brokering a deal between Israel and the Palestinians in security controls for the Gaza border crossing in November 2005 has had a positive impact on European perceptions of the US. Current efforts to end violence in Iraq, Palestine and Lebanon will have decisive effect on the future of cooperation in the region.

As far as the WMD issues are concerned, Iran and its nuclear programs constitute a problem for both the EU and the US. This shall be a field of cooperation between the US and the EU to mitigate the possible threat.

Nevertheless, several reservations have been exposed. The term "democratization" of the Middle East is sensitive and must be used carefully. The democratization may not be dictated from abroad, as mentioned before. Also, introducing democracy in a Western way in the Middle East may lead into anti-Western sentiments among the Arabs and the Islamists can win elections, as this has happened in Palestine.

Among other issues, further cooperation of the US in the region must be made with both "Old" and "New" Europe. The experiences of the new European Union member states can be used in the Mid-Eastern reforms programs (like those of Poland).

Finally, the Arab regimes were afraid of the US military interventions in Afghanistan and Iraq as pretexts for the slow implementation of structural economic and liberalization programs. Now, they are preoccupied with regime protection and consolidating their domestic position. We must, however, bear in mind that Arab economic systems are insufficient nowadays. So, radical economic reforms are priorities.

To sum up, the Quartet and BMENA Initiative with its Forum for the Future seem the last "non-lethal" tools of reforms in the Broader Middle East.

Endnotes

[1] T. C. Wittes, Promoting Democracy in the Arab World: The Challenge of Joint Action, The International Spectator 4 (2004), p. 75-88.

[2] See: Summary of the intervention by J. Solana, EU High Representative for the Common Foreign and Security Policy on Regional Issues at the Forum for the Future, Bahrain, Manama, 11 November 2005, EU document S362/05, p. 3.

[3] See: T. C. Wittes 2004 (En. 1).

4 US-EU Cooperation on the Middle East Peace Process, Bureau of European and Eurasian Affairs, US State Department, Washington, DC, 17 February 2005.

[5] US, EU at "Moment of Opportunity" in Middle East, Documents & Texts from the Washington File, Bureau of International Information Programs, US Department of State, 20 June 2005.

[6] This was sharply visible during the war in the Balkans during the 1990s.

[7] See K. Archick, European Views and Policies Toward the Middle East, CRS Report for Congress, RL31956, 21 December 2005, p. 11 f.

[8] K. Archick 2005 (En. 7).

[9] P. Hilder, Democracy and the Middle East, <http://www.gathering.typepad.com/DemPapers-middle-east.pdf>.

[10] R. A. Schnabel, The Future of Transatlantic Relations, 11 March 2004, p. 1-4.

Human Security – Transatlantic Approach?

12

Controlling Discriminatory Profiles in Intelligence-Led Policing: Can Article 14 of the European Convention on Human Rights do what the US Equal Protection Clause cannot?

Aaron Baker[*][T]

> Intelligence-led stop and searches have got to be the way ... We should not waste time searching old white ladies. It is going to be disproportionate. It is going to be young men, not exclusively, but it may be disproportionate when it comes to ethnic groups. (Ian Johnston, Chief Constable of the British Transport Police)[1]

Introduction

The phrase "intelligence-led policing" seems to beg for an ironic witticism, but it describes a weapon of the "War on Terror" used in deadly earnest by the state, with significant repercussions for the human rights of Muslims, Arabs, and South Asians. Intelligence-led policing ended in the shooting death of the innocent Brazilian electrician Jean Charles de Menezes in a London Underground station on July 22, 2005;[2] it was subsequently used by the UK Home Office to defend the use, in the London Underground, of stop and search profiles that resulted in the disproportionate stopping, searching, questioning, and detention of people of Muslim or South Asian appearance.[3] Intelligence-led policing gave sanction to the rounding up and secret, indefinite imprisonment without charge of hundreds of Muslim and Arab men in the United States after the September 11, 2001 attacks.[4] On the other hand, intelligence-led policing also contributed to the foiling, in early August 2006, of a plot by alleged Muslim extremists, resident in England, to destroy, simultaneously, ten or more jet airliners bound from the UK to the US by smuggling aboard liquid explosives.[5] Anti-discrimination protections must come to terms with intelligence-led policing, in a way that both controls it and respects its efficacy in appropriate circumstances.

Although "intelligence-led policing" means a lot of things – including, obviously, the use of tips, informants, and surveillance to identify individuals engaged in, or preparing for, criminal activity – it appears also to mean that as long as the police have information suggesting that a terrorist act is more likely to be committed by, say, an Asian than a non-Asian, it is not discrimination to subject individual Asians to more "policing" than individual non-Asians. If counter-terrorism officers decide not to detain, search, and question a white man, but instead to detain, search, and question a similarly situated, attired, and accoutered Arab man because he is Arab, intelligence-led policing means that they have not used ethnicity as a criterion for police attention, but instead have relied on the extent to which the individual matches an intelligence estimate that has Arab men as more likely perpetrators of the particular kind of crime under investigation. In short, intelligence-led policing justifies racial and religious profiling, which are not acknowledged as discriminatory so long as police disproportionately target minority individuals because, on the basis of some intelligence, police consider members of their minority group more likely to be guilty of a crime, rather than because they do not like those groups and wish to harass their members.[6]

Counter-terrorism officials in the United States and the United Kingdom, arguably the two most significant protagonists in the "War on Terror", have responded to the events of September 11, 2001 and July 7, 2005 with an increasing resort to the use of racial and religious profiles based on "intelligence".[7] I place the word "intelligence" in quotes not because I assume that officials use it disingenuously, but because even ingenuous reliance on intelligence, to the effect that most people who commit a certain crime have a certain ethnicity, leads to less favorable treatment of an individual with that ethnicity because of his membership in that group, not because of any act he is thought or known to have committed. The "intelligence" is not about the individual – the police will generally have only one relevant piece of intelligence about a stopped-and-searched individual: his apparent ethnicity – and yet the state will claim that it did not stop the individual because of his race, but because of their "intelligence." This sleight-of-hand offers a stern test of protections against state discrimination, in that it can exploit a superficial jurisprudential conception of discrimination as something that is done, rather than something that is experienced.[8] Moreover, the use of such "intelligence" to justify a stop and search or detention can look like, at the same time, both a least restrictive alternative from the perspective of police with no other ideas, and an overbroad, under-inclusive, and arbitrary distinction to those stopped, searched, or detained, an arguably disproportionate percentage of whom are innocent and never charged.

In light of the challenges that intelligence-led profiling poses to constitutional provisions against government discrimination, this paper discusses the extent to which, and why, Article 14 of the European Convention on Human Rights (ECHR), as applied in the UK through the Human Rights Act 1998 (HRA), has a greater potential to control such racial and religious profiling in a counter-terrorism context than does the Equal Protection Clause of the 14th Amendment to the US Constitution. My contention is, in essence, that (1) Article 14 has been less chipped away at by judicial manipulation of the definition of discrimination than has the Equal Protection Clause ("EPC"), meaning that judges are less trammeled in their ability to find that *prima facie* discrimination has occurred and (2) Article 14 provides the judiciary with the tool of proportionality, making it harder for discrimination to stand up to scrutiny. Section II below explains why this comparison contributes to the profiling debate in both the US and the UK. Section III introduces the Article 14 analysis and sets out its strengths in comparison to the EPC. Section IV argues for a particular approach to the application of Article 14 proportionality to profiling, a practice with which Article 14 has yet to grapple. Finally, Section V will illustrate the impact an Article 14-style analysis would have on EPC jurisprudence by subjecting US cases to Article 14 scrutiny.

Why Compare the Article 14 ECHR and Equal Protection Clause approaches to Profiling?

It might seem at first that I make this comparison in an effort to persuade colleagues in the US to push for European-style proportionality to become a doctrine openly adopted by US courts in equal protection cases. I am neither so quixotic nor so insensitive to the transatlantic differences in legal traditions that might make such a move impossible or undesirable. For US colleagues I only seek to explain (1) how the Article 14 ECHR and HRA approach differs from the US approach in that it seeks to *protect* against unequal effects, rather than *prosecuting* discriminatory conduct, and (2) how the language of proportionality affects what kind of information courts should consider in deciding whether an instance of profiling constitutes unlawful discrimination. I contend that constitutional equality provisions that are protective are more effective than those that are prosecutorial, and that proportionality is a more robust scrutiny model than is strict scrutiny of suspect classifications; and I believe (although space prevents me from defending this belief here) that if academics and advocates in the US urged upon the courts the logic of protection and proportionality, there is an outside chance that Equal Protection Clause could develop a bit more muscle.

For UK and European colleagues, I want to make an argument for a particularly muscular Article 14 ECHR, whose protective nature is acknowledged and implemented, and which focuses on discriminatory effects, not intentions. I will also explain that one reason Article 14 can do more than the EPC is that strict scrutiny is one-dimensional, while proportionality is two-dimensional. If a US measure discriminates on the basis of a suspect classification like race or religion, Supreme Court jurisprudence requires strict scrutiny; in the absence of strict scrutiny measures very seldom violate the EPC, so a finding of discrimination on the basis of a suspect classification is nearly a *sine qua non* of a successful claim.[9] Strict scrutiny asks whether the measure pursues a compelling state interest in a way narrowly tailored to the objective.[10] This focuses exclusively on the reasons for choosing the measure in question, not its impacts – although as I will discuss later, there is room for the impact of the measure to be smuggled into the question of narrow tailoring.[11] Proportionality on the other hand requires that the measure not impose a negative impact disproportionate to the extent to which the measure advances a legitimate state interest.[12] This sets up a two-sided balancing: the extent to which the interest is compelling and the measure effective in pursuing it (the state's side of the balance) must outweigh the extent of the negative impact (the claimant's side of the balance).

UK observers might note that in practice there is not a great deal of difference between the two, as UK courts mostly just look at the impact in terms of discrimination being bad – and discrimination on the basis of race or religion being particularly bad – so the measure must represent a particularly efficacious means of pursuing a compelling objective.[13] I contend that in doing this UK courts are simply finessing the question of what kinds of impacts should be considered, and how to measure them. UK courts should view the impact side of the proportionality equation as involving an assessment of how far a challenged measure harms affected individuals or groups, transgresses important principles, and causes societal harms by, for example, undermining social inclusion and dignity. A court can only perform this last part of the assessment by considering social sciences evidence: data or studies produced by economists, sociologists, and psychologists, to name a few. In the US, and indeed in the UK, this type of information is sometimes brought to bear on assessments of the efficacy or narrow tailoring of a challenged measure[14], but there is a crucial difference in the effect of applying such information to the impact side of a proportionality analysis. At least in theory, proportionality can lead to the rejection of a measure that is efficacious, narrowly tailored, and pursues a compelling state interest, if it proves to exact too high a cost in individual, group, principle, or social terms. In other words, proportionality has the potential to say "no" to the state even when the state has nothing but really good reasons for what it wants to do.

I see racial and religious profiling in counter-terrorism efforts as furnishing illustrative examples of the kind of measure that might satisfy US-style strict scrutiny, but should nevertheless fail a proportionality assessment under Article 14 ECHR. I do not intend to develop a detailed definition of what I mean by "racial and religious profiling", because I am concerned less with the nature of the phenomenon than with approaches to controlling instances of it.[15] It should suffice to state that I intend to discuss how Article 14 and the EPC would deal with situations where government law enforcement efforts, either in the form of centrally adopted surveillance or intelligence-gathering policies, criteria or guidelines for decision making, or individual decisions by law enforcement agents or police, employ race or religion as an outcome-determinative factor in deciding whom to stop, search, question, arrest, detain, or investigate.[16] "Outcome-determinative" refers to the fact that profiles can include race or religion as one of several factors, but if the profile works in such a way that a person who meets all of the criteria other than the profiled race will not get stopped, but a person who meets the other criteria *and* race will get stopped, this is disparate treatment on the ground of race, and hence *prima facie* discrimination. By calling this *prima facie* discrimination I do not mean to assume that there is anything unlawful or even immoral about it, simply that it technically involves distinct treatment of individuals who differ solely in their race; this only becomes unlawful or immoral if it lacks an objective justification or fails to satisfy the applicable degree of scrutiny. Although the "classic" profiling scenario involves preventive policing, where a profile is used to narrow the field of targets in efforts to identify terrorists before they commit acts of terrorism, I do not exclude situations where (1) counter-terrorism agents use intelligence information about the racial or religious status of a suspected group of putative terrorists or (2) police use eyewitness descriptions of the apparent race or religious garb of the perpetrators of a specific crime. In each case, viewed from the perspective of the stopped, searched, or detained individual, their race or religion was a determining factor in their being stopped, searched, or detained. The presence of intelligence data or an eyewitness account simply makes the profile arguably more reliable, and hence more susceptible to justification, but it does not change the *prima facie* discriminatory nature of the state action.[17]

The following facts make profiling in counter-terrorism efforts particularly interesting: (1) countering the threat of terrorism will almost always represent a compelling state interest[18] and (2) terrorism presents such an amorphous target for law-enforcement efforts that often it seems that the only effective actions the state can take must employ broad generalizations that impose burdens on a great many people and society as a whole.[19] This second fact sets up the scenario in which a state measure pursues a compelling interest, through a means as narrowly tailored as possible without forfeiting its law-enforcement effectiveness, and nevertheless imposes an individual, group and societal burden that is so unacceptable that the method should be rejected even in the absence of a "less restrictive alternative". I contend in this paper that this scenario would have a different fate under Article 14 than under the EPC. For that reason, what I will do next is provide a brief overview of how the Article 14 analysis works, then make some arguments about how Article 14 should be applied under the HRA in the UK, and then look at US profiling cases that got nowhere under the EPC, and assess how they would fare under the analysis I propose. In doing this I do not purport to offer up a fully developed doctrinal model for analyzing racial or religious profiling, but merely to begin a discussion of how a protective approach to controlling state discrimination, that requires any disparate treatment to procure benefits proportional to the individual and social costs imposed by it, can more effectively deal with profiling than a prosecutorial, one-sided scrutiny model.

How the Article 14 ECHR Analysis works

The first thing to note about Article 14 ECHR is that in one important way it is less robust than the Equal Protection Clause. It does not protect against all discrimination by the state, but only against discrimination "in the enjoyment of the rights and freedoms set out in [the] Convention". That means that before Article 14 can apply, the challenged measure must affect another ECHR right. Fortunately for this discussion, most racial and religious profiling in the context of counter-terrorism will engage either the right to liberty (Article 5), to privacy (Article 8), to free exercise of religion (Article 9), or perhaps to freedom of association (Article 11).[20] In truth this claim is somewhat more controversial than I have made it sound, but that debate is for another paper, and it is at least safe to say that a policy of stopping and searching people who look Muslim or South Asian and are carrying a backpack into the London Underground would engage the right to privacy and allow Article 14 to apply.[21]

In other respects, however, Article 14 can apply more broadly than the EPC because it is what I call a "protective" provision, as opposed to what I call a "prosecutorial" one. In other words, Article 14 promises to protect residents of ECHR signatory states from experiencing inequality of treatment, as opposed to promising to identify and punish instances in which state actors transgress the principles of good human rights practice. A prosecutorial anti-discrimination provision seeks to define "discriminatory conduct", and focuses on whether a challenged measure was the product of such conduct. Article 14, on the other hand, attempts to identify unequal treatment resulting from state action – however motivated – and to put a stop to it if its impacts outweigh its benefits to society.

I have defended this conception of Article 14 as a protector extensively elsewhere,[22] but I would like to set out one argument here. There is little "legislative history" of how the Council of Europe arrived at the particular formulation it adopted for Article 14 in 1950, but it is known that the penultimate version put up for debate read "The rights and freedoms defined in this Convention shall be protected without discrimination . . ."; the final version adopted, however, provided that "[t]he *enjoyment of* the rights and freedoms set forth in this Convention shall be *secured* without discrimination . . ." (my italics).[23] This change meant that "instead of the obligations of the Contracting States, the position of the individual concerned is placed in the foreground".[24] Guaranteeing that rights "shall be protected without discrimination" suggested that state actors must not commit discrimination when protecting Convention rights. On the other hand, guaranteeing that the state will "secure" the "enjoyment" of rights without discrimination suggests that Article 14 binds signatory states to see to it that state action does not abridge the equal enjoyment of Convention rights. This makes Article 14 a protector of equality, not a prosecutor of discriminatory conduct.

In the UK, Article 14 falls to be applied under the Human Rights Act 1998 (HRA), which makes almost all ECHR rights directly justiciable in UK courts. Section 6 HRA makes it "unlawful for a [court] to act in a way which is incompatible with a Convention Right", without express authority from Parliament. This prohibition applies to other state entities as well. It means that presumably all legislative and executive acts have been issued subject to this requirement, but institutionally the courts have the final word, because they have the last chance to prevent Convention-incompatible state actions, and the duty to do so.[25] The courts are bound to apply Parliamentary statutes, but s 3(1) HRA requires judges, "so far as it is possible to do so" to read and "give effect" to legislation, regulations, or decisions in a way compatible with Convention rights, even where a natural reading of the law would violate the Convention. Where a measure cannot be read in a Convention-compatible way without going against the manifest intent of Parliament, s 4 HRA requires that the court issue a "declaration of incompatibility", meaning that the court will apply the statute as written, but substantial political pressure will exist for Parliament to amend the offending statute (although it is not obligated to do so). This means that the courts are empowered essentially to change the effects of measures – amend them from what they would have been upon a natural reading – unless the offending effects were consciously intended by Parliament.[26] Clearly, then, whether an act or law amounts to discrimination under the HRA cannot turn on the fact that, for example, a discriminatory effect of a measure was not intended by Parliament, or flowed from a pure motive: such an effect would be found discriminatory and "interpreted" away. Thus, although UK judges lack the power of US judges to "strike down" acts of the legislature, they are explicitly entrusted with assuring that acts of the other branches of government do not have the effect of violating convention rights. The very structure of the HRA, then, makes it a protective, as opposed to a prosecutorial, scheme. It does not seek merely to root out Convention-offending decision making among government actors, but to assure that even reasonable decisions do not unnecessarily encroach on human rights. This makes Article 14 as applied under the HRA an emphatically protective equality provision.

Once invoked, Article 14 forbids "unjustified" discrimination by the state on a non-exhaustive list of grounds that includes race and religion.[27] Discrimination includes less favorable treatment than an analogous comparator (disparate treatment) as well as indirect discrimination, or disparate impact, where a neutral measure fails to treat differently a person who is relevantly different.[28] No particular motive is required – it suffices that the impugned characteristic was a "but for" cause of the differential treatment or impact – although motive can affect whether the discrimination is justified.[29] The typical analysis first discovers whether there has been bare discrimination before engaging in a separate assessment of whether the discrimination was justified, where only unjustified discrimination is unlawful.[30] Justification depends on whether the challenged measure pursues a legitimate state objective, and whether proportionality is satisfied.

How Article 14 ECHR Proportionality should work under the HRA

The doctrine of proportionality entered into European law through German law, which developed a doctrine of proportionality requiring that state acts or measures be (1) suitable to achieve a legitimate purpose, (2) necessary to achieve that purpose, and (3) proportional in the narrower sense: it must not impose burdens or "cause harms to other legitimate interests" that outweigh the objectives achieved by the measure.[31] This formulation has not been adopted wholesale into the jurisprudence of Article 14 ECHR, but the last element, "proportionality in the narrower sense", was incorporated into the Article 14 analysis in the Belgian Linguistics case, which was in fact the first mention of the doctrine of proportionality by the European Court of Human Rights in Strasbourg (ECtHR).[32] The formulation adopted there required "proportionality between the means employed and the aim sought to be realized".[33] It has subsequently been made clear that this requires the rejection of a regulatory distinction that produces "harms to other legitimate interests" disproportionate to the advancement of a legitimate aim secured by the measure.[34] Jurisprudence of the ECtHR has identified "social inclusion" and dignity generally, and racial and religious equality specifically, as common interests of the Contracting States of the ECHR.[35] Proportionality therefore contemplates a situation where the harm of a measure, in terms of the extent of invasion of an individual's rights, or in terms of the damage to common interests in equal dignity and social inclusion, could outweigh the benefits of even a narrowly tailored measure aimed at a compelling interest. Thus, in theory, a profiling policy of searching all people with an Asian appearance carrying a backpack into the London Underground would treat its targets less favorably than similarly situated non-

Asians because they were Asian, and would violate Article 14 if the impact of the searches (on, I contend, the claimants, other Asians, and the interest of social inclusion in general) outweighed the counter-terrorism benefits of the policy, *even if* the policy was narrowly tailored to pursuing the compelling objective of security from terrorist attack.

Of course, for this theory to become a reality will require that UK courts come to grips with what the doctrine of proportionality requires. UK courts, like courts in the US, tend to focus their scrutiny of allegedly discriminatory measures on the quality of the state's decision-making: Did the state mean to affect a Convention right?[36] Did the state mean to distinguish on the impugned ground?[37] Did the state have any less restrictive alternatives to the distinction employed?[38] This last question is particularly troubling, as it allows the impression that proportionality is really no different from strict scrutiny under the EPC. While I concede that at present, most of the time, there appears to be no practical difference, strict scrutiny and proportionality are in fact two very distinct rubrics. There are plenty of cases in which US courts applying the EPC have considered the impacts of discriminatory laws on the individual claimant or society: it is probably as common in US courts as in UK courts.[39] However, when impacts are considered under the EPC, they are factored into the assessment of whether a measure is narrowly tailored. The narrow tailoring required by strict scrutiny of racial distinctions has recently been explained by the Supreme Court in this way: "the purpose of the narrow tailoring requirement is to ensure that 'the means chosen "fit" ... [the] compelling goal so closely that there is little or no possibility that the motive for the classification was illegitimate racial prejudice or stereotype'."[40] This means that at least in theory impacts are relevant only to the extent they call into question the motive or effectiveness of the measure, or the extent to which the state could meet its objectives in a less harmful way.[41] In this analysis negative impacts lack the potential to outweigh narrowly tailored measures that treat people differently on racial or religious grounds. There may be examples of US judges striking down an effective, narrowly tailored discriminatory regulation simply because of its intolerable effects, but there is no place in the EPC rubric for this, so the ratio of the decision will always be expressed in terms of a fit between the measure and the compelling interest. Proportionality, on the other hand, has a place in its rubric for this kind of decision, and gives courts the option openly to declare that an otherwise exemplary law must fall because it results in unacceptable discriminatory impacts.

UK courts have not yet generally availed themselves of this option, but there are exceptions. For example, in "A and Others v Home Secretary"[42] the House of Lords issued a declaration of incompatibility (which ultimately resulted in a change in the relevant law) in part because the mechanism by which the state sought to "narrowly tailor" its interference with rights had impacts that were simply intolerable. In that case the Home Secretary controversially detained, without trial, suspected terrorists who (a) could not be deported and (b) did not have a right of abode in the UK. This meant that suspected terrorists with UK nationality were not detained, and those without UK nationality, but who could not be deported for fear of torture in their home countries, were imprisoned. In order to impose this burden on liberty in contravention of Article 5 ECHR, the government was required to "derogate" from Article 5 on the ground of a national emergency, which it could only do to the extent "strictly required" by the emergency. The government advanced, as one of its reasons for the nationality distinction, the argument that the non-nationals were considered more of a threat, and that therefore the detention of the non-nationals was all that was "strictly required", while detention of the nationals would go beyond what was "strictly required" by the threat. Although this argument satisfied the Court of Appeal, which focused exclusively on the quality of the state's reasoning,[43] the Lords opined, *inter alia*, that even though the distinction was facially on the ground of immigration status, not nationality; and even though the distinction was intended to reduce the impact of the measure; and even though as a result of the distinction the measure was as narrowly tailored to its aim as it could be and still be effective, the invidious effects of treating non-nationals so differently from nationals were simply disproportionate to the counter-terrorism benefits of the scheme.[44]

Although "A and Others" represents an application that illustrates the difference in potential between proportionality and strict scrutiny, it does not demonstrate the true potential of proportionality. The impact in that case was easy for the Lords to understand. They did not need social sciences literature to prove to them that incarcerating non-nationals while letting similarly situated nationals go free brings the law into disrepute, would violate compelling interests in equality and social inclusion, and would likely create resentments among resident non-nationals. They were directed by proportionality to give the impacts a weight, and to balance them against the benefits, so they gave the impacts the substantial weight they obviously deserved.[45] But for proportionality to come fully into its own, courts must be open to having non-obvious impacts proved to them. It is my contention that advocates on behalf of claimants, and perhaps interveners and *amici*, such as human rights advocacy NGOs and equality commissions, must demand that UK courts turn their attention to the "other side of proportionality" in discrimination cases. The proportionality rubric gives advocates a ground for insisting that a court take into account evidence of impacts, regardless of whether this evidence relates to the individual claimant or to the narrow tailoring of the impugned state action. Human rights lawyers in the UK must begin to make what I will call an "Inverse Brandeis Brief" a part of every Article 14 case. At least until UK courts become accustomed to considering the economic, sociological, psychological and other impacts of discriminatory laws, advocates must present evidence and research outcomes from these fields of study to demonstrate that, for example, a given policy of stopping and searching young men of Muslim or South Asian appearance contributes to an unacceptable breakdown of social inclusion. If courts are made to perform the proportionality analysis the way it reads on the tin, they will be more likely to assign a fair weight to the impacts of discriminatory laws.

To those unfamiliar with the HRA and the ECHR the foregoing might sound like so much wishing on a star. Well might one ask, "if the ECHR has not given effect to proportionality in this way after all these years, isn't asking UK courts to give it this effect much the same as asking the Supreme Court to start applying the EPC like a protector and not a prosecutor?" The answer is no, the two are not the same, for two reasons: (1) the margin of appreciation and (2) the HRA. The Strasbourg court has had little opportunity to set any precedent for how domestic courts should apply proportionality because of the very distinct roles of the ECtHR and domestic courts. The role of the ECtHR is to supervise the extent to which signatory states comply with their treaty obligations. An underlying principle of the ECHR is that Strasbourg determines the standard to which human rights must be protected, but the Contracting Parties decide how to deliver this level of protection. In other words, the mode of protection of Convention rights is not expected to be the same throughout Europe. From this principle has emerged the doctrine of "the margin of appreciation," which refers to an area within which Strasbourg defers to the prerogative of the signatory state to strike its own characteristic balance when human rights must give way to overriding state interests. This does not mean that the ECtHR does not impose limits, it simply means that states are allowed to reach different outcomes when applying proportionality, as long as the outcomes are not outside the margin of appreciation.[46] As a result, the Strasbourg court does not really "do" proportionality beyond what is necessary to determine whether the balance stuck by the signatory state exceeds the margin of appreciation. The actual mechanics of proportionality have always been for the Contracting Parties to sort out, and it is for the state to decide whether the legislature, the judiciary, the executive, or some combination thereof, ultimately strikes the balance.[47]

Enter the HRA

Although enacted in 1998, the first judicial decisions did not emerge until 2001. Thus, while the UK has had ECHR obligations for decades, UK courts and advocates have only had about five years to develop a jurisprudence based on the extent and kind of incorporation of Convention rights effected by the HRA.

The HRA is more than a new scheme for applying Convention rights in the UK: it erects a scheme where there was none before, bringing ECHR rights from the background to the foreground, and effectively starting from scratch in domestic precedential terms. Section 2(1) of the HRA requires that UK courts take Strasbourg precedent into account, but it also contemplates and indeed requires that the courts develop a UK understanding of Convention rights to an extent consistent with the baseline established by the ECtHR.[48] Recently the House of Lords indicated that it would not be UK judicial policy to "leap ahead" of Strasbourg.[49] However, for reasons already discussed, there is nothing in the Strasbourg jurisprudence that even gives guidance, much less restraining precedent, for how the UK should give effect to proportionality, except that it must not allow its protection of rights to fall below the requirements of the margin of appreciation. Therefore nothing stands in the way of UK courts paying increasing attention to weighing the impacts of discrimination in a proportionality analysis, and accepting social sciences evidence in aid of assigning a proper weight.

Majoritarians will almost certainly complain that to the extent a signatory state must balance the benefits of a measure against its impacts on social inclusion or equal dignity, surely this should be done by more democratic institutions like Parliament.[50] I cannot hope in this paper effectively to rebut the preposterous but increasingly popular idea that "more responsive to majority pressure" means "more democratic". It suffices for this purpose to note that the HRA does not confer on UK courts the task of reviewing acts of Parliament for evidence that Parliament strayed from good human rights practice; instead, it forbids the courts to act inconsistently with Convention rights except when required to do so by an act of Parliament, in which case they are to issue a declaration of incompatibility. Thus, the courts must assess proportionality *de novo*. That does not mean that they act without deference: they must defer to the superior expertise of specialist executive departments and to Parliamentary expressions of majority policy preference.[51] However, the courts have, if anything, more expertise than the legislature or executive with regard to applying the principles of proportionality.[52] Moreover, they are institutionally better suited to the retrospective fact finding necessary to determine the actual impacts of measures.[53] The HRA requires courts to ensure not only that laws or decisions comply with human rights at the time of their birth, as it were, but that the end result of their interaction with the outside world – with other state institutions, with executive discretion, with the actual lives of individual people, and with the courts – does not ultimately violate human rights.[54] This is the kind of task that can only be completed after Parliament has performed all the balancing it is going to do, and only by a court. Finally, it is simply inconsistent with the very concept of protecting the human rights of minorities to suggest that an openly political decision made by a majority-controlled legislative body is a more legitimate way of deciding when state action encroaches on basic individual rights, or unacceptably under-

mines the inclusion of insular minorities, than a decision made in a forum where there are two parties of equal importance, given equal opportunity to speak and present evidence, and in which decisions are
premised on reasoned argument rather than the numbers for and
against.

Human rights advocates in the UK have an opportunity, while the
HRA jurisprudence begins to take root, yet still appears to change
every few months, to force the "other side of proportionality" into the
forefront of the jurisprudence of Article 14. The proportionality rubric
provides a basis for demanding that courts not only recognize that impacts can outweigh even well-intentioned and narrowly tailored laws,
but that they pay as much attention to assigning a fair weight to those
impacts as they currently do to assessing the quality of challenged legislation. Article 14's character as a protective, as opposed to prosecutorial, anti-discrimination provision is well established.[55] This attrib-
ute, coupled with a robust application of proportionality, makes Article 14 capable of reaching any situation where state action has the effect of exposing people to different treatment because of their race or
religion, and can in effect set the level of scrutiny to which the state
measure will be subjected on a case-by-case basis, depending not on a
one-size-fits-all suspect classification, but on the impacts of the discriminatory measure.[56]

The Impact of Protection and Proportionality
on US Profiling Cases

The Equal Protection Clause does not on its face contain any re-
striction of its field of application to other constitutional rights – it
guarantees equal protection of all the laws – and nothing in its language would lead one to suspect that it offers any less protection from
discrimination than Article 14. As I suggested earlier, however, US
courts have chipped away at the EPC by distinguishing between intentional discrimination (covered) and indirect or "disparate impact" discrimination (not covered).[57] I purposely used the phrase "intentional
discrimination" instead of the phrases "direct discrimination" and
"disparate treatment," generally used in Europe and the US, respectively, to refer to discrimination resulting from differential treatment
on a prohibited ground. I did this because I think that the extent of

discriminatory motive required under the EPC goes beyond what is generally required under direct discrimination or disparate treatment analyses. The Supreme Court, in McCleskey v Kemp[58] and United States v Armstrong[59], has established that before strict scrutiny can apply, the claimant bears the burden of proving intent to discriminate on a suspect ground: it cannot be inferred from the same kind of evidence that can create a rebut-able inference of discrimination in statutory claims of direct or disparate treatment discrimination. This is not only a question of burden of proof: employment discrimination statutes in the UK do not require an ultimate factual finding of conscious intent to discriminate on the basis of race or religion, but generally accept a but-for relationship between the prohibited ground and the differential treatment.[60] The point here is that the EPC not only offers no protection against indirect or disparate impact discrimination (except where the disparate impact together with other evidence is found to disclose the requisite intent), it fails to apply to – and hence requires no heightened scrutiny of measures that employ – arrangements that give rise to disparate treatment on the grounds of race or religion, but are not intended to burden individuals because of their race.[61]

This is an important distinction in relation to Article 14, which will require a justification involving "very weighty reasons" as long as the facts disclose (1) that like cases were treated unlike or (2) that unlike cases were treated alike, and (3) that "but for" the race or religion of the claimant the less favorable treatment or impact would not have occurred.[62] This flows from the fact that Article 14 is a protector whereas, in my dichotomy, the EPC is clearly a prosecutor. Under the EPC jurisprudence, if a state entity acted reasonably, and without discriminatory intent, the unequal or discriminatory impact is irrelevant. This means that there are cases Article 14 can reach that the EPC cannot reach, regardless of whether proportionality is stronger than strict scrutiny.

For example, in United States v Travis, the Sixth Circuit US Court of Appeals held that where law enforcement officers use race as one of a list of criteria on the basis of which to decide whom to interview, no EPC implications arise: "when officers compile several reasons before initiating an interview, as long as some of those reasons are legitimate, there is no Equal Protection violation".[63] The court in essence viewed the police as not intending to distinguish on the basis of race, but on the basis of satisfying a profile sincerely calculated to nar-row-down the field of suspects. The fact that white individuals who met all of the criteria other than race would not be interviewed eluded the EPC analysis altogether. Under Article 14, however, that fact would lead to the conclusion that the state conduct at issue resulted in less favorable treatment on the ground of race, and must be justified.[64]

A more powerful illustration of the full potential of Article 14 is provided by Brown v City of Oneonta,[65] where the Second Circuit US Court of Appeals held that no race discrimination had occurred when the police used race as part of a neutral policy of stopping and search-ing persons who matched an eyewitness description. The police in a small college town had an eyewitness account to the effect that a bur-glary had been committed by a young African-American male, who allegedly received a wound to the hand in a struggle with the victim.[66] The police reacted by interrogating every black student in the local college (roughly 75) and "stopping and questioning non-white persons on the streets and inspecting their hands for cuts".[67] The litigation arose from outraged African-American residents of the town who complained that the whole investigation was a massive violation of their civil rights. The US Court of Appeals for the Second Circuit, however, ruled that the entire incident arose from the use by the police of a race-neutral policy: "to investigate crimes by interviewing the victim, getting a description of the assailant, and seeking out persons who matched that description."[68] Thus the fact that "but for" their race the claimants would not have been interrogated or stopped and searched (for cuts) did not prove discrimination in the absence of evi-dence that there was a racial motive behind the policy. As a result of the finding that no race discrimination had occurred, no strict scrutiny was applied, with the predictable result that no violation of the EPC was found.

It should be clear by now that under Article 14, provided that the interrogations, detentions, and physical examinations were found to involve rights to privacy or liberty under the Convention,[69] a justifica-tion incorporating proportionality would be required on the facts of Brown v City of Oneonta. Because white people, similarly situated in every relevant respect (young, male, and walking down the street or young, male, and attending the local college) were not stopped, exam-ined or interrogated, and because the claimants would not have been treated less favorably than those white people but for the fact that they were black, *prima facie* discrimination would have been established, and Article 14 would call for a justification of the state action.[70] This is not, however, the only way in which Article 14 would get a firmer purchase on the case than would the EPC. The blanket stopping and interrogation of young black men could offend the principle of proportionality and hence fall afoul of Article 14, whereas it would almost certainly satisfy strict scrutiny, had it been applied.

This point is well illustrated by Bernard Harcourt's strong critique of the reasoning in Oneonta. Harcourt takes the court to task for assuming that a profile based on eyewitness testimony differs in kind, rather than degree, from a profile based on, for example, an alleged statistical probability that a Muslim or South Asian man is more likely to be planning a terrorist attack than other people entering an airport. In either case, he observes, the law enforcement officers consciously use the race of targets as a reason to stop and interrogate them, and the eyewitness case differs only because the police employed an arguably more valid predictor, "where race functions sufficiently to narrow down the suspect pool".[71] Harcourt argues that the court should have treated the case as one of race discrimination requiring strict scrutiny. Tellingly, however, he appears to assume that the mass stops and interrogations in Oneonta would have satisfied strict scrutiny. His quarrel was not with the result, but with how the court got there. His claim was that the extent to which a particular kind of information "narrows down the suspect pool" is a matter of the effectiveness of the measure, and whether it is "narrowly tailored" to achieving the compelling state interest. If it reliably and significantly narrows the pool, it is narrowly tailored to its objective. This is consistent with the orthodox approach under the EPC, which does not take into account the extent of the impact of the measure as a separate consideration. The requirement that a measure be narrowly tailored takes impact into account, but only insofar as it can be shown that the state could achieve its aim with less impact, and thus that the challenged measure was not, in fact, narrowly tailored. The Oneonta profile could satisfy strict scrutiny because (1) there were only four pieces of information offered in the eyewitness statement (young, black, male, cut), (2) using these would narrow down the field significantly, (3) dropping anyone of the traits from the list would render the profile ineffective, and (4) not searching everyone who had the relevant characteristics would not be effective. The state could not more narrowly tailor its investigative technique and retain its effectiveness in pursuing the compelling state interest in apprehending burglars.[72]

Unfortunately, nowhere does the EPC jurisprudence require the court to ask if the impact was so unacceptable that the state should drop the technique altogether. As I suggested above, had the Oneonta case made it to strict scrutiny, a US court might well be moved by the breadth and notoriety of the investigatory sweep to rule that the plan was not narrowly tailored to the objective of catching the alleged burglar. However, the logic would be strained. What is it about the challenged investigation that did not "fit" the interest of crime prevention? If the interests of society required that the burglar be apprehended, and there was not a single lead other than the race, gender, age, and wounding of the suspect (and assuming there were good reasons to believe that the burglar came from and remained in the vicinity), the method seems to fit the objective like a glove.[73] The police could not very well check just half of the young black men because that could easily deprive the investigation of 100 % of its effectiveness. One could argue that the impacts of the mass interrogations would undermine future law enforcement efforts and thus were not narrowly tailored, but that is a fudge: what really bothers one about the case is not one's fear for the future success of law enforcement but the simple, gut-level wrongness of treating every young black man in a small American town as a potential criminal. The act itself is just so wrong and divisive, so destructive of social inclusion for reasons unconnected to law enforcement objectives, that it simply should not be tolerated. Thus the need, imposed by the EPC rubric, to weave such intolerable impacts into the narrow tailoring analysis requires sympathetic courts to engage in embarrassing pettifoggery to get to the "right" result, and allows unsympathetic courts simply not to see the problem.

An EPC analysis performed by the US Supreme Court as currently constituted could quite easily wave the Oneonta investigation through strict scrutiny, assuming that there really were no less restrictive means of pursuing the investigation effectively, and of taking useful advantage of the eyewitness account. And of course, in fact, it never got to strict scrutiny because somehow separating black students out from white classmates in identical situations in every respect except skin color did not amount to racial discrimination under the EPC. On the other hand, provided that the stops and interrogations would be found to implicate the right to privacy under Article 8 of the ECHR, Article 14 would find discrimination, and require the state to proffer a proportionality justification complete with "weighty reasons". This proportionality justification could, and I have argued should, fail because the impact, on individual rights, group rights, and society in general, of interrogating every young black man in a small American town simply outweighs the state's interest in catching one small-time burglar. Proportionality could, for example, take into account what have been referred to as the "social meaning" of profiling, and the "racial (or religious) tax" exacted by it from minority groups.[74] Proportionality would not treat all policing objectives as having the same "compelling" weight, but would ask on a case by case basis whether the law enforcement aim at issue justified the burden imposed. Following that rubric even the Oneonta court would find it hard to conclude that the need to find people to question about a thwarted burglary outweighed the social and individual impacts of the police's sweep of the town.

Conclusion

Law enforcement efforts to uncover terrorist plots and to prevent terrorists from bringing weapons or explosives into public places or transportation networks can always be characterized as pursuing a "compelling state interest". The fact that counter-terrorism officers have so few avenues for identifying who might perpetrate these acts means that police will often have no effective alternative means of pursuing that interest other than, for example, stopping and searching young, South Asian or obviously Muslim men carrying backpacks into the London Underground. In the face of this kind of challenge the Equal Protection Clause seems a very crude tool. Once an objective clears the one-size-fits-all "compelling" threshold, it triggers a one-sided "narrowly tailored" analysis which scrutinizes the measure or act only from the perspective of the state or the police, offering no place in its framework for a nuanced balancing of the interests of the state against the interests of affected minorities and against burdens on the social fabric. The Equal Protection Clause as currently applied simply has no way to deal with regulatory or enforcement distinctions driven by (at least consciously) neutral intentions, that nevertheless cause individuals or groups to experience unequal treatment under the law. By comparison, Article 14 of the ECHR seems custom made to tackle racial and religious profiling in a counter-terrorism context. It applies to any state distinction that burdens the equal enjoyment of rights, regardless of government intention. It can prohibit as unjustified the use of lazy, unimaginative, or insensitive law enforcement techniques whose social costs outweigh their counter-terrorism benefits, even if they are the only, and thus by definition the lest restrictive, techniques the police can think of. In short, it makes it possible, if the evidence supports a finding that using a generalized racial profile in a given case only modestly advances law enforcement aims and profoundly undermines social inclusion, to tell the police that if they can come up with nothing better than to stop and search every young Arab or South Asian man then they must search everyone until they think of something more effective and less divisive.[75]

This will of course only happen in the UK if judges in that country begin to take greater notice of social science evidence in assigning a weight to the "other side of proportionality" – the costs to the individual, group, or society as opposed to the importance of the state interest and the efficacy of the means used to achieve it. This comparison helps show the importance of Article 14's potential to make impacts and social costs a fundamental part of the state discrimination analysis in the UK. It also shows the relative weakness of the Equal Protection Clause analysis. It is unlikely that Equal Protection jurisprudence will be strengthened any time soon by the adoption of European proportionality, with the necessary concomitant jettisoning of decades of suspect classification and strict scrutiny precedent. However, it is not too much to hope, I think, that the Equal Protection Clause conception of discrimination could mature over time. If presented with the argument often enough, even judges can begin to see that what the claimant experienced is as important, or more so, than what the state actor did; that we routinely subject each other to discrimination whether we mean to or not; and that equal protection must be protective.

Endnotes

* I would like to thank the United Kingdom Arts and Humanities Research Council for its support, in the form of a research leave grant, of the preparation of this chapter.

[1] I. Johnston, in the wake of the July 7, 2005 bombings in the London Underground; V. Dodd, Asian Men Targeted in Stop and Search, Guardian Unlimited (August 17 2005) at <Hhttp://www.guardian.co.uk/attackonlondon/ story/0,16132,1550470,00.htmlH>, last checked August 8, 2006.

[2] Pete Walker, Q & A: the De Menezes Investigation, Guardian Unlimited (July 17 2006) at <Hhttp://www.guardian.co.uk/menezes/story/ 0,,1822504,00.htmlH>, last checked August 8, 2006.

[3] V. Dodd 2005 (En. 1).

[4] American Civil Liberties Union, Sanctioned Bias: Racial Profiling Since 9/11 4-5 (1994).

[5] C. Whitlock and D. Linzer, Stakeouts, Tips and Wiretaps Led to Arrests, The Washington Post, August 11, 2006.

[6] See, e. g., Washington v Davis, 426 U.S. 229, 239 (1976); Brown v City of Oneonta, 221 F3d 329, 337 (2d Cir 2000); United States v Travis, 62 F3d 170, 174 (6th Cir 1995); United States v Weaver, 966 F2d 391, 394 n 2 (8th Cir 1992), cert denied 506 US 1040 (1992).

[7] D. Moeckli, Discriminatory Profiles: Law Enforcement After 9/11 and 7/7, 5 European Human Rights L Rev 517 (2005).

[8] A. Baker, Comparison Tainted by Justification: Against a "Compendious Question" in Article 14 Discrimination, Public Law 475 (2006) (hereinafter "Comparison"); A. Baker, Article 14 ECHR: a Protector, Not a Prosecutor, in H. Fenwick, G. Phillipson and R. Masterson (eds.), Judicial Reasoning and the Human Rights Act 1998 (Cambridge: Cambridge University Press, 2006) (hereinafter "Protector"); A. W. Alschuler, Racial Profiling and the Constitution 2002, U Chi Legal F 163 (2002), p. 184.

[9] Adarand Constructors, Inc v Pena, 515 US 200, 237 (1995).

[10] Grutter v Bollinger, 539 US 306, 326 (2003).

[11] See infra notes 36-41 and accompanying text.

[12] A and Ors v Home Secretary [2004] UKHL 56, para 50; Ghaidan v Godin-Mendoza, [2004] UKHL 30, para 133.

[13] See, e. g., Board of Governors of St Matthias CE School v Crizzle [1993] ICR 401.

[14] See, e. g., Grutter v Bollinger, 539 US 306, 327-333 (2003); R (Carson) v Secretary for Work and Pensions [2003] EWCA Civ 797, paras 61-71.

[15] See, e. g., infra n 16 and M.-F. Cuellar, Choosing Anti-Terror Targets by National Origin and Race, 6 Harv Latino L Rev 9 (2003), p. 11; D. A. Rami-

rez et al, Defining Racial Profiling in a Post-September 11 World, Am Crim L Rev 4 (2003), p. 1202-1207.

[16] This is a definition similar to the one set out in S. R. Gross and D. Livingston, Racial Profiling Under Attack, Columbia L Rev 102 (2002), p. 1413, 1415, although they exclude race-focused investigations based on eyewitness descriptions of alleged perpetrators, because this does not involve a 'global judgment about a racial or ethnic group as a whole.' I see no point in quibbling over the definition, because what I am interested in is how constitutional equality provisions deal with the use of race to narrow the pool of investigation targets, and I do not consider that the quality of judgment employed by state actors should factor into the analysis of whether *prima facie* discrimination—differential treatment—has occurred, but should form part of its justification.

[17] B. Harcourt, Rethinking Racial Profiling: A Critique of the Economics, Civil Liberties, and Constitutional Literature, and of Criminal Profiling More Generally, Chicago L Rev 71 (2004), p. 1275, 1345.

[18] A. W. Alschuler 2002 (En. 8), p. 183-184.

[19] American Civil Liberties Union, Sanctioned Bias: Racial Profiling Since 9/11 (1994).

[20] See, e. g., A. Baker, The Enjoyment of Rights and Freedoms: a New Conception of the "Ambit" under Article 14 ECHR, Modern L Rev 69 (2006), p. 714.

[21] A. Baker 2006 (En. 20).

[22] A. Baker 2006 (Comparison) (En. 8); A. Baker 2006 (Protector) (En. 8).

[23] K. J. Partsch, Discrimination, in The European System for the Protection of Human Rights, in R. S. J. Macdonald, F. Matscher and H. Petzold (eds.), 1993, p. 575.

[24] K. J. Partsch 1993 (En. 23).

[25] See, e. g., F. Klug, The Human Rights Act – A "Third Way" or "Third Wave" Bill of Rights, European Human Rights L Rev 361 (2001); I. Leigh, Taking Rights Proportionately: Judicial Review, the Human Rights Act and Strasbourg, Public Law 265 (2002), p. 282-286; J. Jowell, Beyond the Rule of Law: Towards Constitutional Judicial Review, Public Law 671 (2000); M. Elliott, The HRA 1998 and the Standard of Substantive Review, Cambridge L J 60 (2001), p. 301; P. Craig, Administrative Law (4th ed, 1999), p. 546, 556-557, 561.

[26] A. Kavanagh, The Elusive Divide between Interpretation and Legislation under the Human Rights Act 1998, Oxford J Legal Studies 24 (2004), p. 259, 274-277.

[27] Belgian Linguistics (1968) 1 EHRR 252, 283.

[28] Thlimmenos v Greece (2001) 31 EHRR 411.

[29] R (Gillan) v Commissioner of Police for the Metropolis, [2006] UKHL 12, para 44

[30] Ghaidan v Godin-Mendoza, [2004] UKHL 30.

[31] Lord Hoffmann, The Influence of the European Principle of Proportionality upon UK Law, in E. Ellis (ed.), The Principle of Proportionality in the Laws of Europe (1999), p. 107. Lord Hoffmann is a Law Lord in the UK House of Lords.

[32] M.-A. Eissen, The Principle of Proportionality in the Case Law of the European Court of Human Rights, in R. S. J. Macdonald, F. Matscher and H. Petzold (eds.), The European System for the Protection of Human Rights (1993), p. 140.

[33] Belgian Linguistics (1968) 1 EHRR 252, para 10.

[34] A and Ors v Home Secretary [2004] UKHL 56, para 50; Ghaidan v Godin-Mendoza, [2004] UKHL 30, para 133.

[35] East African Asians v UK (1973) 3 EHRR, EComHR; East African Asians v UK, Application 4403/70 (1995) 19 EHRR CD1, EComHR; Thlimmenos v Greece (2001) 31 EHRR 411; Hoffmann v Austria 17 EHRR 293.

[36] R (Douglas) v North Tyneside MBC [2004] HRLR 14, paras 56, 60.

[37] R (Carson) v Secretary for Work and Pensions [2005] UKHL 37 (issued as a joint opinion with the case of R (Reynolds) v Secretary for Work and Pensions).

[38] R(Marper) v Chief Constable of South Yorkshire Police [2004] UKHL 39 paras 28-31.

[39] Grutter, 539 US 306, 333-343; Metro Broadcasting, Inc. v. FCC, 497 U.S. 547, 630.

[40] Grutter, 539 US 306, 333.

[41] Grutter, 539 US 306, 333.

[42] 2004 UKHL 56.

[43] A and Ors (CA) [2002] EWCA Civ 1502, paras 47, 56, 103, 153.

[44] A and Ors [2004] UKHL 56, para 53.

[45] I wish to observe at this point that one of the most significant reasons that constitutional equality provisions do not achieve the potential I imagine them to have is that many judges, in the US and the UK, do not give discriminatory impacts the weight that I would give them. I cannot think of any legal arguments that will persuade all people to assign to all competing interests the same value I assign to them. The point is that I am aware that no matter how strong or weak the rubric of scrutiny is, there will be cases where I think the impacts are intolerable or disproportionate, but the court does not agree. My argument in this paper is simply that the proportionality rubric gives advocates a ground for demanding that a court take into account evidence of impacts, and that this will make it more likely that courts will assign them a fair weight.

[46] Fleshing out the contours of Strasbourg's margin of appreciation falls outside the scope of this paper. For a thorough discussion, see Y. Arai-Takahashi, The Margin of Appreciation Doctrine and the Principle of Proportionality in the Jurisprudence of the ECHR (2002).

[47] See, e. g., Unison v United Kingdom, [2002] IRLR 497; Schmidt and Dahlstrom v Sweden, 1 EHRR 632, paras 34-36 (1976).

[48] R. Masterman, Section 2(1) of the Human Rights Act 1998: Binding Domestic Courts to Strasbourg? Public Law (2004), p. 725, 727; D. Bonner, H. Fenwick and S. Harris-Short, Judicial Approaches to the Human Rights Act, 52, Int'l & Comp L Quarterly (2003), p. 549, 553.

[49] R (Marper) v Chief Constable of South Yorkshire Police [2004] UKHL 39.

[50] See, e. g., A. Young, Judicial Sovereignty and the Human Rights Act, Cambridge L J 61 (2002), p. 53.

[51] A and Ors [2004] UKHL 56; Ghaidan [2004] UKHL 30.

[52] See En. 51.

[53] See, e. g., O. Fiss, Forms of Justice, Harvard L Rev 93 (1979), p. 1, regarding the institutional suitability of courts to the task of weighing public policy concerns against individual rights; I. Leigh and L. Lustgarten, Making Rights Real: the Courts, Remedies, and the Human Rights Act, Cambridge L J 58, p. 509, 522-526, arguing that judicial review procedures in the UK at the time of the enactment of the HRA were not up to the task of coping with the kind of justification inquiry called for by the HRA.

[54] Ghaidan [2004] UKHL 30, para 22 ('the compatibility of legislation with the Convention rights falls to be assessed when the issue arises for determination, not as at the date when the legislation was enacted or came into force'); Ian Leigh, Taking Rights Proportionately: Judicial Review, the Human Rights Act and Strasbourg, Public Law (2002), p. 265, 282-286; P. Craig, Administrative Law (4th ed, 1999), p. 546, 556-557, 561.

[55] Thlimmenos v Greece (2001) 31 EHRR 411; Petrovich v Austria (1998) 33 EHRR 307; Gaygusus v Austria (1997) 23 EHRR 364; Belgian Linguistics (1968) 1 EHRR 252. See also: D. Feldman, Civil Liberties and Human Rights in England and Wales (2nd ed, 2002), p. 144; S. Livingstone, Article 14 and the Prevention of Discrimination in the European Convention on Human Rights, European Human Rights L Rev 1 (1997), p. 25, 32-33; S. Grosz, J. Beatson and Peter Duffy, Human Rights: The 1998 Act and the European Convention (2000), paras C14-20-C14-23.

[56] I leave it for another paper to explore the potential under Article 14 for some uses of profiling to be more likely to pass muster than under the EPC, because the impact is sufficiently light as to be outweighed by less than a compelling state interest.

[57] See, e. g, Washington v Davis, 426 US 229, 239 (1976).

[58] 481 US 279, 292-293 (1987) (holding that statistical proof of a strong correlation between race and subjection to the death penalty could not support an inference of discrimination in the absence of proof that "the decision makers in [this] case acted with a discriminatory purpose").

[59] 517 US 456, 458-459 (1996) (finding that proof that every person prosecuted for the relevant offence in the relevant year was African-American could not furnish evidence of discriminatory prosecution, in the absence of proof that at least one similarly situated white person was not prosecuted).

[60] James v Eastleigh Borough Council [1990] 2 All ER 607.

[61] United States v Travis, 62 F3d 170, 174 (6th Cir 1995).

[62] A. Baker 2006 (Comparison) (En. 8); East African Asians v UK (1973) 3 EHRR, EComHR; East African Asians v UK, Application 4403/70 (1995) 19 EHRR CD1, EComHR; Thlimmenos v Greece (2001) 31 EHRR 411.

[63] United States v Travis, 62 F3d at 174.

[64] See, e. g., A and Ors [2004] UKHL 56, para 53.

[65] 221 F3d 329 (2d Cir 2000).

[66] 221 F3d at 334.

[67] En. 66.

[68] En. 66. at 337.

[69] In R (Gillan) v Commissioner of Police for the Metropolis, [2006] UKHL 12, paras 25, 28, 44 the UK House of Lords found that a stop and search, even if it lasted for several hours, did not necessarily violate the Article 5 right to liberty or the Article 8 right to privacy, but specifically noted that discriminatory stops and searches would be another matter (which the judges reserved for a more appropriate case).

[70] A. Baker 2006 (Comparison) (En. 8).

[71] B. Harcourt 2004 (En. 17), p. 1345.

[72] But see A. W. Alschuler, Racial Profiling and the Constitution 2002 U Chi. Legal F. (2002), p. 163, 184 (2002), arguing that calling the Oneonta sweep "narrowly tailored" would not "survive the laugh test". The tone of Alschuler's discussion suggests that he really means that it should not survive the laugh test, but I contend that in the hands of the same judges who found the sweep not to amount to discrimination, a finding of narrow tailoring is not even a stretch.

[73] See, e. g., R. R. Banks, Race-Based Suspect Selection and Colorblind Equal Protection Doctrine and Discourse UCLA L Rev 48 (2001), p. 1075, 1082, 1108-1124.

[74] See A. W. Alschuler 2002 (En. 72), p. 207-223.

[75] See, e. g., A and Ors [2004] UKHL 56.

13

Rethinking the Threats to Human Security: Implications for Global Governance

R. Scott Fosler

In the six decades since World War II, billions of people around the globe have lived with the threat of instant annihilation from nuclear weapons. Over that period, more than three billion people have died, but not a single one of them from a nuclear blast.[1] Most of those billions of deaths resulted from a wide variety of causes that cut life short of what has become the normal life expectancy in modern society.

The point here is not to discount the threat of nuclear weapons, which is deadly serious. To the contrary, one reason, aside from luck, that the human race has escaped nuclear catastrophe in the years since the first use of nuclear weapons in 1945, is precisely because the consequences are so terrible that the nuclear powers have devoted considerable attention and resources to determining ways in which any further use of nuclear weapons could be avoided. On the other hand, the experience of the past sixty years also demonstrates that even if humans succeed in containing what may appear to be the most frightening threat of the era, they remain exposed to a wide variety of other hazards, including long-standing threats that never went away, new threats that can emerge with little warning, and old threats that can take new form or otherwise become more urgent.

The contrast between the chronic anxiety over some threats that occur rarely if ever, and the nonchalance or ignorance regarding other threats that are constantly causing death, injury and destruction, or threaten to do so in the future, is a reflection of the discontinuities that characterize our age. Never before in human history have so many people lived such long, secure, and prosperous lives. And never before have so many people died of preventable causes, suffered anxiety over so wide a range of threats unlikely ever to occur, and been ignorant of – or ignored – knowable, serious, and largely preventable threats that could cause them great harm.

We live in a time when the real potential for disaster hovers in un-settling tension with the unprecedented security enjoyed by unsur-passed numbers of humans. For most of the world, the prime "secu-rity" threats today are not so much those of "national security" in the way that term has been understood in the past – armed conflict be-tween states – but rather are comprised of a more motley and shadowy array of dangers, some of which are fiendishly difficult to get our minds around. This has created a condition of profound disorientation regarding the nature of the threats that humans confront across the globe, and the ways in which they attempt to deal with them.

The Good News

By the broadest, average indicators, human life at the beginning of the 21st century is more secure than it has ever been. Consider the fol-lowing global developments:

- Despite the unprecedented violence and death of the 20th century, the human population grew faster than ever. Today, at six and one-half billion souls, it is larger than it has ever been, and still growing.
- Over the past three decades, the political violence that dominated the earlier 20th century peaked, and – contrary to popular percep-tion – declined. By the beginning of the 21st century, the relative magnitude of political violence and death around the world was the lowest it had been in centuries, a feature of what has been characterized as "the most free, most peaceful, and most stable in-ternational community in human history".[2]

- People are living longer than ever before. The average human life-span was 63.8 years in 2002, the longest it has ever been, and it is projected to reach 76.6 years by 2050. This is due principally to the fact that child mortality has been reduced in all parts of the world.
- People are healthier than ever. Human nutrition has improved because there is an abundance of food, enough for everyone. Many deadly diseases, such as smallpox, have been eradicated, diminished, or are now more successfully treated. Living conditions are cleaner, healthier and safer than ever. People lead longer work-lives and longer and more active retirements.
- The material standard of living is higher than it has ever been in human experience. In the last four decades of the 20th century average world-wide incomes increased even as the population doubled, thanks to rising productivity and per capita economic growth. In the last two decades of the 20th century, the number of people existing in extreme poverty dropped by 30 %, from one-and-a-half billion to one billion. Unprecedented economic wealth has provided the resources for more people than ever before to make full use of the capacity to live longer, healthier, more flourishing lives.

So with all this good news, why do so many people now feel so anxious or fearful?

Anxiety and Disorientation

There appear to be five principal reasons for the continuing, or heightened sense of threat that many people feel throughout the world.

First, and most obviously, the positive overall indicators are broad and based on averages, and therefore mask significant variations. Rich people living in safe neighborhoods in stable countries are naturally less likely to feel threatened, or to be exposed to genuine risks, than poor people living in dangerous neighborhoods in chaotic countries. Two major regions of the world, sub-Sahara Africa and the Middle East, are conspicuous exceptions to the overwhelmingly positive constellation of trends. And people who live in places subject to sudden new threats, such as terrorism, understandably remain anxious until the new threat is more reliably calibrated and confronted.

Second, some of the positive trends contain troublesome implications. For example, while the unprecedented population growth of the past century is an indication of the human species' success in surviving and reproducing, it has also created enormous strains on earth's natural environment.

Third, some of the troublesome implications in the positive developments have risen to the point of genuine threat, while qualitatively new threats have also emerged from the new world humans have created. For example, population densities have caused the collapse of vital natural support systems in some regions of the world, and in others have created conditions that give rise to other threats, such as new infectious diseases. And powerful new technologies that have given humans enormous new power over their lives have themselves created new threats. Most significantly, weapons of mass destruction are now more accessible and can be used by small groups of people to cause death, injury and destruction on a massive scale. This new "asymmetry" in the use of powerful and deadly technologies is not only a very real threat, but one that tests both human cognitive capacity and institutional ingenuity as never before.

A fourth explanation may result from what Jürgen Habermas refers to as the "dialectic of progress", in which the solution to one set of social problems invariably gives rise to a new set of problems.[3] An apparent corollary is the human tendency to forget how much more arduous life was before the old problems had been solved, and to focus instead on the aggravations and challenges posed by the new problems. There is a corresponding tendency for citizens of more prosperous societies to become increasingly preoccupied with comparatively small problems and complaints, and to exaggerate some threats while ignoring or denying others based on their own individual calculus of values, risk and inconvenience.

And a fifth explanation is that the accelerating pace of change and the mounting complexities of modern life, have created new uncertainties, some of which involve genuine threats that are more dangerous than they are perceived to be, and others of which can create the perception of being a greater threat than they really are. A "threat" is a combination of the probability an event will occur, its possible and probable consequences, the threatened subject's vulnerability, and the subject's perception of all these factors. And herein lies one of the principal sources of the current disorientation. Our society does, indeed, confront very real and serious threats, some of which are potentially more devastating than any posed in past human experience. And yet, as the past sixty years demonstrated for the three-and-a-half billion people who lived and died with the constant threat of nuclear annihilation, it is possible that in our lifetimes the threats we dread the most will never materialize.

Given these forces of disorientation, it is not surprising that people today perceive and react to threats along the full continuum of human emotion and judgment: from a sane refusal to be troubled by trivial or highly improbable incidents; to stubborn and lethal denial of impending dangers; to wise avoidance of counterproductive preemptive action; to alert but cautious attention and preparation; to risky procrastination; to chronic, paralyzing, self-defeating – and in some instances, justifiable – alarm; to timely, energetic, skillful and innovative preventive or corrective action; to ill-informed, ill-advised, poorly executed, and counterproductive preemptive or retaliatory action; and on to panic and self-immolation.

The heightened sense of threat from terrorism in the West, and especially in the United States, has altered conventional feelings and thinking about the nature of threats to security more generally in the world today. In some ways, that shakeup was long overdue. There is no question that the threat of terrorism is real, serious, and potentially devastating. Terrorists such as Osama bin Laden and Al Qaeda have been clear about their intent to wreak destruction and havoc on the West, and have demonstrated their ability to do so. The potential destruction and disruption that could be caused by terrorists' use of weapons of mass destruction include massive casualties, places made inhabitable for decades, and economic and social disruptions that could seriously alter life in the West and elsewhere. Indeed, in the most extreme cases, conceivably scores or even hundreds of millions could be killed, democratic society with civil liberties would prove to be impossible, and civilization as humans have known it and hoped it would become, not just in the West but in the world at large, could be fatally impaired.

In other ways, however, the sudden preoccupation with terrorism has skewed beliefs about personal and societal security in ways that are not helpful to understanding and dealing more effectively either with terrorism, or with the wider range of threats confronted in the West and throughout the world. While the potentially catastrophic threat of terrorism should not be denied, it needs to be put in appropriate context, along with other serious, and not so serious, threats. Misunderstood threats, misplaced fears, misappropriated resources, and miscalculations of strategy and action, can all end up creating greater vulnerability, and increasing rather than decreasing real threats to security. The positive constellation of trends over the past half-century suggests that life in most of the world has been getting dramatically better and that political violence of all kinds, including terrorism, has been declining. The gravest mistake would be to not recognize and ally ourselves with those positive trends, to fail to nurture them, to act in a way that could disrupt or reverse them, or to be diverted from effectively addressing the most serious threats we confront.

Toward An Orienting Framework

In short, we need a different framework to account for perplexing trends and the different kinds and orders of threat they pose, a framework that accounts for the new destructive potential of human activity, the real underlying forces that are shaping life on the planet (both positive and negative), the altered scales of time and place, the interdependencies among numerous factors, and the fundamental challenges to human cognitive capacity and collaboration in dealing with the real and apparent risks posed by these new and continually changing circumstances.

With the intent of moving towards such an orienting framework, this paper begins to sort out some of the principal threats to human security according to three different orders of threat, including:

- First-order existential threats that directly imperil human life and core values;
- Second-order environmental threats that jeopardize the physical environment from which first-order threats emerge; and

–   Third-order institutional threats that undermine the human capacity to address both first-order existential and second-order environmental threats, and in some cases constitute threats of their own.

After highlighting key features of each of these three orders of threat, the paper will then suggest some implications for global governance.

First-Order Existential Threats

First order threats are existential in the sense that they directly threaten human existence, either for individuals, groups, or societies. These are the threats we commonly associate with "life and death," or "life, limb, and property," or "death, injury, and destruction." They are forces that can immediately terminate life, inflict mortal injury, irreparably disable, create excruciating or paralyzing pain, cause life-threatening disruptions or dislocations, or attack core values that people hold as dear as life itself (that is, values for which they would be willing to give their lives, and in that sense are "existential values").

Forces of Nature

Historically, humans have been increasingly successful in protecting themselves against extremes of heat, cold, wind, water, drought, fire, collision, earthquake, and volcano. However, the 150,000 people killed in the Asian tsunami of 2004, the 50,000 killed in the Pakistani earthquake of 2005, and the 6,000 killed in the Indonesian earthquake of 2006, all attest to the continuing threat from the forces of nature. And the 1,800 people killed by Hurricane Katrina along the Gulf Coast of the United States in 2005 demonstrated that not even residents of the wealthiest countries can necessarily escape devastating blows from a wrathful nature. Among the 15 worst threats to Americans in 2003, the US Department of Homeland Security ranked two types of natural disasters, a major earthquake as the 9th and a major hurricane as the 10th worst.[4]

Often the losses caused by natural forces result from people exposing themselves to predictable natural dangers, by living in nature's high danger zones (such as living on a coast vulnerable to hurricanes), by failing to take adequate precautions (such as constructing buildings that will not withstand hurricane force winds), or by causing or permitting natural buffers to be lost (such as marshes, islands, and vegetation that can reduce the force of a hurricane). A critical question now is whether human activity has been changing climate in a way that might increase the violence or unpredictability of some natural forces.

Disease

Disease is by far the leading cause of death, injury, and disability and is likely to remain so. Infectious diseases, the most lethal kind for humans, were the cause of some 57 million deaths worldwide in 2002.[5] Modern society has been quite successful in reducing, treating or eradicating many infectious diseases over the past century, especially those that are most lethal to children. This is the principal reason child mortality has dropped so dramatically, and, in turn, why average life expectancy has increased. The life expectancy for those who reach the age of 70 has increased very little over the past 150 years. But since there are many more people that age, the numbers of elderly, and their proportion of the population, have grown substantially.[6]

However, infectious diseases such as malaria, measles, and tuberculosis remain a serious problem in developing countries. Of an estimated 11,250,000 children under 5 years old who died from infectious diseases worldwide in 2002, 98 % lived in developing countries. Malaria alone infects as many as 2 billion people around the globe, mostly in developing countries, and causes an estimated 1 – 3 million deaths per year world-wide. As many African children die of malaria every eight months – about 150,000 – as the total number of people who died in the 2004 Asian tsunami.[7]

The fact that people are living longer means that more people are now suffering from degenerative diseases such as heart disease, stroke, and cancer that are associated with aging or life-styles involving smoking, alcohol, drug use, poor diet, and lack of exercise. This is especially the case in the developed countries, which have had the greatest success in fighting infectious disease. In 2000, the leading eight causes of death in 38 member states of the World Health Organization, most of which were developed countries, were all diseases, and accounted for nearly half of all deaths in those states. And most of these were diseases characteristic of more affluent societies.[8] Twelve of the 15 leading causes of death in the United States in 2003 were diseases, and the first four, all "affluent" diseases, accounted for nearly two-thirds of all deaths in the United States that year.[9]

Meanwhile, there are indications that infectious disease may be on the rebound. For example, after declining and stabilizing in the first part of the 20th century, the US death rate from infectious disease doubled between 1980 to 2003. Perhaps more troubling, some 35 new infectious diseases emerged in the last three decades of the 20th century, a rate considered by epidemiologists to be unprecedented in the history of medicine,[10] These include E. coli, Legionnaire's disease, hepatitis C, and HIV/AIDS. In 2003, Severe Acute Respiratory Syndrome (SARS), and in 2005 avian flu, were found to have infected humans, both for the first time documented. These developments have renewed concerns about the threat of virulent new pandemics.

The emergence of new and potentially deadly microbes has increased the threat of epidemics and pandemics. Influenza kills hundreds of thousands of people worldwide each year, including some 36,000 each year in the United States alone. Worldwide flu pandemics have occurred about three times a century for the past several hundred years. Health officials are concerned that yet another flu pandemic, possibly spreading a more lethal virus such as the H5N1 avian strain (bird flu), might be in the offing. The AIDS pandemic is testament to the potential for a new and deadly microbe to emerge and spread rapidly throughout the world. Deaths resulting from HIV/AIDS were estimated to be between 2.5 and 3.5 million worldwide in 2003, accounting for about 5 % of all deaths. About 5.3 million new HIV infections occur each year, 90 percent in developing countries.[11]

Genetics and Synthetic Biology

The life sciences have increased the human capacity to manipulate life in ways never before possible, especially since the unraveling of the human genome. In 2003, a molecular geneticist created the first live, fully artificial virus in a lab. Using standard equipment and chemicals and a genetic code acquired for free over the Internet, he assembled hundreds of tiny bits of viral DNA purchased online to create a variation of the virus that causes polio, but one different from any known naturally evolved virus. Such artificial viruses can be useful in making safer vaccines to protect against the natural viruses they resemble. Since that first artificial pathogen was created, rapid advances have been made in the technology of engineered microbes and novel ways to make them. It is possible that thousands of scientists worldwide by now have used similar methods, and that the process could soon become a relatively simple technical procedure. The new technology promises to help find new and powerful ways of preventing and curing diseases, and thereby saving and improving lives. But it also significantly increases the threat that engineered pathogens could be unleashed, intentionally or by accident, with the potential for massive disease and death.

Nathan Myhrvold, a physicist who is CEO of Intellectual Ventures and former chief technology officer for Microsoft, has noted that it is now possible for a person with modest education in biology and molecular biology to develop a germ that could kill tens of thousands, millions, and even billions of people. The technology required to make deadly pathogens is much less a barrier than the technology required to make a nuclear weapon. Biologists have discovered millions of possible combinations of new germs, including some that are more toxic, infectious, and lethal than small pox or anthrax. Myhrvold says that knowledge about these possibilities is not widespread, in part because they are so horrific that even those knowledgeable about them tend to be in a state of denial. The consequence is that most people either do not know about these potentially devastating pathogens, or do not take the threat seriously.[12]

Accidental Death and Injury

Millions of people die every year from accidents, including motor vehicle collisions, poisoning, drowning, fire, smoke, and work-related and home accidents.

An estimated 300,000 people each year die of fire-related burns and some 400,000 by drowning, a high proportion of both in developing countries.

Motor vehicle accidents alone each year cause an estimated 1.2 million deaths and as many as 50 million injuries worldwide, losses that are projected to double by 2020 if current trends hold. Some 85 % of road deaths and injuries occur in low and middle income countries,[13] Substantial progress has been made in curbing traffic deaths and injuries in the developed countries. In the United States, traffic fatalities have been declining for several years, falling to 42,636 in 2004, although they were up slightly in 43,200 in 2005 [14]

Meanwhile, the developed world continues to discover more deeply embedded sources of accidental death and industry. For example, a 2000 report by the US Institute of Medicine (IOM) estimated that medical errors of all sorts in the United States cause as many as 98,000 deaths each year, more than were caused by highway accidents and breast cancer combined.[15] And a 2006 IOM report estimated that medication errors harm 1.5 million people and kill several thousand each year in the United States.[16]

Human Violence

Over one-and-a-half million people died worldwide in 2000 as a result of human violence, that is, people intentionally killing people. Suicide was the principal source of lethal human violence, accounting for fully one-half of the total (815,000), and homicides were the second largest source with nearly a third (520,000). War-related deaths came in a distant, if not insignificant, third, accounting for somewhat less than one-fifth (310,000) of all deaths from human violence in the world that year.[17] (So much for Max Weber's proposition that "a state is a human community that (successfully) claims the monopoly of the legitimate use of physical force within a given territory."[18])

Deaths resulting from suicide and homicide varied widely by region. Overall, the politically volatile Middle East had a lower incidence of violent death by homicide or suicide than any other region in the world in 2002. Homicide rates were nearly three times greater than suicide rates in North and South America and Africa. And suicide rates were more than double homicide rates in Southeast Asia and Europe, and nearly six times greater than homicide rates in the Western Pacific.[19]

Patterns of personal violence[20] also varied widely within regions and countries.

In the United States in 1999, African-American youths aged 15 – 24 years were twice as likely to be victims of homicides than Hispanic youths in that age group, and over twelve times more likely than their counterparts among Caucasian, non-Hispanic youths.[21] Homicides in the United States declined by 30 % between 1979 – 1998,[22] and continued declining into the 2000s. However, preliminary FBI statistics indicated that homicides rose nearly 5 % in 2005, which some experts took as a sign that the long-term decline in homicides may have bottomed out, and could be heading back up.

Worldwide indicators compiled by the Human Security Centre of Canada show that, contrary to popular perception, organized political violence of all kinds has been declining over the past several decades. And this was the case with nearly every category of organized political violence, including wars between states, armed conflicts within states, and conflict involving non-state actors, such as terrorists. The average number of battle-deaths per conflict per year has been declining since the end of World War II, and the overall number of armed conflicts around the world has declined by more than 40 % since the early 1990s. The number of refugees declined by some 45 % between 1992 and 2003, largely because of the declining number of wars. Five out of six regions in the developing world experienced a net decrease in core human rights abuses between 1994 and 2003.[23]

There was one glaring regional exception to this overall positive trend. As political violence declined in every other region of the world, the bloodshed in sub-Africa increased. At the beginning of the 21st century, most armed conflicts were taking place in sub-Saharan Africa, and more people were being killed in armed conflicts there than in the rest of the world combined [24]

Violence Between States

The end of World War II brought to a conclusion the bloodiest half-century in history. Some of the positive trends in political violence date from that point (including the decline in the average numbers of battle-deaths). The six decades following the end of World War II constituted the longest period of uninterrupted peace between the major powers in centuries (allowing for the chronic tensions between the United States and Soviet Union during that period and the various proxy wars that were fought by and with other states as a part of their rivalry).[25] International crises, which often foretell war, declined by more than 70 % between 1981 and 2001.[26] Major international arms transfers declined in dollar value by 33 % between 1990 and 2003, and global military expenditures and troop numbers also dropped sharply in the 1990s.[27]

The overriding factor accounting for the dramatic reduction in interstate violence over the past three decades has been the reduction in conflict among states in the Western world. Europe and its various spin-offs had been the principal source of state violence afflicting the world for the previous five centuries. Intensive rivalries among the European powers were frequently manifested in outright warfare among themselves, and were also projected on a global scale as they competed for markets, colonies, and political control throughout the world. World Wars I and II represented a kind of climax of this interstate European rivalry, engaging Europe's spin-offs societies and colonies throughout the world, including the United States.

Following World War II, the European states embarked on a serious effort to restructure the relations among themselves in a way that would minimize if not eliminate future military conflict. To this end, Jean Monnet's vision of peace through institutional integration, beginning with the European Coal and Steel Community and leading to the European Union, has been fulfilled, at least in part. Monnet's broader vision extended beyond Europe. At the end of his memoirs, he wrote: "the [European] community itself is only a stage on the way to the more organized world of tomorrow".[28] Ironically, the European transformation was helped along by the specter of nuclear war, and the standoff between the United States and the Soviet Union. The Cold War stayed cold largely because the nuclear powers came to recognize that they had little to gain and potentially much (if not all) to lose by engaging in nuclear warfare.

In the post-World War II era, the European imperial states were compelled to give up their overseas empires, the acquisition and main-tenance of which had been a principal source of global violence, both among the imperial powers themselves and between them and their colonies. The collapse of the European empires also created condi-tions of instability that fostered violence, including among political, ethnic, and religious groups in the former colonial territories. The end of the Soviet Union in 1989 more or less completed the dismantling of the last of the great European empires, but the consequences of Europe's global influence over the past few centuries will be long-lasting.

There is, of course, no certainty as to how long the absence of wars between major countries might last. Increasing competition for scarce resources continues to offer one source of contention and potential conflict among major powers. And the emergence of large countries such as China and India as significant world powers could alter the in-ternational equation in both dangerous as well as hopeful ways. In the meantime, wars among smaller, as well as between large and small states, have continued, albeit it at a comparatively lesser scale. The re-cent bloody conflicts that have occurred in Africa and the Middle East, and the continuing instability of those regions, are cause for con-cern. Much of that instability is grounded in ethnic and religious ten-sions that do not respect conventional state borders. The hopeful signs are that several traditionally war-like states and ancient rivalries have successfully found more constructive paths through economic en-gagement and democratic inclinations, and that even some chronically hostile states with the capacity for devastating one another have dem-onstrated their ability to refrain from doing so over unusually long stretches of time until their hostilities could ease.

Organized Political Violence Within States

Organized political violence within states, including a state's violence against its own citizens, was an increasingly grave threat in parts of the world during the first two-thirds of the 20th century. This form of violence includes the targeted killing of individual political enemies, more sweeping "politicides," genocide, ethnic cleansing, military coups, civil war, torture, and terrorism.

However, in recent decades, the Human Security Centre data show that in almost every one of these categories of political violence largely within states, the trends have been decidedly positive. Since the end of World War II, the number of military coups and attempted coups has declined.[29] In 2004, the 25 armed secessionist conflicts under way was the lowest number since 1976.[30] To be sure, the bloodshed in Congo, Rwanda, Srebrenica, Sudan and other places has been horrendous. But worldwide the overall number of genocides and politicides since World War II peaked in 1988 and by 2001 had plummeted 80 %.[31]

Political Violence by Non-State Actors

Non-state actors have been a threat ever since they were defined by the rise of states 5,000 years ago. Pirates, gangs, terrorists, private militias, tribal warlords, revolutionaries, rebels, and insurgents have existed in various forms ever since, and continue to do so today. Here again, the indicators suggest that even the extra-state violence associated with the modern versions of such entities has been on the decline in recent years. The difference today is that such non-state actors may have access to modern technology and weapons, including potentially weapons of mass destruction, which gives them an unprecedented asymmetrical edge in being able to disrupt and lethally damage complex modern societies.

As note earlier, terrorism had appeared to be declining along with other forms of political violence over the past decade or so, until just a few years ago, when terrorist attacks suddenly spiked upwards [32] The data on overall terrorism trends are less than clear. Some datasets show an overall, continuing decline in international terrorist incidents from the early 1980s through about 2004. Others suggest a dramatic rise in the number of high-casualty attacks since 9/11. And still others indicate the spike began in 2003 after the US led invasion of Iraq. Since it was invaded in 2003, Iraq has accounted for a high proportion of terrorist incidents and deaths related to terrorism around the world, as well as for the reported annual increase in terrorist incidents.[33]

According to the US National Counterterrorism Center (NCTC), in 2005 there were 11,111 terrorist attacks worldwide, a nearly fourfold increase over 2004. Some 8,299 terrorist attacks were reported in Iraq in 2005, or about three-quarters of the total worldwide.[34] About one-half of all terrorist attacks worldwide in 2005 resulted in loss of life. More than 14,600 noncombatants were killed in terrorist attacks in 2005, a majority of them in Iraq, and 80 % in the Near East and South Asia. The number of "high fatality incidents" around the world, excluding Iraq, decreased between 2004 (a year in which terrorists killed hundreds in Russia and Madrid) and 2005. Most fatalities were attributed to armed attacks and bombings. None occurred in the United States or involved weapons of mass destruction.[35]

One interpretation of these data is that world-wide terrorism had been in a long-term decline – along with virtually other form of political violence – until the US-led invasion of Iraq, at which point it suddenly spiked back up. In fact, the spike in global terrorist attacks could be accounted for by the sudden number of terrorist attacks in Iraq, which was obviously a consequence of the invasion. A logical conclusion might be that the invasion of Iraq essentially turned around a downward trend in global terrorism, sending it dramatically upward. That, of course, raises the policy question as to whether it was wise to invade Iraq and create a world center of terrorism in a country where there had been little or no documented terrorist activity (quite aside from the broader question of the invasion's role in destabilizing the entire Middle East). That policy question is clouded in part by issues of definition.[36]

Conventional Weapons

Weapons of mass destruction (WMD) have increased the potential for human violence multifold, but in the meantime conventional weapons have been developed and used over the past century with increasingly deadly consequence without recourse to WMD. Between nine and ten million people were killed in World War I, testament to the growing lethality of "conventional" weapons (supplemented with some use of chemical gas weapons) in the modern era. But nearly all of those died were the military combatants of states at war. During World War II, nearly 60 million people died, including an estimated 36 million in Europe, a substantial proportion of which were civilians, including the millions gassed in the Nazis death camps (which might be defined as the use of a chemical weapon of mass destruction).[37]

Over the course of the twentieth century airpower transformed concepts of "conventional" war by making it possible to deliver ever larger numbers of increasingly powerful conventional explosives by aerial bombing and missiles. Massive air raids using conventional bombs caused more death and destruction in both Europe and Asia than the two 15 kiloton nuclear bombs the United States dropped on Hiroshima and Nagasaki.[38] Jet planes increased in speed, size, and range; rockets became cheap and ubiquitous; missiles increased to inter-continental range and developed sophisticated guidance systems; helicopters increased their fire power and capacity to deliver ground combat forces; and precision bombing vastly improved.

The United States military demonstrated during its invasion of Iraq in 2003 the capacity of a comparatively small armed force to deliver rapid, massive, and precision-targeted conventional explosives with deadly effect. The US Air Force has large conventional bombs with high explosives (such as GBU-28 "bunker-busters") capable of knocking out deeply entrenched underground facilities, and reportedly has developed a tactic of rapid sequential delivery of such massive bombs to achieve a concussive impact equal to a tactical nuclear weapon that is intended to reach unusually well entrenched underground facilities (such as those that may house facilities used to make nuclear weapons). The artillery North Korea has installed along its southern border could probably destroy the South Korean capital of Seoul (only a few miles from the border) and most US troops in the northern regions of South Korea, even after being attacked.

Small arms remain lethal. Most of the casualties associated with genocides, civil wars, guerrilla warfare, and insurgencies have been caused by knives, hatchets, machetes, hand guns, rifles, mines, and various sorts of "improvised explosive devices" (IEDs). IEDs are essentially homemade bombs and booby traps that use dry, liquid, and plastic materials to make explosives, often fashioned with great ingenuity and sophistication and sometimes triggered by remote control.

Used by suicide bombers, terrorists, and insurgents, IEDs were the cause of 62 % of all American combat deaths, and 72 % of all American wounded, in Iraq in 2005.[39] Shoulder-fired missiles, which typically weigh less than 40 pounds and are small enough to fit in a golf bag, have a range of up to 23,000 feet and pose a particular threat to both civilian and military aircraft. In 1998 a Congo Airlines Boeing 727 was downed by Tutsi rebels firing a shoulder-fired missile, killing all 41 people on board. Tens of thousands of shoulder-fired missiles are unaccounted for around the world.

Nuclear Weapons

Over the two decades following World War II the explosive yield of a given amount of weapons material increased by a factor of a million, and it became possible to deliver nuclear warheads over intercontinental distances at speeds forty times faster than World War II aircraft.[40] The fact that no nuclear weapons have been used since World War II has caused a certain complacency about their potential danger.

The Cuban missile crisis of 1962 is recalled as a moment when a nuclear exchange between the United States and the Soviet Union was narrowly avoided. But we have since learned that the world came closer to nuclear conflagration on that occasion than is generally realized. It turns out that the United States had faulty intelligence in believing that the Soviet missiles in Cuba were not armed with nuclear weapons. Had President John F. Kennedy ordered an invasion of Cuba to dismantle the missiles, as he was urged to do by every one of his military advisors, Soviet commanders had instructions to launch their nuclear armed missiles against the United States, causing an estimated 90 million American deaths and probably provoking an all-out nuclear retaliation by the United States against the Soviet Union.[41]

The brush with nuclear conflagration during the Cuban missile crisis motivated the major powers to evolve a de facto global nuclear regime that provided a measure of stability and reduced the risk of accident or miscalculation in the use nuclear weapons.

From the 1960s to the present, the United States and Russia have maintained a nuclear balance of "mutual assured destruction" (MAD), in which the nuclear strike forces of both countries were capable of surviving a nuclear attack from the other and delivering a devastating nuclear retaliation inflicting "unacceptable costs" (i.e. each side possessed a deterrent "second strike" capability). (The United States and Russia agreed in 1994 not to target each other, but their missiles can be re-armed and launched in a matter of minutes.) In the meantime, strenuous efforts were made to dissuade other states from acquiring nuclear weapons, leading to the Nuclear Non-proliferation Treaty (NPT).

To date, the global nuclear regime that evolved over the course of the Cold War has been successful, certainly by the measure of having prevented the use of nuclear weapons. However, it is under stress from several source.

In the first place, the Nuclear Non-Proliferation Treaty (NPT) appears to be breaking down. The number of nuclear powers has increased beyond the core group of five major states (the United States, Russia, China, Britain, and France), to include India, Pakistan, and Israel. In recent years, North Korea has developed an embryonic nuclear weapons capability. And by 2006 Iran had developed the capacity to enrich uranium to an energy-generation grade (3.6 % enrichment), and seems intent on continuing the development of its capacity for enrichment to a weapons-grade uranium (90 % enrichment).

Meanwhile, although Article 6 of the NPT commits the existing nuclear powers to move towards the significant reduction and eventual elimination of their nuclear arsenals, in fact they have not done so (aside from the rather haphazard deterioration of the Soviet/Russian nuclear arsenal). The United States retains a stockpile of about 6,000 strategic nuclear weapons, each about 330 kilotons (compared with the Hiroshima and Nagasaki atom bombs of 15 kilotons). Of these, 2,000 are warheads on 15 minute alert for launch from land-based Minuteman missiles or sea-based nuclear submarine missiles. A half-dozen other states collectively retain thousands of strategic nuclear weapons that could be launched in minutes with intent, by miscalculation, or by mistake, or which might be obtained and used by terrorists.

These factors all threaten to destabilize the basic tenet of deterrence on which the de facto nuclear regime is based, that is, the belief that any use of nuclear weapons could be answered by a massive "second strike" retaliation. With multiple actors it becomes increasingly difficult for any one country to be certain of the capacities, intentions and actions of the others. The complications grow when the nuclear states are of different sizes and cultures, and controlled by regimes with strikingly different politics, ideologies, and command structures (which can make it difficult to know who actually controls the nuclear weapons within a given country). The picture is further clouded by the entry of terrorists and other non-state actors with increasing access to nuclear weapons, because it will be easier to buy them, purloin them, or simply accept them from a willing donor. Terrorists who are driven by apocalyptic ideologies and belief in martyrdom are less likely to be deterred by the probability of their own destruction (and could conceivably be motivated by that possibility), and lacking a clearly defined home territory, they are also more difficult to target for nuclear retaliation. Perhaps the greatest challenge to the viability of deterrence is that the emergence of multiple nuclear actors with complex and shadowy relationships among themselves could make it difficult to detect which party actually launched a nuclear strike, and which parties may have been complicit in the launch, so that they might be targeted for retaliation.

Ironically, the equation of deterrence could be further destabilized by the rising nuclear supremacy of the United States. With the steady deterioration of Russia's nuclear arsenal, it is no longer certain that Russia retains a second strike capacity. Such a change could create insecurity on the part of Russia and tempt the United States to consider a more aggressive use of its own nuclear capability (including the threat, if not the intent, to use nuclear weapons), or otherwise to engage in riskier international actions. It could also motivate secondary nuclear powers such as China to develop their own second strike capability, potentially instilling a new nuclear arms race and otherwise further destabilizing the existing nuclear regime.[42]

The increasing instability of the global nuclear regime has caused several experts to warn of a rising nuclear threat. Former US Secretary of Defense William Perry has predicted a better than 50 % probability of a nuclear detonation within the United States within a decade. Prof. Graham Allison of Harvard's Kennedy School of Government has made essentially the same calculation.[43] Former US Senator Sam Nunn has warned repeatedly that insufficient progress has been made in securing nuclear weapons, especially in Russia, to guard against their falling into the hands of terrorists or hostile states.[44] In 2003 the

US Department of Homeland Security (DHS) ranked the detonation of a 10-kiloton nuclear device in the central business district of a major city as the worst threat facing the United States. (DHS rated a radiological attack by a "dirty bomb" as the 11th worst threat.) Russian nuclear weapons expert Valery E. Yarynich has warned that a deterioration in the "negative controls" used by the United States and Russia has significantly increased the possibility of nuclear weapons falling into the hands of terrorists, as well as the risk of an accidental or unauthorized launch.[45] Former US Secretary of Defense Robert S. McNamara, has characterized the US and NATO nuclear strategy as "immoral", "illegal", "bizarre", "dangerous", and "militarily unnecessary", and has warned that unless the United States takes the lead in radically changing nuclear strategy, "I guarantee that the combination of nuclear weapons and human fallibility will inevitably lead to the nuclear destruction of nations".[46]

Some of these and other strategic experts and political leaders have called for a radical reduction in nuclear arms by all countries. McNamara would reduce the US arsenal from thousands to hundreds of strategic nuclear weapons. Those calling for a reduction to zero include the late US Army General Andrew Goodpaster, former US Secretary of Defense Melvin Laird, and former German Chancellor Helmut Schmidt.[47] Others counter variously that there is really little practical alternative other than to attempt to reinforce the system of deterrence; that the experience of the past sixty years demonstrates the value of nuclear weapons in limiting war among nuclear states; that the key to the viability of deterrence is non-proliferation; and that deterrence would still be possible with additional nuclear actors.

Chemical Weapons

The 1899 Hague Convention prohibiting the use of "poison or poisoned weapons" was violated in World War I. The 1925 Geneva Protocol once again banned the use of chemical weapons in war, although it did not prohibit their manufacture and stockpiling. Italy, a signatory of the Geneva Protocol, used mustard agent during its conquest of Abyssinia (Ethiopia) in 1935/1936. The Nazis first used gas (initially carbon monoxide from the exhaust of motor vehicles) to kill people as part of their adult euthanasia program. It was from this program that the Nazis developed gas chambers, later using Zyklon B, to mass-murder Jews and other "enemies of the Reich". Iraq's Saddam Hussein used chemical weapons against Iranian troops in the 1980's, and again against his own Kurdish population in the 1988 Anfal extermination campaign.

The first known use of chemical weapons by terrorists occurred in Japan, where Aum Shinrikyo cultists used sarin to kill 19 people and injure some 3,000 others in two incidents in 1994 and 1995. The United States and Russia continue to maintain large stockpiles of chemical weapons, which they have reduced only slightly on the ground that they may be required for use against terrorists. In 2002, the Russians attempted to use gas against the Chechen terrorist who seized a Moscow theater, and in the process killed 127 of the hostages.[48]

Biological Weapons

A biological weapons attack occurred in the United States in 2001 (a few weeks after the 9/11 terrorist attacks) when anthrax was sent through the US mail, killing five people and injuring others. Al Qaeda is known to have sought bioweapons, and has recruited experts, including microbiologists. In 2005, the US Department of Homeland Security ranked biological terrorism as the second (aerosolized anthrax) and fourth (pneumonic plague) worst threats facing the United States.

The US government has radically stepped up funding for defenses against known bioterrorism. Such defenses include vaccines that can inoculate against dangerous pathogens, special sensors that can detect them, and drugs that can treat them. However, all of these defenses are directed at known, natural pathogens. To date, they apparently have not addressed unknown natural pathogens, or artificial pathogens that have been, or could be, invented by humans. Some experts believe it is unlikely terrorists would use engineered microbes as weapons if only because ordinary natural germs could have a devastating impact with far less cost and expertise required. However, Henry Crumpton, Coordinator for Counterterrorism for the US Department of State, has characterized an attack on the United States with a synthetic biological weapon as his "worst nightmare. A nuclear explosion, he explained, "can be contained", but an invented or modified biological pathogen can spread from person to person with no way to contain it.[49]

As noted earlier, it is now possible for a person with modest education in biology and molecular biology to develop synthetic germs. Engineered microbes could be used not just by terrorists, but by a scientist or biological hacker working alone or in a small group, driven by ideology, personal bitterness, mental illness, or even sheer recklessness. It is plausible that such a person carried out the anthrax attacks of 2001.

Mega-catastrophe

One of the reasons people become complacent about potentially serious threats is that they have been subjected to so many exaggerations and false alarms over the years about the imminent perils facing the planet: nuclear conflagration, overpopulation, mass famine, lethal plagues, global cooling (before global warming), ecological collapse, chronic war, social anarchy, and so on. The iconic example is Paul Ehrlich's prediction in "The Population Bomb" (1969) that the world was confronting run-away population growth, at about the same time world population growth rates were declining, and that this would lead to world famine, at about the same time world per capita food production was beginning to soar due to the Green Revolution. Science fiction has regularly imagined apocalyptic scenarios, and Hollywood revels in converting them into cinematic "chicken little" hysteria warning that the sky-is-falling. Like the villagers who stopped responding to the boy who cried wolf once too often, woe-weary people simply tune out the prophecies and become skeptical about any prediction of peril. In the folk fable, after all, the sky did not fall. On the other hand, the wolf finally did come.

The challenge of sorting out the various threats and assigning them some reasonable probability of occurrence and consequence, therefore, becomes all the more difficult when we move from mere catastrophes to mega-catastrophes. Some mega-catastrophes are events that have happened in the past and we know will almost certainly happen again, but probably not any time soon, such as an asteroid hitting the earth. Still other possible mega-catastrophes are theoretically possible but highly improbable, such as a high-energy particle accelerator that creates hyperdense "'strange matter"capable of attracting nearby nuclei in such mass as to compress the entire planet into a dense sphere less than 100 meters in diameter. And still others are theoretically possible and highly improbable, but somewhat less distant than they may have seemed just a few years ago. For example, it seems theoretically possible that global warming could release vast quantities of methane (now contained beneath melted ice caps and permafrost) that could rapidly accelerate the warming process and create a dense cloud layer over the earth, which could in turn block heat from the sun and thereby cause global temperatures to plummet, plunging the earth into a deep freeze.

These and other such mega-catastrophes may seem either far-fetched, or so improbable as to not be worth our attention. But some serious and thoughtful people do worry about them. Richard A. Posner, a judge on the US Court of Appeals for the Seventh Circuit (and popularly characterized as a conservative), believes that the government is not doing nearly enough to address such possibilities.[50] Sir Martin Rees, Britain's Astronomer Royal and a professor at Cambridge University, does not worry about an asteroid hitting the earth, but believes there is no better than a fifty-fifty chance our present civilization will survive to the end of the 21st century. Rees worries that science and technology, always a mixed blessing, are progressing at breakneck speed and likely to produce new capacities, even more dangerous than nuclear weapons, that are either inherently catastrophic or likely to be misused – accidentally or intentionally – by humans.[51]

Second-Order Environmental Threats

Second-order threats are those related to the physical environment in which humans live, and from which first-order existential threats emerge. The physical environment can be conceptually divided into three parts: the natural physical environment from which humans evolved; the artificial physical environment created by humans; and the hybrid physical environment that results from the interaction between the natural and the artificial ones.

The natural physical environment is comprised of two distinct but interrelated spheres. The physiosphere constitutes the basic material of the cosmos of which the earth is comprised. And the biosphere, which emerged from the physiosphere, is comprised of life, and the interactive biological and geological support systems on which human life depends. The biosphere is the habitat of life on our planet, an interacting web of rock, soil, water, air, plants, and animals. It hovers at the outer edge of the Earth's crust, reaching down several miles into its oceans and up into its atmosphere. Beneath it lies the earth's molten core with temperatures that exceed several thousand degrees. Beyond it lies the vacuum of space, with temperatures that approach absolute zero. Life as we know it can live unassisted only within its narrow and precariously balanced boundaries.

In the process of attempting to reduce the natural risks inherent in life in the biosphere, humans have created an artificial physical environment, the "built environment" and its associated technical apparatus that has altered the natural physical environment. The artificial transformation of nature has brought enormous benefits to humans, and, by and large, has reduced the threat of natural forces. But it has also created new kinds of threats. One has been to undermine aspects of the natural environment on which humans depend for their own prosperity, health, and survival. Jared Diamond has documented processes by which severe environmental degradation historically has led to social collapse.[52] Another kind of threat emerges directly from the artificial environment itself. Buildings can collapse and create more opportunities for people to fall and injure themselves. Tools and machines can cause injury in both their production and in their use, and misuse. Weapons, of course, are designed with the intention of killing, maiming, and destroying, and can do so not only deliberately, but also as a result of miscalculation or accident.

Since the emergence of culture as a major force in human experience some 50,000 years ago, human artifice has interacted with the natural environment in increasingly intricate and profound ways. In the past two hundred years, the scale and impact of the artificial environment has grown to the point where it is not only interacting with natural forces in powerful and unpredictable new ways, but may also be altering some of the fundamental properties of natural forces.[53] The new hybrid physical environment appears to have emergent properties and rules of its own. Its various elements – including both natural and artificial (i.e. human made) elements – interact among themselves in ways that humans do not fully understand. Some of these interactions have been demonstrated to be threatening, while others clearly pose threats, although their probability of occurrence and consequence remain uncertain.

Human Population

A prominent feature of the physical environment, and a threshold factor in human security, is the size and age of the human population itself.

In 2006, world population was estimated to be 6.5 billion and growing at an average annual rate of 1.1 per cent, for a net addition of about 74 million people per year. The growth rate and the absolute numbers of people added to the population each year are both lower than they were in the mid-1990s, when global population growth probably peaked. The principal cause of slowing population growth is the declining fertility rate (i.e. the average number of live births per woman in her lifetime). As humans improve their economic situation they tend, on average, to have fewer children. With worldwide economic growth and rising living standards, fertility rates have fallen almost everywhere, causing population growth rates to slow, and in some countries, such as Japan, to turn negative, so that the population is actually declining. If the recent trends in fertility continue, the global human population is expected to level off at somewhere between 9 and 12 billion people by the end of the 21st century, and then possibly begin to decline. In the meantime, the human population will continue to age.[54]

Human Conditions

A second prominent feature of the physical environment affecting human security, in addition to population size and age, is the basic condition of the human population. This involves a number of interacting factors, including the health of the population (and therefore its susceptibility to disease and ability to provide for itself), the geographical distribution of the population (including location, local natural resources, population densities, and racial, ethnic, and cultural features), and the various economic, social, cultural, technical, and political systems that shape human behavior and interaction.

Health depends fundamentally upon nutrition. A substantial part of the human population suffers from malnutrition, which weakens the body and makes it more vulnerable to disease and other environmental stresses and threats.

One form of malnutrition is undernutrition or hunger, which results from an insufficient basic food intake to provide the energy and nutrients people need for good health and productive lives. In 1999 – 2001 some 17 % of the total population of developing countries, or about 798 million people, suffered chronic hunger.[55] That was actually a substantial improvement. The total number of chronically hungry people declined by about 18 million from 1990 to 2000, and their proportion of the population declined even more significantly since the total population of the developing countries increased by some 662 million over that decade. These aggregate improvements have resulted from dramatic increases in per capita food production throughout most of the world, along with a reduction in the number and percentage of people in poverty, especially in Asia. In Africa, by contrast, the number of undernourished people increased, and in some African countries their proportion of the population also increased.[56]

Malnutrition can also result from over-consumption of food, which in turn can cause obesity and associated diseases such as diabetes and heart disease,[57] which are growing problems in more affluent countries. Obesity is thought to be associated with anywhere from 100,000 to 300,000 deaths per year in the United States.[58]

Human health is also affected by the immediate physical environment in which people live. For example, an estimated two million children in the developing world die each year from respiratory diseases, many of which are linked to indoor air pollution caused by open fires used for cooking and heating and often fueled by toxic animal dung. And lack of access to clean water is also a major cause of death and poor health (as discussed later). In the United States each year an estimated 130,000 people die from diseases linked to outdoor air pollution.

A substantial number of deaths each year are attributable to human behaviors that are largely matters of personal choice, such as the excessive or inappropriate use of alcohol, tobacco, and drugs, the lack of exercise, and risky behaviors that lead to injury, as well as diet (including over-eating, or eating unhealthy food).[59] However, personal behavior can be conditioned by social, cultural, and economic factors. In that regard, the good news is that such conditions have been generally improving throughout most of the world, both developed and developing, over the past half-century. Rising average incomes have permitted increasing numbers and proportions of people in most countries to eat more nutritious food and have access to better health care, while expanding literacy and education have given them greater information about how to gain access to such resources and to make the best use of them. At the same time, rising affluence also expands access to substances and behaviors that can be harmful to health, and the culture of consumerism, including ubiquitous entertainment and adverting that promotes the material life, can create powerful incentives to engage in unhealthy behavior.

Such interacting factors can also play a role in the spread of disease and the risk of epidemics and pandemics. For example, the rapidity with which the SARS (Severe Acute Respiratory Syndrome) virus spread in 2003 from its apparent place of origin in southeast Asia to spots around the world, demonstrated that modern air travel and mobility can spread a lethal disease in a matter of days, if not hours (even though the SARS outbreak was successfully contained). And HIV/AIDs has been spread through unsafe sexual practices, intravenous drug injections, and inadequate medical treatment.

The case of Congo demonstrates the interaction of factors that can produce a lethal physical environment that shapes the human condition. A particularly vicious brand of European (Belgian) imperialism and post-colonial political instability set the stage. Congo's longtime dictator Mobutu Sese Seko (who renamed the country Zaire) exploited the country's mineral wealth of gold and diamonds to enrich himself and his cronies, thereby entrenching a deeply corrupt government and keeping the country poor. All these factors exacerbated chronic malnutrition, which in turn undermined health and made people especially vulnerable to such chronic diseases as malaria, measles, diarrhea, and tetanus, all of which are otherwise easily preventable and treatable. Children were especially vulnerable to these forces, resulting in high infant mortality. These problems were exacerbated by political violence, originally caused by inter-state tensions which was transformed into civil war. Years of fighting and instability continued to undermine the country's critical infrastructure and exacerbated conditions that caused malnutrition and disease. The International Rescue Committee, a nonprofit organization, estimated that four million people died in Congo between 1998 and 2005 as a direct result of the fighting and of the conditions it caused or exacerbated. It estimated that nearly half of those deaths, almost two million, were children under the age of 5.

Public Systems

Public systems designed to serve benign human purposes can also pose risks in their own right. Death and injury that result from "accidents" associated with public systems are typically considered to be unintended. However, an expectation and tacit acceptance of some rate of tolerable human death and injury are built into the design and/or de facto operating standards of most public systems. In the United States, it is expected that each year about 45,000 people will die in traffic accidents. Another 100,000 Americans are expected to die each year in hospitals from medical mistakes. And as a consequence of personal behavioral choices influenced in part by the public systems that shape commerce, communication, and human mobility and interaction, 400,000 Americans are expected to die each year from tobacco use, 300,000 from poor diet and inactivity, 100,000 from alcohol use, 30,000 from disease-related sexual behavior, and 20,000 from illegal drug-use. In commercial air travel, by contrast, the expectation is that there will be zero fatalities, and that standard is generally met in the United States, as it is in most countries.

The chronic death rates in some public systems does not go unnoticed, and in fact efforts to reduce fatalities and injuries have often had substantial success. For example, such safety features as air bags, safety belts, infant car seats, and snap-on helmets (for motor cyclists) have substantially reduced traffic fatalities and injuries. Major causes of traffic fatalities include the failure to use such devices, as well as driving under the influence of alcohol.[60] A 2006 study of inattention and distraction by automobile drivers in the United States found that nearly 80 % of automobile crashes involved drivers who were distracted or drowsy. Cell phones were one source of distraction (accounting for about 7 % of all crashes or near crashes) for all age groups, demonstrating yet again that new beneficial technologies can also pose new kinds of threats.[61]

Critical Infrastructure

The failure of critical infrastructure – such as airports, seaports, energy facilities, transportation and communications systems, and water supply – can result both directly and indirectly in death, injury and loss, and therefore is a source of both first-order and second-order threats. Energy infrastructure, for example, is critical in supporting the normal functioning of modern society, including systems that are a matter of life and death.

Energy infrastructure now constitutes a vast, interconnected global network that includes thousands of land-based oil wells and offshore platforms, hundreds of refineries, mammoth coal mines and cut and cover operations, extensive underground gas storage, thousands of hydroelectric plants and their associated reservoirs, hundreds of thousands of miles of major oil and gas pipelines, thousands of ships and hundreds of major ports to transport oil, coal, and liquid natural gas, thousands of power plants (using oil, coal, gas, and nuclear energy), hundreds of thousand of miles of high-voltage electric power transmission lines, millions of miles of electric power distribution wires, and millions of miles of natural gas pipelines. By 2006, this global energy infrastructure was extracting, shipping, refining, and retailing 86 million barrels of oil per day through a single, global, integrated, complex oil system, partly free-market and partly controlled by states. In 2006, about 40 million barrels of oil crossed oceans on tankers everyday, a volume some project will rise to 67 million barrels by 2020.[62]

This global energy complex was not designed to guard against sabotage, and is highly vulnerable to terrorist attack. There are several key chokepoints along the major transportation routes used by ships bearing oil and liquefied natural gas, as well as other vital and valuable cargo, and these are vulnerable to attack by terrorists and hostile states: the Straits of Gibraltar at the western Mediterranean channel to the Atlantic; the eastern Mediterranean (which carries about 65 % of Europe's energy and a large percentage of other seaborne trade flows); the Suez Canal linking the Mediterranean to the Red Sea; the Bab el Mandeb Strait, at the entrance to the Red Sea; the Bosporus Strait, a critical export channel for Russian Caspian oil; the Strait of Malacca, which carries 80 % of the oil imported by Japan and South Korea and about half of the oil imported by China.[63] Osama bin Laden has referred to such critical infrastructure, especially related to energy, as the "hinges" of the world's economy, and Al Qaeda on occasion has threatened to attack them.[64]

The global energy complex was designed to guard against normal and cyclical forces of nature, but only up to a point. For example, the offshore oil industry in the United States traditionally has built facilities to withstand a "hundred year storm". In the summer of 2005, two "hundred year storms", hurricanes Katrina and Rita, hit the Gulf Coast just a few weeks apart, crippling the enormous energy complex of wells, pipelines, and refineries in the Gulf of Mexico. The oil and gas facilities themselves actually survived the hurricanes reasonably intact, and were almost immediately prepared to resume production once the storms had passed. However, they were unable to do so mainly because the storms had knocked out the electrical energy generation and transmission capacity on which the oil and gas industry depend to operate their production facilities.[65]

Human Interaction with the Natural Environment

People require space, food, water, energy, and other resources, and generate waste and other by-products, and therefore invariably have an impact on the natural environment. However, the actual impact caused by human population depends on the average per-capita impact (resource use and waste generation) of all humans in a given region, and in the world, and that, in turn, is a function of human behavior and technology, which is highly variable over time and space. Early stages of industrialization tend to create certain kinds of environmental pollution, such as particulate emissions that create smog and raw sewage that goes untreated and pollutes water supplies. Most Western societies have successfully addressed such environmental problems as their economies have moved into the post-industrial stage. However, each citizen of the US, Western Europe, and Japan on average now consumes 32 times more of some resources, such as fossil fuels, and generates 32 times more of some wastes, such as greenhouse gas emissions (principally carbon dioxide), than do inhabitants of poor countries.[66] The much larger populations of poor and developing countries moving from the agricultural into the industrial stage of development have been repeating the environmental pollution patterns of the West. So they are likely both to clean up the severe pollution problems they are now experiencing, and also to create new pressures on the environment similar to those now generated by richer countries.

Land

Humans have transformed the land surface of the earth by hunting, mining, cutting down (and replenishing) forests, growing crops, building cities, and spreading animal and plant species from one place to another. This reconfiguration of the land has brought unprecedented benefits to humans, and it has also caused stresses on the land and its associated natural resources. There are numerous accounts of how misuse of the land historically has caused serious environmental degradation and occasionally social collapse, many of which have continuing lessons for the present.[67] Contemporary concerns also include additional ways in which misuse of the land poses potentially serious threats.

For example, epidemiologists believe that patterns of land use and activity may have played a role in the rapid emergence of new infectious diseases in recent decades. The combination of dense human populations in close contact with dense animal populations that are husbanded to meet the rising demand for meat and protein from a large and growing human population creates an ideal environment for the rapid evolution of new strains of microbes that are lethal to animals and humans alike. Such is the concern about the emergence of new strains of avian flu among the poultry farms and markets of Southeast Asia.

Large and densely developed urban regions can also act as heat traps, both by generating their own heat (as a byproduct of energy consumption) and by converting natural land that reflects solar heat into hard surfaces (such as buildings and roads) that absorb it instead. In the summertime, such urban heat traps can raise temperatures to levels that threaten the health and life of people not equipped to protect themselves (by good health, good sense, or good air conditioning). They can be particularly dangerous during unusually severe heat waves.

Fresh Water

There is currently sufficient fresh water in the world to meet all the domestic, industrial, and agricultural needs of the world's population. But access is highly uneven, owing both to the location and condition of water supply. In 2000, an estimated 1.1 one billion people lacked access to a safe and affordable domestic water supply, and an estimated 2.4 billion people lacked safe affordable sanitation.[68] Over two billion people are infected with water- or soil-borne parasitic diseases (such as bilharzias and helminthes), with 300 million suffering serious illness. A range of water pollutants affects health, including high arsenic levels in water from deep wells, which affects 50 million people in Asia.[69] Poor sanitation and pollution of the water supply caused an outbreak of cholera in Angola in the winter of 2006 that killed over one thousand people within four months and infected tens of thousands more.[70]

Glaciers are estimated to contain as much as 70 % of the world's supply of fresh water. Some 300 million people in northwest China, and millions more in Nepal and northern India, rely on the snowmelt from Himalayan glaciers for their water supply. Consequently, evidence of the accelerating retreat of glaciers in the wake of rising global temperatures (which tend to be intensified at the higher altitudes where glaciers are located) is a growing concern in those areas directly dependent on glacial melt-water.

Oceans

Oceans are a major source of food and protein, and absorb excesses of human-caused carbon dioxide, nitrogen dioxide and heat. Over the years, numerous studies and commissions have reported on the continual degradation of the world's oceans, bays, and estuaries, and virtually all have called attention to the urgency of taking immediate action. In 2003, a study funded by the Pew Charitable Trusts reported that "there is a consensus that our oceans are in crisis and that reforms are essential",[71] a view reinforced by other studies since then.

The ocean is harmed principally by excesses in taking resources out of it, and by excesses in using it as a repository to dump waste.

Excessive exploitation of ocean resources has been driven by a combination of rising demand for fish and protein and improved technology. The consequence has been a major depletion of marine life. Modern fleets use fishing lines and drift nets 50 miles long. Fine mesh nets pick up virtually everything in their path, including species that have little value to fisherman, but are important parts of marine ecology. According to some estimates, populations of several species of big fish (such as tuna, swordfish, and shark) have been reduced by as much as 90 %.[72] As bigger and more accessible fish dwindle, fishermen go for more exotic and less accessible bigger fish. For example, Chilean sea bass, currently a hot item in trendy North American restaurants, mature at about age 30 and live to as long as 100 years. If such fish are killed before maturing and reproducing, the entire species is endangered.[73]

As modern commercial fishing has depleted stocks closest to the coasts, commercial fisherman have moved increasingly into the high seas. Numerous experts have expressed concern that the exploitation of vulnerable deep-sea habitats threatens both known and unknown species and ecosystems, and that protection is required to prevent irreparable damage beyond what might have already occurred. The UN Division for Ocean Affairs and the Law of the Sea has proposed a moratorium on deep sea exploitation for consideration by the UN General Assembly in the fall of 2006.

The ocean is used as a repository for a wide variety of human-generated waste. Urban pollution in the form of storm water runoff carries an estimated 10.9 million gallons of motor oil every eight months – the equivalent of the Exxon Valdez spill in Alaska – from American streets alone into bays and oceans.[74] Rural pollutants in the form of agricultural chemicals flow into streams and rivers that reach bays and oceans. Together, these waste products have created dead zones high in nitrogen levels that kill marine life. In 2004, some 150 such dead zones had been identified,[75] including one in the Gulf of Mexico off the United States coast that has grown to the size of the state of New Jersey.[76]

The ocean has been absorbing a substantial proportion of human generated carbon dioxide (as much as one-third, by some calculations), which is altering the ocean chemistry by, for example, increasing its acidity. Higher acidity, in turn, is believed to be damaging not only choral, but also marine life with external shells, including organisms that form the base of the ocean food chain.

Biodiversity

There is wide agreement among biologists that life on earth today is in the process of the sixth known mass extinction.[77] The last one occurred 65 million years ago, with the extinction of the dinosaurs. Extinction is a normal part of biological evolution and natural selection. However, while past mass extinctions appear to have been caused by catastrophic non-biological natural events (such as climate, volcanoes, and asteroids), today's mass extinction is the result primarily of human activity.

The threats to animal and plant species (biodiversity) come in many different forms, including the direct over-harvesting of species, habitat destruction, habitat fragmentation, invasive species, disease, pollution, climate change.[78] These threats can interact and reinforce one another. For example, climate change can alter the temperature range and seasons of a given habitat and thereby disrupt nesting times and flowering times, and habitat fragmentation can block the migration of species to regions where the temperature range is more favorable.

It is not clear at this point what the consequences of the mass extinction will be for basic human survival systems. The water and land are likely to continue to team with life, but the species that survive and prosper may be comprised of a more restricted and homogenized array of organisms. Alternatively, emergent species adaptable to the new environment may or may not be favorable to the overall environment, or to humans. It is also possible that the dynamics of natural selection – which Darwin identified as the mechanism that drives biological evolution – could be fundamentally altered.[79] In essence, evolutionary success on earth in the future could be determined by how well species adapt to the new hybrid physical environment comprised of conditions and forces humans have caused but have yet to clearly identify, and whose dynamics remain a mystery. Some experts believe that even if the magnitude of the extinction can still be curbed, there is little humans can any longer do to reverse the new trajectory of human-influenced evolution on which life on earth is now headed.[80]

Atmosphere

The atmosphere is vital to life in providing oxygen for animals, carbon dioxide for plants, a shield against harmful solar rays, a blanket that keeps the earth warm, and a repository for certain waste products generated by human activity.

Human activity can affect the atmosphere in several ways. The emission of toxic gasses can cause air pollution directly harmful to humans. Particulate matter, in addition to being directly harmful, can also block solar rays from getting to the earth's surface thereby causing atmospheric temperatures to cool, a condition known as "global dimming". The chemical action of chlorine and bromine released by gases such as chlorofluorocarbons (CFCs) depletes the ozone layer, forming "ozone holes" which permit the penetration of higher levels of harmful ultraviolet solar rays that are believed to increase the risk of skin cancer and cataracts in humans, to reduce crop yields, and to harm sea life. CFCs have been used in aerosol sprays and cooling equipment, including refrigerators and some air-conditioning systems. Growing "ozone holes" were observed over Antarctica about 30 years ago and were later discovered elsewhere in the earth's atmosphere, including over Africa, Asia, southern Australasia, Europe, Latin America and North America. And the emission of so-called "greenhouse gases", such as carbon dioxide and methane, can trap heat from the sun that is reflected back from the earth before it can escape into space, and thereby cause the atmosphere to warm. Humans have been generating all of these kinds of emissions.

Few people doubt the harm done by the toxic emissions and particulate matter, which produce effects that are directly irritable to the human senses, like smog and other noxious air, and which people can thus literally see and feel. The damage done to the ozone layer by chlorofluorocarbons (CFCs) was not something people could literally see or feel, but they could easily understand that one consequence could be increased skin cancer, and the scientific evidence of expanding "holes" in the ozone layer was also graphic and compelling. There has been considerable success in reducing each of these sources of atmospheric damage. Smog-causing emissions have been substantially reduced in much of the developed world. And the Montreal Protocol of 1987 led to the reduction of CFCs and the healing the ozone holes. The levels of ozone-depleting substances appeared to peak in 1992 – 1994 in the troposphere and later in the 1990s peaked in the stratosphere, and the ozone layer was predicted to recover to pre-1980 levels by 2050.

But little has been done with regard to greenhouse gases, which have remained controversial, in part because their impact and potential dangers are far more difficult to demonstrate. There is little doubt among climate experts that global warming is occurring. Evidence demonstrates that the earth's global average temperature rose about half a degree centigrade from 1900 to 1940, was stable between 1940 and 1980, and resumed rising during the 1980s.[81] The past decade was the hottest on record worldwide. Predictions of future global warming over the course of the 21st century range from 1.5 to 4.5 degrees centigrade.

There is some degree of uncertainty as to the cause, or causes, of global warming. A variety of factors can affect global temperatures. Some of these are entirely natural, including volcanic emissions, cyclical climate phenomena such as El Nino and La Nina, and especially the variable intensity of solar rays caused by the tilt of the earth's axis. The earth's axis "tilts" in relation to the sun, altering the angle at which the sun's rays strike earth as it revolves around the sun, and thus causing changes of seasons. It also "wobbles" in a way that can periodically change the range of temperatures on earth. A natural cycle of ice ages has occurred fairly regularly over the past eight hundred thousand years, with each cycle lasting about a hundred thousand years. In each cycle, the ice age itself lasts about ninety thousand years, followed by a warm interglacial period that lasts about ten thousand years. The last ice age ended about 12 thousand years ago, when a predictable warm period began, the one we are now living in. Assuming that the warm period was the interglacial segment of the natural cycle, we are probably overdue for the onset of another ice age that would eventually bury the northern half of North America and Europe under massive ice sheets, as occurred in past ice ages. It is possible a new ice age has already begun. Or, given the margin of difference in past cycles, a new ice age may not begin for another two thousand years.

There are also possible human contributions (anthropogenic) to global warming, such as greenhouse gas emissions (including carbon dioxide, methane, and other gases) and the previously mentioned urban heat traps. There is a strong scientific consensus that carbon dioxide, generated principally through the burning of fossil fuels, is a prime contributor to global warming. Before the 20th century, and dating back at least 650,000 years, the levels of carbon dioxide in the atmosphere had never surpassed 300 parts per million. In 1958, for the first time carbon dioxide was recorded as having reached 310 parts per million in the atmosphere, and by 2005 it had reached 380. Some current projections show it rising to 600 by 2050. The correlation among three factors – the human generation of carbon dioxide emissions through the burning of fossil fuels, the rising carbon dioxide levels in the atmosphere, and the acceleration of global warming – strongly indicates that human activity is a cause of rising average global temperatures.[82] The Intergovernmental Panel on Climate Change (IPCC) concluded that there was a "discernible" human influence associated with the rise of global average temperatures.

Still other factors can affect global temperatures in a variety of ways, altering or masking the effects of primary factors. The "global dimming" effect caused by particulate matter in the atmosphere may have helped cool the earth in the twentieth century, thus possibly masking the full measure of the warming trend. It is also possible that oceans' absorption of heat may be masking the full effect of global warming, and that once the ocean's limit for absorbing heat has been reached (relative to the air), the warming of the atmosphere could accelerate.

While there is substantial scientific agreement that average global temperatures have been increasing, and that human-caused carbon dioxide emissions is a likely contributor, there is greater uncertainty about the likely impact of global warming. Some experts predict the impact it will be slight, and that it could even be positive by, for example, lengthening the growing season in colder regions. And some have suggested that if it turns out that another ice age is about to occur, global warming might even dampen its effect. Possible negative consequences include melting glaciers, rising sea levels, negative impacts on agriculture in certain regions, extended and more severe summer heat waves, more frequent and intense storms, and changing ecosystems for plants and animals, some of which could contribute to the extinction of species, and others of which could facilitate the emergence of unfavorable species of plants and animals, including new diseases.

The evidence is compelling that that glaciers are melting and that global warming is the cause. Evidence on the extent and cause of sea level's rising is more mixed. There is reliable documentation (and reasonably accurate measurement) demonstrating that sea levels have been rising since at least the early 1800s to the present. Since the Industrial Revolution and its generation of carbon dioxide did not get into full swing until well into the 19th century, it seems doubtful that human activity could have been the cause of rising sea levels in the early part of that century. However, the rate of rising sea levels appears to have been accelerating over the past fifty years. Since that period coincides in time with the rapid increase of carbon dioxide in the atmosphere, the acceleration of global warming, and evidence of glacial melting, it is widely believed that at least the recent rise in sea levels is probably due in part to global warming caused by the emission of carbon dioxide gasses.

Global warming of the earth could have highly variable impacts in different regions of the world (which is why many scientists prefer to call the phenomenon "climate change"). For example, for any given incremental increase in global average temperature, meteorologists generally believe that the polar regions are likely to experience greater increases than those nearer the equator (and there is evidence that this is occurring). Relatively higher polar temperatures, in turn, could affect the circulation of air and water. One concern is that higher polar temperatures could melt enough fresh glacial water to interfere with warm ocean currents, such as the Gulf Stream, that play a major role in warming some land areas, such as Europe, thus causing those regions to become cooler. Consequently, "global warming" could mean that some places on earth become much warmer than the rising global average temperature, while others may actually become cooler. There is a growing consensus that the biggest losers from climate change are likely to be regions in tropical latitudes, such as India and Africa, where agriculture will suffer and infectious diseases, such as malaria, are likely to increase.[83]

The net sum of these various trends, bodies of evidence and arguments appears to be the following: it is now accepted by most scientists that there is a very high probability the earth's atmosphere is warming; that glaciers are melting; that sea levels are rising at an accelerating pace; and that these changes are driven at least in part by greenhouse gas emissions (principally carbon dioxide) that result principally from the human burning of fossil-fuels. There is somewhat less agreement regarding the magnitude and timing of global warming, as well as the types, magnitudes, and consequences of climate change it might produce. Predictions range across outcomes that are beneficial, benign, inconveniences, seriously negative, and potentially catastrophic.

In light of these considerations, to do nothing about global warming is a high-stakes gamble. It is not just betting the farm, betting the firm, or betting the family fortune. It is betting the planet. Part of the gamble lies in ignoring the likelihood that humans are having a potentially profound effect on a vital planetary life support system without understanding how it works or what impact it might have. On the other hand, some experts (including some former skeptics of global warming) have concluded that it is too late to curb carbon-dioxide emissions sufficiently to stop global warming and climate change, and that whatever steps humans might take to slow the increase, they should also prepare to adapt to the consequences.

Third-Order Institutional Threats

Third-order threats have to do with the institutions that humans rely upon to protect themselves from first-order existential threats and second-order environmental threats – that is, to protect themselves from harm, and to generate, manage, sustain and/or renew the human-made systems and the physical environment on which life depends.[84] The "institutional threat" includes both the threat to institutions – forces that would cause the institutions to malfunction or otherwise fail to perform – and the threat of institutions – that is, institutions that are employed to attack other human institutions, or which are harmful in their own right to the people they are supposed to serve.

There is substantial conceptual and semantic confusion in definitions of "security" and in the design and operation of security-related institutions. As a result, there is also frequently a corresponding confusion, and a great deal of complicating (and often unacknowledged) overlap among security institutions in threat definition and assessment, strategies, functions, organization, and capacities. The threshold institutional challenge is to define "security" and "security threats" in a manner that is conceptually clear, accurate in depicting reality, capable of gaining necessary understanding and support, and conducive to the effective design and operation of the institutions created to address those security threats.

For most states, "security" traditionally has focused on violent threats, including hostile states, internal personal and political violence, and the forces of nature. Heightened concern with non-state actors, and especially terrorism, has caused a major shift in the missions of traditional security institutions in some countries, such as the United States, which had viewed itself as being largely free of serious terrorist threats prior to September 2001. Meanwhile, concern about the resurgence of infectious diseases and the potential for pandemics has raised the institutional profile of agencies concerned with public health. Mounting environmental concerns have caused many states to raise the importance of institutions concerned with environmental protection. The critical infrastructure on which modern societies depend have become increasing security concerns, because of their vital importance and inherent complexity, because of the inherent dangers they pose to the people they are intended to serve, and because of their vulnerability to both natural and human disruption. All of these inter-acting security-related institutions are dependent on the security and effective functioning of the underlying economic, social, and political systems they are designed to serve.

Following are some of the major categories of institutions concerned with various kinds of "security", along with comments on how changing definitions have been reshaping security-related institutions, principally in the United States.

Human Security

The traditional concern with "national security" has focused on defending the state, or the nation-state, from external threats. But since political violence in recent decades has occurred more within state than among them, some institutions – particularly some international agencies and non-governmental organizations – have been increasingly concerned with "human security" more generally defined as the security and well-being of people as individuals and their associated communities, regardless of their political affiliations.

One prominent view holds that human security includes hunger (malnutrition), disease, natural disaster, poverty, and ecological devastation. Those who hold that broader view note that these factors account for more deaths than do outright violence. The 1994 Human Development Report published by the UN Development Program, for example, articulated such a broad conception.[85] A comparatively narrower view of human security typically focuses on such violent threats to individuals and their immediate communities as civil war, genocide, the displacement of populations, ethnic cleansing, terrorism, and torture.[86] UN Secretary-General Kofi Annan, for example, has characterized the narrower human security approach as being concerned with "the protection of communities and individuals from internal violence".[87] Many of the factors that threaten human security (whether in the broader or narrower sense) are interrelated, especially when they are concentrated in the same place, as is the case in poor countries. So the broader and narrower views are complementary.

National Security

"National security" refers broadly to a country's overall physical security against attack, and so generally encompasses a state's top political leadership, strategy advisors, diplomatic corps, intelligence agencies, armed forces[88], and public safety agencies. In the United States prior to 9/11, "national security" was more or less synonymous with "national defense", since it was assumed that the US Department of Defense would defend the nation against outside attacks. The White House National Security Advisor worked through the National Security Council on behalf of the president to coordinate the various federal agencies concerned with "national security". Following 9/11, when it became clear that this apparatus was not sufficient to keep enemies from penetrating US borders and attacking US territory, the concept of "homeland security" emerged as a way of focusing policy and institutional missions and capacities more intensively on security at and within national borders. But the distinctions and overlap between "national security" and "homeland security" have yet to be clearly defined in the United States, and conceptual and organizational confusion persists.[89]

Homeland Defense

"Homeland defense" usually refers to that part of the function of "national security" and "national defense" that focuses specifically on defending the national territory, and is consequently also a part of, or a complement to, "homeland security". For example, NATO defines "homeland defense" as "the military's role in preventing and defending against terrorist attacks on the territory of Alliance members". [90] This would apply to such missions as defending national territory against outside attacks, including especially those involving weapons of mass destruction, preventing WMD proliferation, and preventing illegal trafficking in weapons. NATO forces, which draw on the combined country military forces of NATO members, have a substantial war-fighting capability, more in fact than NATO believes it needs for potential conventional war-fighting missions. But they lack some specific capacities required for such "homeland defense" functions as medical support, engineers, military police, and transport units.[91]

Homeland defense and homeland security together encompass the protection of critical infrastructure, including energy facilities, airports, and seaports; guarding maritime approaches; defense against future missile threats; prevention and management of terrorist incidents; and reacting promptly to WMD use. This presents something of a challenge to NATO, since such functions require close coordination with national governments, which usually include resources engaged in "homeland security" that are considered by states to be important elements of national sovereignty.

Homeland security

"Homeland security" refers to protecting the "homeland," which usually means the national territory. In the United States until 9/11, the term "homeland security" was rarely heard or used officially in connection with government organization. The conceptual and terminological confusion regarding the meaning of the term was converted into organizational confusion with the creation of the US Department of Homeland Security (DHS), which consolidated some two dozen operating agencies from other federal departments. While DHS was conceived as the lead federal agency to address the heightened concern with terrorism, its operating agencies deal principally with border control issues and emergency management. DHS does not include several of the most important functions and agencies that protect the US homeland from terrorism, including all of the country's armed forces (excepting the Coast Guard), all of its intelligence agencies, and all of its law enforcement agencies.

Intelligence

National intelligence agencies traditionally have had the responsibility of obtaining (through both overt and covert means) and analyzing information considered vital to "national security", especially with regard to the intentions, capacities, and activities of other states. Since 9/11, the intelligence function in the United States have been expanded and redirected toward terrorist activities.[92]

These shifts have heightened the tension between security and civil liberties. Those who place the priority on fighting terrorism favor giving police and criminal justice agencies greater authority to engage in secret surveillance and to apprehend and hold suspected terrorists without formal charges or court hearings. Those who place the priority on civil liberties complain that such latitude is a threat to privacy and personal protection against abuse of power and arrest and incarceration without due process.

The need for increased international liaison and exchange of intelligence information regarding terrorism has further complicated these issues. For example, in 2004, over the objection of the European Parliament, European Union nations agreed to provide US authorities with 34 items of personal information on airline passengers departing Europe for the United States (including name, address, credit card details, etc). In May 2006, the European Court of Justice ruled that those EU nations acted without the requisite legal basis.

Counterterrorism

Counterterrorism typically refers to all functions required to protect a country against terrorism, including detection and surveillance of terrorist plots and networks; interdiction that involves the disruption, apprehension, arrest, incarceration, questioning, prosecution, and disposition of terrorist suspects; the prevention and mitigation of terrorists attacks by hardening targets and reducing vulnerabilities; and immediate response to terrorist attacks These functions typically involve a wide array of intelligence, military, and law enforcement agencies concerned with foreign and domestic counterterrorism intelligence, surveillance, investigation, and interdiction, as well as agencies concerned with border security, infrastructure security, and emergency management.

The interface between intelligence agencies and police and law enforcement agencies in the detection, surveillance, investigation, and interdiction functions is especially challenging, and handled differently in different countries. In the United States, the Department of Justice has been given a major role in counterterrorism, with the Federal Bureau of Investigation (FBI), which is located within the Department of Justice, undertaking a major transformation in its mission from a nearly exclusive focus on criminal justice to a preponderant focus on counterterrorism. This new mission runs counter to the FBI's traditional criminal justice culture, with its focus on catching criminals after a crime has been committed, and gathering sufficient evidence to convict them in a criminal court. Effective counter-terrorism focuses on detecting and investigating potential terrorists before they have committed a terrorist act, not only to prevent the act from occurring, but also to gain information and understanding into the nature of terrorist networks and future activities. The FBI has struggled with this change.

Emergency Management

"Emergency management"[93] addresses hazards that range across a continuum typically defined by their causes, including natural forces, accidents, personal violence, and political violence (generally following the definitions of these terms presented earlier). Some emergency management regimes dispense with the question of what caused the incident, and simply assume responsibility for addressing "all hazards", whatever their cause may be.

Emergency management functions traditionally focused on responding to incidents after they have occurred in order to save lives, rescue victims and limit damage to property. A broader view of emergency management encompasses a continuum of functions that extend its concern to before the incident occurs and more extensively afterwards, in a kind of cyclical approach to preventing disasters and reducing their impact. This continuum of functions includes: mitigating if not preventing potential disasters; preparing to respond to them before they occur; responding to an incident (the traditional emergency management function); and assisting victims and communities in recovery, preferably in a way that will help prevent similar disasters in the future. A comprehensive "all hazards" approach, which includes terrorist attacks, takes emergency management further into the pre-incident stages of counterterrorism that attempt to prevent terrorist attacks from occurring, and to mitigate their consequences should they occur by hardening targets and reducing vulnerabilities and negative consequences.

The emergency management function is organized in a wide variety of ways from place to place. Typically the principal responsibility is lodged with "first responders", such as police, fire, rescue, and medical treatment (formally named "emergency management specialists" typically have a combination of rescue and medical treatment skills), which are likely to be employed by various combinations of local, provincial, "state", and national government agencies. In some countries, military services play a major supplemental role, and in some cases a primary role, in emergency management.[94] The heightened attention to terrorism in the United States has prompted a call for a more proactive role for police to be not just "first responders" to an incident after it occurs, but also "first preventers" engaged in detecting, investigating, disrupting and deterring terrorist activities before they occur.

One of the most controversial features of the new US organization for "homeland security" was the decision to include the Federal Emergency Management Agency (FEMA) in the newly created Department of Homeland Security, which some critics felt compromised the independence and effectiveness of emergency management while distracting the secretary of homeland security from focusing on counterterrorism. This issue came to a head with the government fiasco in dealing with Hurricane Rita, which hit Florida and the Gulf Coast (including New Orleans) in the summer of 2005.[95]

Public Safety

The "public safety" function in the United States traditionally has encompassed police, fire, and emergency response agencies, the "first responders" in emergency management who are now being enlisted to become "first preventers" in the fight against terrorism. Public health agencies are increasingly viewed as part of the public safety cluster of functions because of the rising importance of their roles in fighting pandemics and bio-terrorism. An intersecting public safety cluster links police to "law enforcement and criminal justice".

Law Enforcement and Criminal Justice

Public law and order in the United States traditionally has linked the interrelated police and legal prosecutorial functions of crime prevention, response, investigation, criminal apprehension, incarceration, and prosecution. These functions typically encompass police agencies, other criminal investigators, prosecutors, and government legal representatives.

The shift of resources in the US criminal justice system away from traditional crime toward fighting terrorism has placed a double stress on conventional police forces at the state and local level. On the one hand, they are expected to expand – not shift – their own missions to become "first preventers" in the fight against terrorism while continuing to address conventional crime. And on the other hand, in their conventional crime-fighting they are losing logistical support from the federal criminal justice system, including the FBI, which has been shifting its resources and attention from crime to terrorism. All of this has raised concerns about traditional public safety related to crime, especially as government statistics suggest that violent crime may be on the rise in the United States after a long period of decline.

Health Security

"Health security" straddles the line between first- and second-order threats. The constellation of public health functions (including responsibility for hospitals, clinics, disease control, water supply, and public sanitation) are among the "first responders" in addressing serious outbreaks of disease, in managing epidemics and pandemics, and in detecting and responding to bio-terrorism. And they are also on the frontline in addressing the more deeply rooted causes of disease that account for the preponderance of human death and disability.

Environmental Protection

"Environmental protection" (and "environmental security") tend to focus narrowly on the safety of the natural environment. Part of the institutional challenge to environmental security has to do with the interdependence among multiple factors that affect the safety of the natural environment, including urban development, agriculture, natural resource consumption, and alien species as well a wide variety of point and non-point source pollutants that contaminate the air, water, and land. Taken one at a time, each of these factors appears to be manageable. However, when viewed interactively, as they function in reality, the overall challenge is quite formidable,[96] the more so when the new capacities for genetic manipulation and artificial pathogens are added to the mix.

Security Support Institutions

Security support institutions are those whose functions are not necessarily viewed as addressing frontline security concerns, but are nonetheless vital to the performance of institutions that do. The importance of critical infrastructure is reflected in frequent references to the security of numerous facilities, including "airport security", "energy security", etc.[97] "Corporate security" generally refers to the security of an organization's vital assets, including its data, information systems, facilities, and employees. Since information equipment is increasingly mobile, concerns about "mobile security" have also arisen. The emergence of globally integrated enterprises has raised a new generation concerns for businesses, whose global supply chains and institutional supports are increasingly vulnerable to economic, financial, political, and terrorist disruption.[98]

Individual "personal security" in the modern world encompasses a wide range of security-related functions for which people now look to institutions, beyond the conventional concern with physical security from violence.[99] A complex array of public, private and nonprofit institutions at all levels, from community to global, are involved in providing such functions. And since a nation's capacity for physical, social, and cultural security ultimately depends on the strength of the economy, "economic security" in the modern world is integral to all other security concerns.[100]

General Purpose Governance Institutions

In the end, the principal responsibility for institutions that address human security concerns rests with the general governmental and political institutions of individual states. Of course, this has always been true for traditional "national security" and "public safety" concerns. But as security-related issues have become ubiquitous, complex, and interdependent, the capacity of general purpose government to address them, individually and interactively, has become an urgent security issue in its own right.

The main burden of this general institutional challenge ultimately falls on the top political leadership and professional cadres in the various branches of government (executive, legislative, and judicial). These are the organs of government that define security-related missions, design the institutional structures to pursue them, appropriate the funds required to staff and equip them, select the leadership to manage them, adopt the policies to guide them, supervise their execution, and provide the oversight to hold appropriate organizations and people to account for their performance. These are the essential security-related institutional tasks of political and governmental leadership. And in an increasingly interdependent world, states rely more than ever on inter-state cooperation to address a wide array of mutual security concerns.

Implications for Global Governance

The challenges posed by these three orders of security threat – existential, environmental, and institutional – have several implications for global governance.

Defining Global Governance

Global governance is the process by which people throughout the world, working principally through various institutions, determine and pursue ends and means that have global implications.[101] By this view, global governance does not refer to a narrow set of institutions (and certainly not to "world government"), but rather to the cumulative result of a multitude of decisions and actions by people and organizations throughout the world that have global impact. Since the world is highly interdependent, it is inescapable that many actions in any one country are likely to have far-ranging consequences that affect other countries. The central governance issue is whether or not such actions will be guided (by authoritative institutions, professional standards, cultural norms or personal habit) in a manner that the net impact is positive for individuals, for groups, for states, and for the world as a whole. De facto global governance, therefore, is a reality; the only question is whether it is done well or poorly, and who benefits and pays the costs.

States constitute the institutional building blocks of de facto global governance. The territory of the globe is now almost completely divided among states, and while each state governs its own parcel of the global territory, the collection of states taken together provides the institutional foundation for governance of the planet as a whole. Therefore, the effectiveness of global governance in the first instance depends on the effectiveness of governance in each of the individual constituent states.

States continue to interact among themselves principally according to formal and informal rules of international law and international relations that have evolved over the centuries. These include explicit interstate treaties, agreements, and organizations, as well as tacit cooperation among states. Since World War II, the nations of the world have constructed an expanding constellation of international institutions, grounded in a core cluster of organizations including the United Nations, World Bank, and International Monetary Fund. This institutional core, in turn, has generated a wide array of more specialized organizations (such as the World Health Organization, World Trade Organization, World Meteorological Organization, etc.). An even broader institutional constellation includes similar types of international regional organizations, as well as a growing constellation of non-state actors (such as business corporations, and not-for-profit, non-governmental organizations, or NGOs) that are active both domestically and on the global stage.

All of these groups – government, business, non-profit/NGO, civic – are forming complex networks of interaction within their own sectors as well as with the other sectors, producing a multitude of interweaving trans-state networks.[102] At times elements of this thickening web of relationship behave in a manner largely independent of states themselves, forming new kinds of extra-state and supra-state players with a degree of "sovereignty" in their own right, and therefore increasingly free of direct state accountability.

For some purposes, this de facto system of global governance seems to work quite well, especially if the task is precisely defined and enjoys substantial political support from all the actors involved, such as in delivering the mail or sharing weather data. For other purposes, however, the de facto global governance system works quite poorly, or not at all, or even counterproductively. As a consequence, such critical threats as disease, terrorism, nuclear proliferation, reducing the potential for nuclear catastrophe, preventing and containing armed conflict, and reversing the degradation of the physical environment, are not being addressed in a timely and effective fashion. Five principal implications for global governance emerge from the foregoing sorting out of threats to human security.

Comprehensive, Cross-boundary Approaches

First, few, if any, of the most critical first-order existential threats or second-order environmental threats can be effectively or reliably addressed by any one institution, any one sector, or any one state, acting alone.

Virtually all the critical first-order threats – disease, pandemic, weapons of mass destruction, political violence, and terrorist attack – require the sharing of information and coordinated action across institutional and political boundaries, including across national boundaries.

For example, national health agencies learned during recent outbreaks of potentially dangerous pathogens that effective action to detect and contain a potential pandemic requires vigilance on the part of national, regional, and local health agencies in all countries where initial outbreaks are most likely to occur; the rapid sharing of information up-and-down the intergovernmental chain within countries as well as with counterpart health agencies among countries; and rapidly coordinated action to trace the connections and travel patterns of people who may have been infected with the pathogen in order to locate those people and impose quarantines as required. Cross-boundary co-operation is also required in the development and stocking of vaccines to protect populations and prevent the spread of disease, in the development of treatment capacity for those already infected, and to inform the public as to how they can best deal with a potential or actual outbreak.

Similarly, liaison among the intelligence agencies of countries allied in fighting terrorism has proved to be both essential and effective in detecting and disrupting terrorist cells, plans, and activities. National leaders have also recognized that to stop terrorists from gaining access to fissile material requires securing existing nuclear facilities in all countries where they exist. In 2002 leaders of the G-8 countries (US, UK, France, Germany, Japan, Italy, Canada, and Russia) initiated a Global Partnership Against the Spread of Weapons and Materials of Mass Destruction, principally to secure and/or dismantle nuclear military facilities in the former Soviet Union. However, progress has proved to be slow, in part because of classic interstate disputes between Russia and countries funding the effort over such issues as taxation, liability, and site access.[103]

Second-order environmental threats require a similarly comprehensive, cross-boundary approach. This is especially the case for environmental resources located in geographical areas that cross national boundaries. For example, protection of the ecosystems of endangered species that cross political borders requires international cooperation. The 2004 Convention on the International Trade of Endangered Species (CITES), signed by over 150 countries, recognizes this need in attempting to integrate the numerous actions required to protect such ecosystems, including international treaties, prohibitory laws and regulations, land protection, bio-reserves, sustainable-development programs, litigation, and policy advocacy.[104]

Global Commons

Second, several high priority first- and second-order threats are integrally associated with global commons that can only be protected and managed through effective institutions and processes of global governance. A commons is a resource – typically a material resource of the physical environment – that all members of the community depend upon for their livelihood or survival. The "tragedy of the commons" occurs when members of such a community use the common resource as they please without concern about the impact on its sustainability, so that eventually the common resource is diminished or lost, to the disadvantage of all.[105] Among the classic global commons are those having to do with the planetary physical environment upon which all humans depend for survival, including the atmosphere, the oceans, and the planet's biodiversity.

Global warming has all the classic signs of the tragedy of the commons.[106] The atmosphere is viewed as a resource available to everyone, with no sense of exclusive or collective ownership. So anyone can use it, and engage in behavior that generates more greenhouse gases, without having to pay the direct cost of that use. The "tragedy of the commons" in this case is that there is insufficient incentive for individuals to account for the changes in the atmosphere that result from their contribution of greenhouse gases, with the result that that common resource – the atmosphere – is diminished in its capacity to absorb greenhouse gases in a manner that protects the earth from excessive heat and consequent unfavorable climate changes.

The principal global effort to curb greenhouse gases is the Kyoto Protocol on Climate Change, which took effect in February, 2005. While it is a significant first step, the Kyoto Protocol's impact on curbing carbon dioxide will be trivial for two reasons. One is that the policy actions stipulated under the treaty will not be sufficient to significantly curb or reverse the growth of carbon dioxide or other greenhouse gases. And the second is that it does not include either of the two principal contributors of carbon dioxide, the United States and China.

The United States in recent years has accounted for about 21 % of the world's greenhouse gas emissions, and is expected to increase its overall volume about one-third by 2025. By that year, China is projected to double its volume of greenhouse gas emissions, and will account for about 25 % of the world's total, surpassing the United States as the world's leading contributor (even though the United States would still have a higher per capita generation). No serious progress will be made in curbing greenhouse gas emissions unless these two countries participate.

Global Public Goods

Third, in addition to protecting the global commons, an array of global public goods is required to effectively address critical threats of all three orders: existential, environmental, and institutional.

Global public goods include global public order and international security (including international law and the capacity to prevent and contain conflict), global emergency management, global economic growth and stability, global regulatory regimes for the protection of global commons, global critical infrastructure (such as transportation, communications, and energy), global public health (in the prevention and treatment of disease, and regulation of such critical health-related activities as synthetic biology), and global environmental protection.

The emergence of globally integrated enterprises as new units of international business has increased the importance of providing global public goods required for corporate security and prosperity in a highly interdependent – and insecure – global economy.[107] International business leaders may turn out to be in the vanguard pushing for more effective and integrative global governance institutions, because many of them recognize the importance of global public goods to the security and prosperity of their businesses. Some business leaders have begun to formulate a global agenda to "reform health care and education, secure the world's trade lanes and electronic commerce, train and enable the displaced and dispossessed, grapple with environmental problems and infectious disease", and address other challenges of globalization.[108] Foremost among the global public goods required for business investment and economic growth are global security and order, since businesses are not likely to invest anywhere where they are not reasonably confident that their investment will be secure.

Global Institutional Scope

Fourth, international and global institutions in general lack the authority, scale and scope of coverage required to address the issues of global commons and global public goods, and to more directly address first-order existential and second-order environmental threats in a comprehensive fashion.

None of the critical global commons has an institutional regime with adequate scope and authority. But for a few of the key global goods, an appropriate scope may within reach. For example, states and corporations have been slowly building a more comprehensive and integrated global energy network, but important gaps remain. The Paris-based International Energy Agency (IEA), created in response to the 1973 Arab oil embargo, links the industrialized countries in an effort to coordinate policies and actions to protect the global energy system, and in particular oil supplies.[109] Daniel Yergin has urged that the principles of energy security on which this institutional structure is based be expanded to include recognition of the full global dimension of the energy security system, and that both China and India should be fully engaged in it.[110]

Global Institutional Capacity

Fifth, the institutional capacities required to address these and other tasks of global governance are in many instances inadequate or altogether missing.

If states are to be the institutional building blocks of a de facto global governance network, they need an upgraded set of capacities required to perform in a complex, fast-paced, interdependent, and uncertain world.[111] This is a threshold requirement for effective global governance, and requires that nations such as the United States first address the kinds of deficiencies and tensions in the design and operation of their own security institutions as described in the previous section. An even more fundamental security capacity problem is the fact that many countries of the world lack the institutions and capacities to perform the elemental functions of statehood, much less more complex security functions. If nation-states are the building blocks of global governance, then such "fragile" states constitute major gaps in its foundation. The World Bank has classified 71 states as "fragile"(over one-third of the world's total number of states), based on levels of violence, instability, and wealth. While most of the world's functioning states have come to understand that shoring up fragile states through "state-building" or "nation-building" is critical to collective regional and global security, and therefore in their own self-interest, there remains much debate as to how this can best be done.[112]

Just how fundamental the institutional capacity problem can be, both for fragile states and international organizations, was demonstrated by the response to the cholera epidemic that broke out in February 2006 in Luanda, the capital of Angola. In the first place, public water supplies and sewage systems were inadequate or nonexistent. The Angolan central and local governments attempted to compensate through a system of commercial water delivery in which tanker trucks drew water directly from rivers that were contaminated by fecal-laden sewage and sold it to residents in slums not served by piped water supply. Government, working with UNICEF, provided chlorination tablets at pumping sites in order to purify the water, but they lacked the staff to assure that the tablets were properly used. According to observers with Doctors Without Borders, a non-profit organization on the scene, at the time of the outbreak only about 10 % of the commercial water trucks were estimated to be using the chlorination tablets properly, or at all. Once the epidemic broke out, the government appeared to make little effort to provide safe, free drinking water to residents, and so the epidemic continued to spread.[113]

At the other end of the scale, there is a need to continually upgrade even the well-established and sophisticated institutional capacities of national governments and international organizations to address new types of global security challenges. For example, national governments and international agencies have developed a substantial capacity for managing global financial flows, as demonstrated in recent years by the comparative stability of international finance and an expanding global economy. Over the past two decades, however, international financial interactions have become increasingly voluminous, rapid, interdependent and complex, raising concerns about financial and monetary security. The integration of capital markets across international borders can improve the efficiency of financial capital allocation and better distribute risk, but it can also increase the risk of instability unless global financial markets are effectively structured, regulated, and managed, and the institutional capacity and authority exists to resolve serious financial imbalances and manage crises when they arise. The threat of financial instability has been further increased in recent years by such structural changes in global financial markets as "growing reliance on over-the-counter derivative instruments and markets, the growth of credit derivative markets, and the capital market activities of insurance and reinsurance companies".[114] Continual attention is required to assure that appropriate institutional capacities are in place to deal with such developments.

Perhaps the most urgent capacity need is for institutional arrangements that can more effectively prevent, contain and quell violent conflicts among states, and can also do so for political violence within states that involve atrocities or that might otherwise spread across national borders. Over the past several decades international organizations and various coalitions of states have demonstrated substantial success in efforts at curbing atrocities, resolving conflicts, and peacekeeping. There have been conspicuous failures, to be sure, in strategy, execution, and inaction. But viewed in historical perspective, such as in comparison with the record of the League of Nations and the failure of international collective security arrangements in the years between the First and Second World Wars, recent international efforts have shown serious intent and accomplishment.

Still, the institutional capacity for international collective security remains weak, both in comparison with rising international norms and expectations for peace, security and human rights, and given the high stakes involved in addressing an array of unusually dangerous regional and global threats. The principal forum and instrument for international conflict prevention and resolution, the United Nations, has obvious limitations in its governance structure, resource base, and operational capacities, most of which are inherent in the institutional design the great powers fashioned for that body. Meanwhile, the ad hoc nature of the typical international responses to critical conflicts and brewing tensions is, while understandable in the context of traditional international relations, are totally inadequate for addressing the range of potentially serious threats that confront the international community.

Conclusion

The only way these security issues of global governance are likely to be addressed is through the leadership of the major nations themselves. For a half-century following the Second World War, the United States spearheaded a coalition of leading nations to fashion and implement a vision for building such a constellation of international institutions and relationships, one that served the United States' own interests as well as the broader interests of virtually all nations in shaping a world with more effective processes of global governance.

At the beginning of the twenty-first century, the United States departed from that historic institutional vision and leadership role in favor of a more stoutly unilateral approach to international affairs.[115] By the middle of 2006 the American occupation of Iraq was well into its fourth year, sectarian violence in that country was chronic, Iran continued to push ahead with its uranium enrichment program, instability in the Middle East was increasing, American military capacity was stretched thin around the globe, and world opinion of the United States was at an all-time low. There have been indications that the American leaders who took the country in the more unilateralist direction were having second thoughts about it. However, it is unlikely that the same leadership would be able to successfully resurrect the former agenda for building international institutions and relationships even if it was genuinely inclined to do so. Consequently, any recommitment of the United States to a serious effort to building the institutions required for effective global governance in order to address the existential, environmental, and institutional threats we confront will probably have to await the arrival of new national political leadership. In the meantime, perhaps other nations that recognize the urgency of this agenda might step forward to pick up the leadership responsibilities that the United States, at least for the present, has foregone.

Endnotes

[1] Some people who survived the atomic blasts in Hiroshima and Nagasaki died later from causes traced to injuries and radiation poisoning suffered in those attacks. Since then, there have been no nuclear weapons used in anger, and no reported deaths from the explosions of nuclear testing, although there have been suspected deaths that resulted from radiation from those explosions.

[2] W. R. Mead, Foreign Affairs (May/June, 2006), p. 142.

[3] J. Habermas (Trans. T. McCarthy), Communication and the Evolution of Society, (Boston: Beacon Press, 1979), p.164-165.

[4] US Department of Homeland Security (DHS), National Planning Scenarios (Washington, D.C.: US Department of Homeland Security, 2003.

[5] A. Mills and S. Shillcutt, Communicable Diseases (Copenhagen: Consensus, 2004).

[6] National Vital Statistics Report 53 (2004), Number 5.

[7] A. Mills and S. Shillcutt 2004 (En. 5).

[8] World Health Organization (WHO), World Report on Violence and Health (Geneva: World Health Organization (WHO), 2002).

[9] The four leading causes of death in the United States in 2003 were: heart disease (28.0 %), cancer (22.7 %), stroke (17.5 %), and chronic lower respiratory diseases (5.2 %). Source: D. L. Hoyert, M. P. Heron, S. L. Murphy, and H.-C. Kung, Deaths: Final Data for 2003, National Vital Statistics Reports 54, No. 13 (Washington, D.C.: National Vital Statistics System, National Center for Health Statistics. Centers for Disease Control and Prevention, US Department of Health and Human Services, 2006), p. 5.

[10] P. Epstein, associate director of Harvard Medical School's Center for Health and Global Environment, has characterized the rate at which infectious diseases emerged since the 1970s as "without precedent in the history of the annals of medicine", quoted in the Baltimore Sun, May 2003, p. 10A.

[11] A. Mills and S. Shillcutt 2004 (En. 5).

[12] Charlie Rose TV Program, Nov. 17, 2004.

[13] Global Commission on Road Safety, Make Roads Safe: A New Priority for Sustainable Development (Geneva: World Health Organization, 2006).

[14] US National Highway Traffic Safety Administration (NHTSA).

[15] Institute of Medicine, To Err Is Human (Washington, D.C.: National Academy Press, 1999).

[16] Institute of Medicine, Preventing Medication Errors (Washington, D.C.: National Academy Press, 2006).

[17] World Health Organization (WHO) 2002 (En. 8), p. 7, Table 1.

[18] M. Weber (translated and edited by H. H. Gerth and C. Wright Mills) From Max Weber: Essays in Sociology (New York: Oxford University Press, 1958), p. 78.

[19] World Health Organization (WHO) 2002 (En. 8), p. 7.

[20] Personal violence includes both self-directed violence (suicide and self-abuse), and interpersonal violence. WHO defines interpersonal violence to include family or partner violence involving children, a spouse, a partner, or the elderly, and communal violence involving acquaintances or strangers, which includes youth violence, random acts of violence, rape or sexual assault by strangers, and violence in institutional settings such as schools, workplaces, prisons and nursing homes, World Health Organization (WHO)

2002 (En. 8), p. 4. Personal violence can result in death, injury, and temporary or permanent physical, mental, or emotional disability and related losses in things of value.

[21] World Health Organization (WHO) 2002 (En. 8), p. 7.

[22] National Vital Statistics Report 2004 (En. 6).

[23] The Human Security Centre, Human Security Report 2005 (Canada: British Columbia University, 2005), p. 1.

[24] The Human Security Centre 2005 (En. 23), Figures 1.2 and Figure 1.9.

[25] J. Mueller, Retreat from Doomsday: The Obsolescence of Major War (New York: Basic Books, 1989), p. 1.

[26] Human Security Report 2005 (En. 23), Figure 1.5.

[27] Human Security Report 2005 (En. 23), Figure 1.10.

[28] R. Cooper, The Breaking of Nations: Order and Chaos in the Twenty-First Century (London: Atlantic Books, 2003), p. 151.

[29] Heidelberg Institute on International Conflict Research, Conflict Barometer 2004 (Heidelberg: Institute on International Conflict Research, 2004). .

[30] M. G. Marshal and T. R. Gurr, Peace and Conflict 2005, Center for International Development and Conflict Management (College Park, MD: University of Maryland, 2005), p. 1.

[31] Human Security Report 2005 (En. 23), Figure 1.11.

[32] Human Security Report 2005 (En. 23), p. 1.

[33] Human Security Report 2005 (En. 23), Figure 1.12.

[34] The US National Counterterrorism Center (NCTC) defines terrorist attacks as "premeditated, politically motivated violence perpetrated against noncombatant targets". The NCTC defines "combatants" as "military, paramilitary, militia, and police under military command and control in specific areas or regions where war zones or war-like settings exist". Diplomats and other nonmilitary government "assets", as well as civilians, are considered noncombatants for counting purposes. The NCTC acknowledges that its definition of such terms as "terrorist attack", "combatant", and "noncombatant" are "open to interpretation". But in Iraq, such incidents – defined as those resulting in 10 or more deaths – have increased since the invasion of 2003. In 2005 there were 3,500 such attacks in Iraq, up from 866 in 2004. About one-half of all terrorist attacks worldwide in 2005 resulted in loss of life.

[35] These figures were compiled and reported by the United States National Counterterrorism Center (NCTC) and released with the annual State Department "Country Reports on Terrorism".

[36] The principal definitional question is the extent to which the attacks recorded in Iraq were the actions of "terrorists" engaged in "terrorism", as opposed to "combatants", "insurgents", "militias" or other types of non-state actors engaged in some form of "insurgency" or other form of violence. To the

extent the latter is the case, then Iraq's real contribution as a significant new source of global terrorism is probably not quite as great as the NCTC figures suggest. And if those attacks turn out to have been the initial stages of an Iraqi civil war, then perhaps they will be retroactively reclassified as "civil war related attacks" and their contribution to the overall global terrorism count in those years will be even further diminished (which, of course, will leave open the question of what impact an Iraqi civil war might have in exacerbating global terrorism).

[37] A. C. Grayling, Among the Dead Cities: This History and Moral Legacy of the WWII Bombing of Civilians (London: Walker, 2006).

[38] A. C. Grayling (En. 37).

[39] J. Barry, M. Hastings and E. Thomas, Iraq's Real WMD, Newsweek (March 17, 2006), pp. 22-29.

[40] J. D. Steinbruner, Principles of Global Security (Washington, DC: Brookings Institution Press, 2000), p. 6.

[41] R. S. McNamara, former US Secretary of Defense, University of Maryland School of Public Policy, College Park, Maryland, USA, October 8, 2004. Robert S. McNamara was US Secretary of Defense under Presidents John F. Kennedy and Lyndon B. Johnson.

[42] K. A. Lieber and D. G. Press, The Rise of US Nuclear Primacy, Foreign Affairs (2006), p. 42-54.

[43] , G. T. Allison, Nuclear Terrorism: the Ultimate Preventable Catastrophe, New York Times.

[44] S. Nunn and M. Flournoy, A Test of Leadership on Sea Island, Washington Post (June 8, 2004), p. A23.

[45] V. Yarynich, The Ultimate Terrorism, The Washington Post (April 30, 2004), p. A29.

[46] R. S. McNamara 2004 (En. 41).

[47] R. S. McNamara 2004 (En. 41).

[48] S. L. Knobler, A. A. F. Mahmoud and L. A. Pray (eds.), Biological Threats and Terrorism: Assessing the Science and Response Capabilities: Workshop Summary, Forum on Emerging Infections, Board on Global Health (Washington, D.C.: National Academies Press, 2003).

[49] Charlie Rose TV Program, Feb. 13, 2006.

[50] R. A. Posner, Catastrophe, Risk and Response (Oxford: Oxford University Press, 2004).

[51] M. Rees, Our Final Hour: A Scientist's Warning: How Terror, Error and Environmental Disaster Threaten Humankind's Future in this Century On Earth and Beyond (New York: Basic Books, 2003).

[52] J. Diamond, Collapse: How Societies Choose to Fail or Succeed (New York: Penguin Books, 2005).

[53] Teilhard de Chardin characterized the emergence of a new human sphere of reflection and conscious invention as the noosphere, from the Greek "noos," referring to mind. Vladimir Vernadsky also embraced the notion of the noosphere, viewing it in part, as did Teilhard de Chardin, as "a sphere of mind", but also incorporating more of the human capacity for altering nature itself.

[54] US Census Bureau. International Program Center. International Data Base.

[55] UN Food and Agriculture Organization of the United Nations (FAO).

[56] Food and Agriculture Organization of the United Nations (FAO), cited by J. B. Behrman, H. Alderman and J. Hoddnott, Hunger and Malnutrition, (Copenhagen: Consensus, 2004).

[57] J. B. Behrman, H. Alderman and J. Hoddnott 2004 (En. 56).

[58] Time, March 27, 2006.

[59] A 1993 study by the Carter Center in Atlanta, Georgia, estimated that two-thirds of deaths are due to six risk factors related at least in part to behavior: tobacco, alcohol, injury risks, high blood pressure, obesity/cholesterol and poor primary care (including prenatal and reproductive care).

[60] D. ElBoghdady and S. Ginsberg, Drowsy, Distracted and Driving: Inattention Contributes to Bulk of Vehicle Crashes, Study Shows, Washington Post. (April 21, 2006).

[61] D. Brown, Saving Millions for Just a Few Dollars: Cost-Effective Health Measures for Poor Nations, Washington Post (April 3, 2006), p. A08.

[62] D. Yergin, Ensuring Energy Security, Foreign Affairs (March/April 2006), p. 69-82, 79.

[63] D. Yergin 2006 (En. 62), p. 82.

[64] D. Yergin 2006 (En. 62), p. 82.

[65] D. Yergin 2006 (En. 62), p. 81.

[66] J. Diamond 2005 (En. 52), p. 495.

[67] J. Diamond 2005 (En. 52).

[68] F. Rijsberman, The Water Challenge, Copenhagen Consensus, May 14, 2004.

[69] F. Rijsberman 2004 (En. 68).

[70] C. Timberg, Cholera Spreading Rapidly In Angola: Almost 1,300 Are Dead; Squalid Conditions Cited, Washington Post (May 18, 2006), p. A16.

[71] J. Eilperin, Ocean Exploitation Surfaces as Crisis Widespread Pollution, Overfishing Spur Presidential Panel to Urge New Rules, Washington Post (October 9, 2004), p. A03.

[72] F. Krupp and P. Benchley, Oceans in Need of a Visionary, Washington Post (August 6, 2004), p. A19.

[73] S. A. Earle, Threats to Biodiversity in Marine Ecosystems, Cosmos Club Symposium on Biodiversity, Cosmos Club, Washington, D.C., April 3, 2004.

[74] J. Eilperin 2004 (En. 71), p. A03.

[75] S. A. Earle 2004 (En. 73).

[76] F. Krupp and P. Benchley, Oceans in Need of a Visionary, Washington Post (August 6, 2004); p. A19. F. Krupp is the president of Environmental Defense, and P. Benchley is an author and ocean conservationist.

[77] J. Diamond 2005 (En. 52), p. 488.

[78] L. Merriam Talbot, The State of Biodiversity, Keynote Introduction, Cosmos Club Symposium "Implications of Biodiversity for Our Life", April 3, 2004.

[79] New drivers of evolution could take a variety of forms: a novel combination of natural selection based on fundamental and residual forces of the natural environment; natural selection based on new natural forces influenced by human behavior; natural selection based on the novel combinations of natural and artificial forces resulting from human behavior; artificial selection of biological species directly contrived by humans; and artificial creation of non-biological agents that interact with natural organisms.

[80] S. M. Meyer, End of the Wild, Boston Review (April/May 2004), p. 20-25. Stephen M. Meyer is professor of political science at MIT and the director of the MIT project on Environmental Politics and Policy.

[81] T. C. Schelling, It's Getting Warmer, The Wall Street Journal (February 23, 2006), p. A16

[82] A. Gore, An Inconvenient Truth (New York: Rodale, 2006).

[83] As noted earlier, some experts have suggested a worst-case scenario in which global warming unleashes a dynamic so powerful that it flips the entire global climate into a deep freeze.

[84] An institution is an incentive system in which a group of individuals who share a common culture and beliefs exhibit predictable patterns of behavior and relationships governed by a stable set of explicit and implicit rules, such as moral codes and routines of practice.

[85] UN Development Programme, Human Development Report (New York: United Nations, 1994), cited by Human Security Report 2005 (En. 23).

[86] In 2005, The Human Security Centre at British Columbia University in Canada, which takes the narrower view, issued Human Security Report 2005 (En. 23), the first of what it intends to be an annual Human Security Report that will comprehensively "map[s] the trends in the incidence, severity, causes and consequences of global violence".

[87] Human Security Report 2005 (En. 23). The Human Security Centre in Canada, which published Human Security Report 2005, takes the narrower view of "human security".

[88] Armed forces include army, navy, air force, coast guard and "special forces" such as the US Army Rangers, Green Berets, and Delta Force, and

Navy SEALs, with functions variously defined as "national defense", "expeditionary" missions, "war-fighting", and "special operations".

[89] The White House organization for the overlapping national security and homeland security functions includes the president and his immediate staff, the National Security Council and the Homeland Security Council (with overlapping staffs), a Domestic Consequences Group, Message Meetings, and daily presidential briefings by the Director of National Intelligence Director (DNI). The DNI oversees a loosely linked series of 15 intelligence agencies located in various federal departments, as well as the independently standing Central Intelligence Agency (CIA). Each of those departments also has other, non-intelligence related security functions, as do the Department of Treasury, the Department of Health and Human Services (including the Centers for Disease Control and Prevention), the Department of Transportation, and other federal departments.

[90] Center for Technology and National Security Policy (2006), p. 1.

[91] See En. 90.

[92] Following 9/11 terrorist attacks on the United States, critics argued that one reason for what was viewed as an intelligence failure was the inability, or unwillingness, of the numerous federal intelligence agencies to share information about terrorist activities. Under the reorganized federal intelligence structure adopted by the US Congress in the Intelligence Reform and Terrorism Prevention Act of 2004, a new Director of National Intelligence (DNI) was charged with integrating the information flows and activities of 15 agencies housed in half-a-dozen federal departments, and the independent Central Intelligence Agency (CIA), which together comprise the federal "intelligence community." The federal departments involved include the Department of Defense (including separate intelligence arms of the Army, Navy, Marines and Air Force, as well as the Defense Intelligence Agency (DIA), the National Security Agency (NSA), which performs analysis of electronic intercepts, the National Imagery and Mapping Agency, the National Reconnaissance Office, which builds and operates satellites, as well as intelligence units of the Special Operations Command, Central Command, Northern Command, and Iraq invasion command); the Department of Justice (DOJ) (including the Joint Terrorism Task Force (JTTF), and a center for terrorism analysis in the Federal Bureau of Investigation (FBI); the State Department (coordinator for counterterrorism); and an intelligence analysis unit in the Department of Homeland Security. Representatives of the 16 federal agencies in the intelligence community meet three times daily (at 8 a.m., 3 p.m. and 1 a.m.) under the direction of National Counterterrorism Center (NCTC), which reports directly to the Director of National Intelligence (DNI), to update the terrorism "threat matrix". The DNI briefs the president each morning on the threat matrix, a function that used to be performed by the CIA.

[93] Various organizational terms that are virtually synonymous with "emergency management" include "disaster management", "catastrophe management", "consequence management", and "crisis response and management". Similarly, "emergencies" are variously "disasters", "catastrophes", "crises", or other disruptive public incidents that have serious consequences.

[94] The "civil-military" function typically involves various combinations of military and civilian government agencies that carry out, often collectively, "civil-military missions" involved emergency management, including international disaster relief, peacekeeping, humanitarian missions, and counterterrorism. There may also be an overlap between "civil-military missions" and other security operations, such as "homeland defense", in those instances when homeland defense capabilities are used in support of support civil-military missions.

[95] Prior to organizational relocation to the newly created Department of Homeland Security (DHS), the Federal Emergency Management Agency (FEMA) had been an independent agency whose "director" had cabinet rank (i.e. similar in status with the "secretary" of a federal "department") FEMA was originally fashioned by the merger of organizational elements of civil defense agencies formed during the Cold War to prepare the civilian population for atomic attack, as well as various agencies that dealt with natural disasters. The newly created FEMA became a dumping ground for political cronies, until a series of major storms and earthquakes in the late 1980s and early 1990s provoked a public outcry for serious reform. The Congress requested the National Academy of Public Administration to recommend a solution to the problem. (Disclosure: The writer was president of the National Academy of Public Administration at the time.) A new national emergency management system was fashioned on a "network" model of governance, in which FEMA, a comparatively tiny agency, became the hub of a national emergency management system involving all sectors of society and all levels of government, addressing "all hazards" across a continuum of functions from mitigation to preparation, response and recovery; National Academy of Public Administration, Coping with Catastrophe (Washington, D.C.: National Academy of Public Administration, 1993). The new system required that the FEMA director be qualified by expertise in emergency management, experienced in running large, complex public institutions and networks, and directly report to the president. By the end of the 1990s the new system was in place and flourishing, and FEMA was hailed as an example of successful government "transformation".

Following his election in 2000, President George W. Bush appointed his campaign chairman, Joseph Albaugh, as FEMA director, and Albaugh publicly disavowed FEMA's recently adopted leadership role in promoting the mitigation of disasters at the state and local level, one of the key elements of the new system. When FEMA was placed in the newly created Department of Homeland Security, Albaugh resigned rather than accept less than a cabinet status. He recommended as his replacement his former roommate, Michael Brown, a lawyer with no previous emergency management experience. Brown headed FEMA during the Hurricane Katrina catastrophe in New Orleans and the Gulf Coast in the summer of 2005, and became the most visible symbol and scapegoat for its mismanagement. After he was fired from his post as FEMA director, Brown in turn attacked his boss, DHS Secretary Michael Chertoff, and the White House, for their complicity in the fiasco.

[96] S. M. Meyer 2004 (En. 80), p. 21.

[97] Others include "port security", "nuclear plant security", "transportation security", "public transit security", "communications security", "electronics systems security", "cyber-security", "information security", "information assurance", and so on.

[98] S. J. Palmisano, The Globally Integrated Enterprise, Foreign Affairs, (2006), p. 127-136. p. 135.

[99] Aspect of personal security include "housing security", "food security", "income security", "pension and retirement security", (which, in the United States, includes "Social Security"), "job security", "education security", and a constellation of "individual rights" (variously characterized as "constitutional rights", "legal rights", "civil rights", "civil liberties" and "human rights").

[100] Some countries rank "societal security" and "cultural security" with "economic security".

[101] For an elaboration of this view of "global governance", see R. S. Fosler, Human Governance and the State: The Global Challenge to Sovereignty, in D. J. Eaton (ed.), The End of Sovereignty? - A Transatlantic Perspective, Transatlantic Public Policy Series (edited by E. Bohne, C. F. Bonser and K. M. Spencer (Hamburg/Münster: LIT-Verlag, 2006), p. 65-78.

[102] A.-M. Slaughter, The New World Order (Princeton University Press, 2004). Slaughter addresses in particular the trans-state networks that have formed among the various counterpart functional agencies of national governments.

[103] S. Nunn and M. Flournoy, A Test of Leadership on Sea Island, Washington Post (June 8, 2004), p. A23.

[104] S. M. Meyer 2004 (En. 80), p. 22.

[105] G: Hardin; The Tragedy of the Commons; Science 162 (1968); p. 1243-1248

[106] G. Hardin 1968 (En. 105).

[107] S. J. Palmisano 2006 (En. 98), p. 127-136, p. 135.

[108] S. J. Palmisano 2006 (En. 98), p. 135

[109] D. Yergin 2006 (En. 62), p. 69-82, p. 75.

[110] D. Yergin 2006 (En. 62), p. 75.

[111] R. S. Fosler, The Global Challenge to Governance: Implications for National and Subnational Government Capacities and Relationships, in The Challenge to New Governance in the Twenty-First Century: Achieving Effective Central-Local Relations, National Institute of Research Advancement of Japan and National Academy of Public Administration of the United States. (Tokyo: National Institute of Research Advancement, 1999).

[112] See, for example, F. Fukuyama, State-Building: Governance and World Order in the 21st Century, in R. Orr (ed.), Winning the Peace: an American Strategy for Post-Conflict Reconstruction (Washington, D.C.: Center for Strategic and International Studies, 2004).

[113] C. Timberg., Cholera Spreading Rapidly In Angola: Almost 1,300 Are Dead; Squalid Conditions Cited, Washington Post (May 18, 2006), p. A16.

[114] G. J. Schinasi, Safeguarding Financial Stability: Theory and Practice (Washington, D.C.: International Monetary Fund, 2006).

[115] Drawing a stark contrast between unilateral and multilateral approaches poses a false choice. There is no incompatibility between taking a multilateral approach that builds international institutions, arrangements, and relationships when it is in a state's interest to do so, and taking a unilateral approach that calls for appropriate independent action when that is in its interest.

Index

List of Authors

Aaron Baker, Senior Lecturer in Law, Durham University, Durham, UK

Jan Bury, Analyst, Polish Institute of International Affairs, Warsaw, Poland

Sławomir Dębski, Deputy Director (acting Director), Polish Institute of International Affairs, Warsaw, Poland

Helen R. Desfosses, Associate Professor of Public Administration and Policy, and African Studies, State University of New York at Albany, USA

R. Scott Fosler, Visiting Professor and Roger C. Lipitz Senior Fellow, Center for Public Policy and Private Enterprise, University of Maryland School of Public Affairs, Chevy Chase, Maryland, USA

Beata Górka-Winter, Research Fellow in Security Affairs, Polish Institute of International Affairs, Warsaw, Poland

Dietmar Herz, Director, Professor of Comparative Government, Erfurt School of Public Policy, Erfurt, Germany

Lukasz Kulesa, Project Coordinator, Polish Institute of International Affairs, Warsaw, Poland

Marek Madej, Analyst, Polish Institute of International Affairs, and Lecturer at the Institute of International Relations, University of Warsaw, Poland

Renée de Nevers, Assistant Professor in Public Administration, Maxwell School of Citizenship and Public Affairs, Syracuse University, Syracuse, USA

Rafael Reuveny, Associate Professor, School of Public and Environmental Affairs, Indiana University, Bloomington, Indiana, USA

Ryszard Stemplowski, Professor, Jagiellonian University, Krakow, Poland

Jaclyn D. Streitfeld, Department of Political Science, University of Illinois, Urbana-Champaign, Illinois, USA

Adrian Zdrada, Analyst, Polish Institute of International Affairs, Warsaw, Poland